BISON
BOOKS

T0386152

JAMES R. WALKER

LAKOTA SOCIETY

EDITED BY
Raymond J. DeMallie

University of Nebraska Press
Lincoln and London
Published in cooperation with
the Colorado Historical Society

Manufactured in the United States of America

First Bison Book printing: 1992

Library of Congress Cataloging in Publication Data
Walker, J. R.
Lakota society.

"Published in cooperation with the Colorado Historical Society."
Bibliography: p.
Includes index.
1. Oglala Indians—Social life and customs. 2. Indians of North America—Great Plains—Social life and customs. I. DeMallie, Raymond J., 1946–. II. Title.
E99.Q3W172 978'.00497 81-14676
ISBN 978-0-8032-9737-1 AACR2

Contents

Illustrations

Preface

This is the second volume of documents about the Oglala Lakotas recorded by James R. Walker during his eighteen-year stay at Pine Ridge Reservation, from 1896 to 1914. The first volume, *Lakota Belief and Ritual,* edited by Elaine A. Jahner and myself, presents the Oglala holy men's perspectives on Lakota life during the buffalo-hunting days. Oglala religion was the focus of Walker's studies and the area in which he made his most important contribution to Lakota ethnography. The present volume presents a complementary perspective, a more secular one, on the structure and organization of traditional Lakota society. The third volume, *Lakota Myth,* edited by Jahner, will be largely devoted to Walker's own imaginative reconstruction of the holy men's secret and sacred lore about the origins and development of the world and man's place in it.

The documents in *Lakota Society* reveal the interdependence of Walker's work with that of Clark Wissler and Charles and Richard Nines. Wissler was the anthropologist from the American Museum of Natural History in New York who both encouraged and financed Walker's studies. The Nines brothers were white men, brought up with the Oglalas, who were fluent in the Lakota language. Indian traders and homesteaders in northern Nebraska, they frequently served both Walker and Wissler as interpreters. In many respects, much of what we know about the traditional Oglala way of life is dependent on the work of these four men.

During the summer of 1902 Wissler made his first visit to Pine Ridge Reservation. He intended to collect museum specimens of art, utensils, clothing, and so forth, and to begin to record information on traditional lifeways as part of a comparative study of plains Indian cultures projected by the American Museum. As the study progressed—beginning with Alfred L. Kroeber's fieldwork among the Arapahos in 1899—specific topics emerged as foci of study: dialects, design symbolism, kinship systems and band structure, mythology, the sun dance, adoption ceremonies, and men's and women's societies and ceremonial associations. The overall plan was to reconstruct a developmental history of plains Indian culture by mapping the similarities and dissimilarities of these elements from one tribe to the next, thereby revealing historical interrelationships. By comparing these static phenomena among the various tribes, they hoped to reconstruct dynamic relationships that would give anthropologists a better understanding of how a homogeneous culture area, like the plains, came to develop from heterogeneous sources. Most of the men who undertook this study were students of Franz Boas, the Columbia University professor who was the preeminent anthropologist of his day. Boas directed anthropological research at the American Museum until 1905, when he resigned and was replaced by Wissler, his student. Boas had already demonstrated the soundness of this type of comparative method by using it in his studies of Northwest Coast Indian cultures.[1]

When Wissler arrived at Pine Ridge in 1902, he met Walker and the Nines brothers and found them invaluable to his work. Wissler himself was not a novice at fieldwork among plains Indians, for he had been working, and was still continuing his studies, with the Blackfeet. He was so impressed with the ability of Walker and the Nines brothers that he gave them the major responsibility for fieldwork among the Oglalas for the American Museum, and he himself only returned for brief summer visits.

Wissler wrote a letter to the American Museum during his first visit to Pine Ridge that explicitly reveals his methods and his reliance from the beginning on his new acquaintances. The letter is dated at White Clay, Nebraska, August 10, 1902:

> . . . I have been quite occupied as we have some old Indians in camp here and [I] am working the two Nines brothers in relays. Dr. Walker also runs in every day and lends a hand. Our whole work here has been in the nature of conferences on the vague and

> inconsistent points so far developed in our work. These conferences are most satisfactory since we have the recognized Indian authorities, Dr. Walker's comprehensive etymological experience, and the linguistic knowledge of Charles Nines, and as all of them have strong individuality, so the conferences sometimes border on the strenuous, making it necessary to "wave the peace pipe" over their heads. C. Nines and Dr. Walker differ fundamentally in their linguistic method so that they clash daily. Walker holds that an analysis of a term into its elements will give its true meaning, while Nines claims that such has only historical value at best, current usage being the sole criterion. So far as I can see, Nines has the best of it, but for various reasons I have tried to keep out of the fight.
>
> As to the informants, they also have "chips on their shoulder." One of them is inclined to use steamroller methods.
>
> So altogether I am having anything but a vacation time. Yet it is the most interesting fieldwork I ever undertook.[2]

Wissler was clearly pleased by the strong interest everyone took in his anthropological studies. Given this level of commitment, the problem was not finding data to record but narrowing down the field of study. From his own fieldwork Wissler primarily recorded information on the symbolism of beadwork and other art forms as an adjunct to the specimens he collected, and on men's and women's societies. He also recorded some myths and notes on miscellaneous subjects. He published a series of short papers on art and myth and a monograph on societies; other material is carefully preserved in his field notes but has not yet been published.[3]

All of Wissler's publications depended heavily on both Walker and the Nines brothers; large sections of "Societies and Ceremonial Associations of the Oglala" (1912) were actually written by Richard Nines, with only minimal editing by Wissler, and other portions were largely contributed by Walker. In the present volume, documents 12–16, 18, and 24–26 were recorded by Richard Nines in 1911 and 1912 in response to Wissler's requests for information on specific topics to complement his monograph on societies.

Wissler left the bulk of the ethnographic study of the Oglalas to be completed by Walker himself. He encouraged Walker to record Lakota ceremonial music, to collect specimens for the museum, to record data on physical characteristics of the Oglalas, and to continue the ethnographic investigations on ritual and myth. With Wissler's encouragement and editorial assistance, Walker prepared a study of Lakota games (1905–1906), a summary of Lakota kinship and social organization (1914), and his major publication, "The Sun Dance" (1917), which includes reconstructions of the sun dance, *Hunka* (ritual adoption ceremony), and Buffalo Sing (girl's puberty ceremony), as well as an important collection of texts and myths.

The material in the present volume covers a variety of subjects on which Walker collected information. Most important in terms of ethnographic significance is Part I, "The Structure of Society," which treats in detail the organization of bands and camps, the manner in which they were formed, and the interrelationships among them. The documents discuss the Lakota governmental system and analyze the distribution of power within society, providing some of the most reliable information ever recorded on the subject and in important ways shaping our understanding of the structure of Lakota society. Previously, only brief summaries of these materials have been available, in the publications of Walker and Wissler. Part I also provides detailed discussions of the structure of the family and kin relationships and includes a very valuable paper on the subject written by Thomas Tyon, an Oglala. These documents correct and expand on material presented by Walker in his "Oglala Kinship Terms." In preparing the latter for publication, the editors at the American Museum so badly disarranged and confused the pieces, and made so many typographical errors, that the published paper is in places nearly incomprehensible. Documents 19–22 present Walker's original material in full.

Part II, "Hunting, War, Ceremony, and Art," presents a potpourri of writings that include valuable information on diverse topics concerning actual day-to-day life in a Lakota camp. Among the subjects touched on are the organization of hunts, the transfer of authority during hunts and during war, the boundaries of traditional Lakota hunting territory, and Lakota beliefs about sexuality. Together with information given in Part I, these pieces provide a much better understanding than previously available of the position and role of women in Lakota society, and thus help to fill a great void in the ethnographic record.

Part III, "Time and History," gives Walker's systematic reconstruction of Lakota methods of measuring and counting time, and presents three winter counts—Oglala calendars that chronicle the Lakota past from 1759 to 1912. No Ears made a copy of his count for Walker, who prepared a translation. Short Man made copies of the pictographs of his count and dictated the captions to Walker, who wrote them down in Lakota and prepared a translation. Iron Crow wrote out his count for Wissler, who recorded a translation evidently made jointly by Iron Crow, the Nines brothers, and Walker. I have reproduced here the Lakota texts in their original form and have made new translations. In addition, Document 31 is an eyewitness account by Beard of the massacre of Lakotas by the Seventh Cavalry at Wounded Knee Creek, December 29, 1890. All of this material is valuable for the insight it gives into Lakota concepts of their own past.

Many of the documents included here present the words of Oglalas directly. Those who contributed materials are listed in Appendix I, "The Authorities." We are particularly fortunate to have these firsthand statements because they help us to understand from Lakota viewpoints. The documents on the structure of society reveal disagreement among informants about the details of the organization of their society and about the past development of subgroups. This is a good reminder that the neat structures which Walker, Wissler, the Nines brothers—and we today—look for may not accurately characterize the traditional Lakota view of their society. The Lakota perspective seems to have been much more flexible, allowing for disparate views that correlated with family, political, and other interests. Again, this is a reflection of the dynamism that is such an important characteristic of Lakota life.

Three of the longest documents in this volume—numbers 22, 23, and 27—are Walker's own synthetic reconstructions of Lakota social organization and family life, everyday camp life and hunting, and art. They are particularly valuable for revealing Walker's overall understanding of the traditional Lakotas, and in very fundamental ways they flesh out the starker documentary accounts presented by individual Oglalas. All of these three documents had their genesis in public addresses given by Walker and reflect his attempts to communicate to the general public his understanding of what the Lakotas of the buffalo-hunting days were like. Representing his interests and imagination, they give us a better insight into Walker himself and help us to evaluate his work.[4]

Unless otherwise noted, all documents are reproduced exactly as they were written, although errors of spelling and grammar have been corrected and long sentences have occasionally been broken up. Paragraphing and punctuation have been provided when lacking in the original, and Lakota words have been italicized to remind the reader that they represent Lakota concepts, not English ones. Tribal names are used in their standard plural forms throughout, both in the editorial material and the documents. Titles for the documents have been supplied when necessary. The names of informants and dates of the documents are given whenever known. The source for each document is indicated after the title by "CHS" (Colorado Historical Society) or "AMNH" (American Museum of Natural History). Editorial additions are indicated by square brackets. Editorial deletions are indicated by three asterisks (* * *).

Acknowledgments

For support and aid in the preparation of this volume of Walker's papers I must first express my gratitude to Elaine A. Jahner, Department of English, University of Nebraska. We have worked together on the project and have freely exchanged ideas. I am especially grateful to Allan R. Taylor and Eli James, Department of Linguistics, University of Colorado, for their critical help in reviewing the translations from Lakota of the winter counts included in this volume. James H. Howard, Department of Sociology and Anthropology, Oklahoma State University, read the manuscript and provided helpful comments, particularly on the sections relating to art and winter counts.

It is a pleasure to express my enduring gratitude to Maxine Benson and Cathryne Johnson of the Colorado Historical Society for their support and cheerful cooperation. Likewise, Stanley F. Freed and David Hurst Thomas, of the Department of Anthropology, American Museum of Natural History, have freely made their resources available to me. Both institutions have granted permission to publish the Walker materials in their holdings, making the present work possible. The Short Man winter count pictographs and the first page of Iron Crow's winter count are used by courtesy of the American Museum of Natural History. The Amon Carter Museum, Field Museum of Natural History, and Indiana University Museum also gave permission to reproduce photographs in their collections.

I wish also to express my indebtedness to the Center for the History of the American Indian, Newberry Library, Chicago, where, as a Fellow, I began the preparation of this volume during the year 1978–79. Without the time that this fellowship allowed for study and contemplation, the present volume would have been much longer delayed. I must also thank the Colorado Historical Society for helping to subsidize publication of this work.

I

The Structure of Society

The material presented here on social organization is especially valuable because there has been so little recorded about this subject for the old Lakota way of life. The first anthropologists with definite interests in the structure of society did not visit the Sioux reservations until the 1930s (notably Haviland Scudder Mekeel, who worked at Pine Ridge in 1930 and 1931, and Donald Collier, who visited Pine Ridge briefly in 1939). By that time the memory of the old social forms had been filtered through more than a half century of reservation life that was dominated by Indian agents (later superintendents) who devoted themselves to every possible means of destroying the old social groupings and of forcing the Lakotas to face the world as individuals, modeled on the image of European immigrants to the plains.[1]

Walker published two accounts of Lakota social life. The first, "Oglala Kinship Terms," prepared at Clark Wissler's request, appeared in 1914. In this he succinctly presented his reconstruction of the structure of Lakota society, as follows:

> Those who speak certain dialects and conform to certain customs and usages are Lakota. The Lakota are allied against all others of mankind, though they may war among themselves. They are *oyate ikce* (native people), and are *ankantu* (superior), while all others of mankind are *oyate unma* (other-people), who are *ihukuya* (considered-inferior). This is the relation of the Lakota to all others of mankind, and if any refuse to acknowledge this relation they are *tokayapi* (considered-enemies), and should be treated as such.
>
> The Lakota *taku-kiciyapi* (consider-one-another-kindred), because they are all either *owe* (of-blood, of-one-blood), or *oweya* (considered-of-blood). The *owepi* are those whose ancestors were *owepi*. The *oweyapi* are those who have ancestors who were *owepi*, but who have one or more ancestors who were *oyate unma* (other people).
>
> The bonds of relationship of the Lakota are stronger between the *owepi* than they are between the *oweyapi*. These bonds depend on the following conditions: The Lakota are divided into seven *otonwepi* (of-own-blood tribal divisions), of which the Tinta-tonwan (Camp-on-plains = Teton) is the principal *otonwe*. The Tinta-tonwan are divided into seven *ospayepi* (divisions), the Oglala being the principal *ospaye* of these seven.
>
> The Oglala are divided into seven *ti-ospayepi* (tipi-divisions = bands); each *ti-ospaye* is composed of one or more *wico-tipi* (camps),

> and each camp is composed of two or more *ti-ognakapi* (husbanded-tipis).
>
> Thus the strength of the relationship of one Lakota to another is in the following order: 1, *ti-ognaka;* 2, *wico-tipi;* 3, *ti-ospaye;* 4, *ospaye;* 5, *otonwe.*[2]

Following this explanation, Walker presents accounts of marriage, divorce, and family relationships, and then discusses Lakota kinship terms. The article concludes with a text by Tyon, badly garbled and rife with typographical errors, and with obvious inaccuracies in the translation.

Walker sent his paper on kinship to Wissler on December 22, 1913, with the following disclaimer: "I am enclosing herewith what I have been able to do in the matter of Oglala terms of relationship. It appears to me to be very small relative to the amount of work and time I have given to it. The Tyon paper I have translated and interpreted in my way." Wissler acknowledged receipt of the paper on January 6, 1914, declaring it impressed him as an "excellent piece of work." Wissler turned the paper over for examination to Robert H. Lowie, the member of the museum staff most knowledgeable about kinship systems. Presumably, the two collaborated in reorganizing Walker's material for publication. In the process the kinship data became garbled and confused, the problem confounded by the idiosyncracies of Walker's translation of the Tyon text. The published article is very difficult to use. Document 20 presents a new translation of Tyon's text, and document 21 brings together the data on kinship terms from the article, correcting garbled spellings and restoring the information to the order in which Walker had originally presented it, that is, arranged in three generational blocks: terms for relatives in generations older than ego, those for relatives in ego's own generation, and terms for relatives in generations younger than ego.[3]

The schematic classification of social groupings that Walker gave in this article indicates the importance he placed on hierarchical classifications. It is unlikely that any Lakota would have generated this classification spontaneously, but by putting together information from many Lakotas, and by discussing the results with them, Walker was able to construct a kind of consensual classification. The result may be taken as representing the

Lakotas' ideal understanding of the ways in which their society was organized, but it must not be assumed that the classification represented on-the-ground social reality. Action of all kinds in Lakota culture ritually tends toward the sacred numbers four and seven, and Lakotas tend to classify in fours and sevens as a conceptual tool. This does not necessarily mean that at any one moment it would have been possible to identify four or seven distinct social groupings at any level of the classification. In fact, at the time Pine Ridge Reservation was first settled in 1879, there do seem to have been seven bands *(tiyošpaye),* at least conceptually. However, these seven units were actually composed of many more camps (see document 3), and the bands soon splintered into many more. The best way to visualize Lakota social groups as they existed on the ground is as parts of a dynamic process, not as a static classification.

Central to Walker's understanding of Lakota unity are language, culture, and blood, all three of which were shared by all Lakotas. In his writings, Walker took an Oglala perspective: when he used the word *Lakota* in its broadest sense, he intended it to include the Dakota speakers (the Santees and Yanktons/Yanktonais) as well as the Lakota speakers (Tetons). The Lakotas were held together as a people by a common language (divided into three or more dialects), by common culture, and by common blood. In speaking of blood as a binding force for Lakota society, Walker's writings are unique among accounts of Lakota kinship and society. It is important to recognize this concept of blood *(we)* as a Lakota one, not a Western one; we do not know enough about the Lakota concept to define it precisely. Surely it is not a simple notion of biological relatedness, for Walker records that women captured from other tribes were counted as Lakotas after they learned to speak the Lakota language, and their children by Lakota men were undifferentiated from other Lakota children (document 22). The notion of blood as a defining factor in kinship must be understood as a metaphor whose contours are not clearly defined in Walker's writings. It is possible that this emphasis on blood reflects more of Walker's own notions of kinship than those of the Lakotas.

Some understanding of the Lakota concept of blood may be gotten from Walker's distinction between two kinds of family relationships: *wico-we,* "they-blood," related by blood; and *wico-un,* "they-usage," related by usage. By "usage" Walker generally meant "customs." These terms, according to Walker, were extended to people who came from other tipis *(oti-toka-hi)* and were also used to designate those dwelling in one's own tipi *(oti-wahe,* "family"). Walker differentiated between these three degrees of relationship as follows. Members of one's own family, related by blood, are designated by the usual kinship terms. Those related by usage are designated by the same kinship terms, to which are added the suffix *-ya,* "considered as." (Presumably this would be used only referentially, not for address.) These *-ya* designations might also be extended to people coming from other tipis, not related by blood, but, according to Walker, "The difference between the terms for *wico-un* and those for *oti-toka-hi* is that the former are permanent while the latter are temporary."[4]

From Walker's discussion we can conclude that kinship terms might be used to designate any member of Lakota society, but that the relationships so designated, unless they were "of blood" or "considered of blood" were not necessarily permanent. Both "of blood" and "considered of blood" relationships were permanent, however, thus indicating that what we from our Western perspective might call real kinship was not narrowly defined by the Lakotas in biological terms, but was defined, rather, by behavior. Even today, among the Lakotas, relatives are people who *act* like relatives and consider themselves to be related.

The second of Walker's publications on Lakota society is a brief section in "The Sun Dance" (1917, pp. 72–78). Here the focus is on political organization. He discusses the origin of the Sioux near Sacred Lake (Mille Lacs, Minnesota), their subsequent division into the Seven Council Fires, and the continued division of each of the Fires *(otonwepi,* divisions) into tribes *(ošpayepi)* and bands *(ti-ošpayepi)*. Walker then discusses the composition of Oglala camps, their councils, chiefs and other officials, and the structure of the formal camp circle.

Most of the materials on which Walker based both of these accounts are presented in the following documents. Consolidating information from many different Lakotas, the documents reveal ranges of difference among the individual informants that are masked in Walker's synthetic published accounts. This merely shows that in their social organization, as in their religion, the Lakotas held in common a series of basic principles and concepts, with each individual person and each individual social unit working out those principles in daily life. Again, Lakota social organization was clearly characterized by its dynamism; it was never static. One strong indication of this emerges from Walker's material; it seems that whenever he asked Lakotas about the structure of their society, he was presented with discussions of the processes by which new bands were formed and new chiefs were recognized (for example, see document 9).

A third published account of Lakota social order is given by Clark Wissler in his monograph "Societies and Ceremonial Associations of the Oglala" (1912), a work strongly influenced by Walker's ideas and by information he provided. Wissler's account, though brief, has become the classic work on Lakota government, covering such topics as the numbers of chiefs and shirt wearers, the appointment of *akicita* as camp police, and the structure of the chiefs' and headmen's societies. Documents 12–16 reproduce the complete texts of some of the interviews on the subject of Lakota government that were recorded for Wissler by Richard Nines and on which Wissler's published account is closely based. Together they represent very nearly all that is known about Oglala government. A careful reading of this material reveals that like Walker, Wissler was quick to classify and categorize his data. Predictably, informants differed on the particulars of Lakota government and on the chiefs' and headmen's societies, and we may better understand the variations in their accounts as reflecting a dynamic political process rather than as a static classification fraying around the edges.

Walker was undecided about the words he should use to refer to Lakota social units. In his writings he used *clan, gens* (or the plural form *gentes),* and *band* completely interchangeably. Apparently he used the word *clan* in his earlier work, thinking the Lakota social system could be analogized to the Scottish clan system. He dropped this in favor of *gens,* following Wissler's suggestion that *gens* was the proper term to be used for groups in which descent was through the father's line, and that *clan* should be used only for groups that traced descent through the mother's line. The use of the term *gens* fit with Walker's observation that children belonged to the father's social group (document 22). However, he also observed that kinship was traced both through the father and the mother, and hence was bilateral. He finally adopted the anthropological usage of the term *band* to refer to such nonunilineal groups. That kinship was not unilineal was a very important observation. In fact, Lakota kinship may be best understood as nonlineal: membership in social groups was determined by residence and choice, not descent. Just as the ultimate test of kin relationship was behavior, so the ultimate test of group membership was residence. This is one more aspect of the flexibility of Lakota culture.[5]

There is a considerable body of material on Sioux social groups, social organization, and migrations, and on the Seven Council Fires, which can be compared profitably with Walker's data. The following discussion is limited to major published sources, emphasizing the Teton groups.

The first extensive account was recorded in 1766 by the British adventurer Johnathan Carver, who provided a list of Sioux groups and some fragmentary notes on government, including references to chiefs and soldiers *(akicita)*. The earliest systematic treatments were recorded on the Upper Missouri River between 1802 and 1804 in the journals of the explorers Lewis and Clark and the fur trader Pierre-Antoine Tabeau. Both journals list names of social groups, chiefs, locations, and other relevant data. Tabeau gives good descriptions of the *akicita*. A comparable account was recorded by William H. Keating on Long's expedition up the Minnesota River in 1823. Together, these sources provide a firm baseline for understanding the organization of Sioux groups during the early nineteenth century.[6]

In 1838 and 1839 the geographer Joseph N. Nicollet collected valuable material on the divisions of the Sioux, with names of chiefs and territories and an account of migrations. The fur trader Edwin T. Denig wrote a very important account, "Of the Sioux," during the mid-1850s, based on his twenty years of residence on the Upper Missouri. He discusses each Sioux group in turn, presenting information on their territories and chiefs. His detailed account of Assiniboin government in *Indian Tribes of the*

Upper Missouri may serve to characterize the Sioux as well. Denig may also have provided the tabular listing of Sioux groups and chiefs recorded by the traveler Thaddeus A. Culbertson in his *Journal of an Expedition to the Mauvaises Terres and the Upper Missouri in 1850.* Much of the information in the geologist Ferdinand V. Hayden's 1862 volume on Indians of the Missouri valley was taken directly from Denig's manuscripts.[7]

A brief account of the divisions of the Sioux appears in the missionary Stephen Return Riggs's 1852 Dakota grammar and dictionary. This was expanded to include information from historical sources for Riggs's 1893 Dakota grammar, edited by James Owen Dorsey. An elaboration of Riggs's account, with new material, was presented in Dorsey's summary papers on Siouan social organization. These sources document the proliferation of bands among the Sioux after they settled on reservations, as well as the lack of strict consensus among the Sioux about the overall structure of their society.[8]

George E. Hyde synthesized early Teton history in *Red Cloud's Folk* (1937) and included a discussion of changing Sioux social organization and political structure that has become a standard reference for historians, although it is now outdated. Harry Anderson compiled a valuable synethesis of material on the social divisions of the northern Sioux (the Saones) in a study published in 1956.[9]

Much of the literature on Oglala bands has been summarized by William K. Powers in *Oglala Religion;* his account includes historical inaccuracies and must be used with care, although his discussion of structural patterns in Oglala social and ritual life is instructive. The good critical review by Loretta K. Fowler of Powers's *Oglala Religion* is helpful, especially in demonstrating Powers's selectivity in dealing with historical sources.[10]

A substantial amount of information has been published on Lakota kinship. The basic terminologies, as recorded during the 1860s, are presented in Lewis Henry Morgan's *Systems of Consanguinity and Affinity of the Human Family* (1871). In 1928 Alexander Lesser synthesized data on all Siouan kinship systems. During the 1930s, Ruth Landes recorded extensive material on kinship behavior among the Santees, and Fred Eggan summarized kinship patterns throughout the plains. In 1937 Jeannette Mirsky published a good summary of Lakota kinship and social structure based largely on the unpublished writings of Ella C. Deloria.[11]

More information on kinship terminologies was presented by Franz Boas and Ella Deloria in their Dakota grammar (1941), and in 1944 Deloria published a vivid account of Lakota social life in her *Speaking of Indians*. In the same year Royal B. Hassrick published the results of his study of kinship on the Rosebud Reservation.[12]

Fred Eggan summarized problems relating to Sioux kinship in two essays, one in 1955, the second in 1966. My account of kinship change among the Lakotas, published in 1979, provides a listing of Sioux kinship terminologies available in both published and unpublished sources.[13]

Finally, *Lakota Tales and Texts,* collected by Eugene Buechel, S.J., includes a great deal of valuable material on both social organization and kinship, written in Lakota, without translation.[14]

Some general observations may help to orient the reader toward the material that follows. The origin story of the Lakotas, as told by Walker in "The Sun Dance" and elaborated on in the forthcoming volume, *Lakota Myth,* asserts that the Lakotas were created beneath the present world. There they lived in happiness until *Iktomi* (Trickster, the Spider) and *Anog Ite* (Double Face Woman) tricked some of them into coming out onto the earth and led them to their first home in the region of the pines near the Sacred Lake. According to Walker's informant Lone Bear, the spirits were angry at the Lakotas for leaving the center of the earth; then the Bear *(Mato)* took pity on them and gave them medicines to care for themselves (Walker, *Lakota Belief and Ritual,* p. 128). Here it was that the people in time divided into the Seven Council Fires.

Students of the Sioux have always interpeted the Seven Council Fires as a historical phenomenon. For example, in the earliest written account (1825), William Keating characterized the Seven Council Fires as "but a noble ruin." He wrote, "They have long since ceased to meet at the same council fire." His interpretation was that at an earlier time the Seven Council Fires had formed a political union that had fallen into decay "like all the Indian nations with whom the White man has come in contact" (he probably had in mind here the League of the Iroquois). The same interpretation of the Seven Council Fires as a historically real social phenomenon has been reiterated by almost every subsequent writer on the Sioux.[15]

The assumption that an earlier confederation known as the Seven Council Fires actually existed is unsupported by the historical documents of earlier times. The Sioux were mentioned by Europeans first in 1640 and nearly continuously thereafter throughout the remainder of the seventeenth and eighteenth centuries. Yet no mention of the Seven Council Fires is to be found, although a fair amount of information about the Sioux can be gleaned from the historical record. From the perspective of written history, the Seven Council Fires must be considered legend, not historical actuality.[16]

This does not invalidate the concept of the Seven Council Fires. It is only a Western idea that history has as its purpose the objective evaluation of real past events. Certainly this concept of history was not shared by the traditional Lakotas. For them—as for most peoples throughout the world—history has as its function the validation of the present. History in a nonacademic sense can be thought of as a moral study, not an objective one. The story of the Seven Council Fires serves to validate the cohesion of the Sioux as a single people; it provides a charter that explains why all these people speaking the same language, sharing the same customs, and having the same blood are spread out over such a wide territory.

To appreciate the value of these accounts of the Seven Council Fires as recorded by Walker, we need to understand them for the statements of social and cultural unity that they are and not dismiss them as poorly remembered history. The historical facts of the interconnections of the various Sioux groups were obviously not of much concern to the Sioux themselves. As Walker noted, he had "heard no legend to account for their division into the gentes and subgentes [tribes and bands]" (document 2).

The most valuable comparable material on the Seven Council Fires is that recorded by Joseph N. Nicollet in 1838 and 1839. Interestingly, he presents detailed classifications of the Sioux divisions, tribes, and bands, but he, too, was unable to record traditions to account for these divisions. The important fact is simply that these seven great divisions of the Sioux shared the original council fire.[17]

The preservation of sacred fire was important for the Sioux. On marches, coals from the previous council fire were carefully preserved and used to rekindle the council fire at the new campsite. The council fire itself was the symbol of the group's autonomy. We may see the fire as symbolic of the Sun, the god *Wi;* all formal deliberations took place around a fire, the coals from which were used to light the pipe whose smoke brought the minds of men into harmony with one another and with the gods. Sharing of a common fire may be seen as one of the integrating symbols of Sioux society.[18]

Similar caution might be expressed about interpreting the names of Lakota social groups. No simple etymological interpretations will serve to give the full range of meaning. Group names were of the nature of nicknames; many of them are of great antiquity, as is attested to by historical records. The difficulty of devising etymologies for some terms (e.g., *Sisiton, Oglala, Titon)* also suggests their antiquity. To understand the range of meanings it is necessary to consider alternate etymologies and explanations of names. For example, although the word *Oglala* literally means "to scatter one's own," the signification is long since lost. Some interpretations suggest that the name refers to the scattering of the Teton bands over the plains, while others relate the name to a specific historical (or mythical) incident of someone throwing or scattering something over someone. Yet the name seems to be embedded in the form "Oujatespouitons" which the French explorer Pierre-Charles Le Sueur recorded as the designation of a Sioux group that visited him at his trading post on the Blue Earth River (in present-day Minnesota) in 1701. The word, of course, was recorded by a Frenchman through an Algonquian-speaking interpreter and hence is far from the original, but Le Sueur translated it as "Village dispersé en plusieurs petites bandes" ("Village dispersed in several small bands"). This account long predates most of the incidents from which the Oglalas are supposed to have taken their name.[19]

The same problems of interpretating names and the variant stories behind these interpretations occur for virtually all Sioux groups. The conclusion must be that the names in and of themselves were of no great importance to the Sioux; what counted was identifying each group vis-à-vis the others. To place too much importance on the names themselves, and to search for definitive etymologies, negates the importance of understanding the names from Lakota viewpoints, in the context of Lakota culture.

One aspect of Lakota social life about which far too little is known is the perspective of Lakota women. Almost nothing has been published from women's points of view about the Lakotas, and little has been recorded about Lakota women in general. Stereotypically, Lakota culture has been presented as dominated by men, with women being of little importance. Walker's materials provide a fair amount of material that may help to increase our knowledge of the role of women. In particular he recorded information about women's rights in marriage and divorce which will help in a small way to fill the largest single gap in our understanding of the old Lakota way of life (see especially documents 17, 19, and 22).

The documents that follow are essentially all by-products of Walker's primary focus on the study of Lakota religion. We are fortunate to have them. They provide abundant material for rethinking our accepted views of Lakota social life.

---

1. Legend of the Camp Circle. John Blunt Horn. (CHS)

Long ago the Lakotas made but one council fire. Then they were all like brothers and made their winter camp on *Ble Wakan* [Sacred Lake], and this was called *Ble Wakan Tonwan* [Sacred Lake Village].[20] Then some wandered so far in the summertime that they did not return to the winter camp, which was made in the place of the pines. These people made their winter camp where the leaves fall in the winter and some made it upon the *tinte* or plains. Then others made their winter camp on *Ble Isan,* or Knife Lake [the Santees]. Then some stayed at the lake in the summertime and ate fish all the time and they stank like fish so they were called *Sin-Sin* [Sisseton]. So there were four council fires.

Then there was war with other Indians and the Lakotas all came together to help each other fight, but there were four council fires. They made the camp circle. Those who lived at Spirit Lake were the oldest camp and they placed their camp opposite the entrance and those from the plains made their camp on both sides of the entrance. (Another version says that the plains people placed their camp on the left and the Knife Lakers on the right and the Slimy Ones [Sissetons] at the entrance.)

After this those at the Knife Lake went to where the leaves fall and made their camp there. They made two council fires. Then some who went to the plains went far away and would not come to help in war. They spoke to the messengers in a rough voice so that the Lakotas called them *Ho He,* or Rough Voiced [the Assiniboins]. But some came to help at council and they placed their camps one on the north side and one on the south side of the entrance to the circle, but they made their council fire on both sides of the entrance. So they were called *Ihank Tonwan* [End Village] and *Ihank Tonwanla* [Little End Village]. Ever since that time there have been seven council fires that would not be extinguished.

---

2. The Seven Council Fires. Antoine Herman and James R. Walker. (CHS)

It is the custom of the Sioux Indians to name a people descriptive of some characteristic or peculiarity of those named as, for instance, they call the Germans *Iaśica,* Bad-Speak; the Negroes *Hasapa,* Black-skin; the Ojibwas *Ḣaḣatonwan,* Camp-at-falls; the Navajos *Śinagleglega,* Make-figured-robes [Striped blankets].

They name themselves, in the Santee dialect, *Dakota,* which is derived from their word *da,* considered, and *koda,* a friend or friends, and it means Considered-friends.[21] The Teton dialect has varied from the Santee according to the natural process of variation of a language which is not written. In the former the sound represented by *l* has taken the place of the sound represented by *d* in the latter, so that the *Titonwan* or Tetons call the Sioux *Lakota.*

They also speak of themselves as *Oceti Śakowin,* a contraction of *Ocetiyotipi Śakowin,* which means the Seven Council Fires, and indicates that they considered themselves as one tribe divided into seven gentes [bands], each gens governed by its own council, and the tribe bound together by a kind of confederacy.[22] According to their legends they were originally all kinspeople, living together under one chief in the regions of the pines [the north], but the writer has heard no legend that accounts for their division into the gentes or that would indicate the exact location of their earliest home. * * *[23]

The only binding force of this confederation was that no one of these clans [bands] should be at war or enmity with any other, though in raids for horses and women and in feuds and reprisals there was at times almost a state of war between some of these clans.[24]

These clans or tribes were:

Mdewakantonwan	Camping at Spirit Lake
Waȟpekute	Leaf Shooters
Waȟpetonwan	Camping among Leaves
Sisitonwan	Camping among Swamps
Ihanktonwan	Camping at the End
Ihanktonwanna	Camping at the Little End
Titonwan	Camping on the Plains

These are the most generally accepted names of the tribes among the Dakotas, but each tribe, except the *Titonwan,* had other names by which they were known, as for instance, the *Mdewakantonwan* were also known as *Kiyuksa,* Violators of a Custom, referring to their taking women in violation of the generally accepted custom of the Dakotas. This is of interest because according to the legends of this people the Campers at Mysterious Lake was the original gens of the Lakotas from which the other six gentes were formed in the manner that will be explained further on.[25]

The Mysterious Lake referred to in this name is the Mille Lacs in Minnesota, situated in the midst of pine forests which extend a short distance southward and terminate along its southern border in a large admixture of deciduous trees, while it extends northwards as the Lakotas believed, indefinitely. They believed that the Mysterious Lake was the center of the world, and north they called *waziyata,* the region of the pines, because no one had been known to find the end of the pine forests in that direction, and according to their stories and myths they extended to the edge of the earth. This indicates that they inhabited this region from remote times, and that the gens occupying this territory was the original from which the other six gentes were formed.

This gens considered themselves the original stock, and that the other gentes were inferior and subordinate to them. When the latter originated the custom of getting their women from gentes other than their own, they continued to take women of their own gens and were thus designated as the *Kiyuksa,* or Violators of the Custom.[26]

When the Lakotas *tonwanyanpi,* or made a camp according to their customs, they did so on the territory they claimed as their hunting grounds, which was established by a common consent, or by conquest, and maintained by force. This territory was generally defined by natural landmarks such as lakes, rivers, hills, prairies, etc., but [the boundaries] were often indefinite, and varied according to the ability of the claimants to extend them or defend them from invasion by others. They varied from place to place for these same reasons. In this manner the Lakotas lost their claim to the territory around the Mysterious Lake to the Algonquins, who, being a canoeing people, were able to move expeditiously about the lacustrine regions of northern Minnesota. Coming from eastward where they were in contact with the white people before the Lakotas were, they had firearms, which gave them an immense advantage in warfare so that they drove the Lakotas from the wooded regions to the prairies in a contest of war which was continual until the U.S. government interfered to make peace between these two peoples.[27]

The original territory occupied by the Lakotas is hardly defined by their stories or legends, but philological reasons indicate that it was confined to the pine regions extending from Mille Lacs, for the first gens originating from the parent gens was the Shooters among the Leaves, which means that they shot among the deciduous leaves of trees; that would indicate that they moved

James Riley Walker, ca. 1909. *Courtesy Amon Carter Museum, Fort Worth.*

Iron Crow, 1909. Photograph by Joseph Kossuth Dixon, taken at the Crow Agency, Montana. *Wanamaker Collection, Indiana University Museum.*

Short Man. Photographer and date unrecorded. *Courtesy Field Museum of Natural History, Chicago.*

First page of Iron Crow's winter count. *American Museum of Natural History.*

southward from the regions of the pines and hunted among the trees with deciduous leaves. The second subordinate gens moved further southward and made their camp among the trees with deciduous leaves. The last of the subordinate gens, the *Titonwan,* left the timbered country altogether and inhabited the plains.

The gentes are given in the order above because in a legend of The Seven Council Fires the camp was established in a circle according to the rank of the several gentes. The oldest and original gens, the *Mdewakantonwan,* were at the west in the place of honor; the next oldest, the *Wah̄pekute,* were at the left of these; the next oldest, the *Wah̄petonwan,* were at the right; the third from the oldest, the *Sisitonwan,* were at the left of the *Wah̄pekute;* the fourth oldest, the *Ihanktonwan,* were at the north side of the entrance to the circle at the east, and the *Ihanktonwanna* were at the south side of this entrance; while the youngest, the *Titonwan,* were at the south side of the circle. They were placed thus to indicate the directions of their territory from the territory of the *Mdewakantonwan,* the oldest of the gentes.

According to the legends of this people, they were originally all kinspeople, with one chief, and lived in one camp. As the writer has heard no legend to account for their division into the gentes and subgentes, it probably was done as such divisions were made in later times, which was as follows.

A man might leave a camp, either voluntarily or driven out, and have his tipi alone, or his friends might leave the camp with him, in which case they *tonwanunyanpi,* formed a camp; or if when he was alone others came to him and camped with him, then they formed a camp and he was the chief of the camp and of the band of people living in it. As long as this camp, band, or subgens remained living in the territory claimed by a gens it was considered a subgens, subordinate to the gens claiming the territory or from which its members were mostly drawn to form the subgens, and the chief of the gens ranked superior to the chief of the subgens. In this way each gens was composed of many subgentes, each with its chief, but the chief of the original gens was the head chief of all the subgentes.

But, if a subgens became numerous and powerful, then it could assume the place of the principal gens and hold the other subgentes as subordinate and its chief would become the head chief of the gens. Or it might take possession of a territory independent of other gentes and become the principal gens of that territory, from which other subgentes would originate, all known under the name of the originating gens.

It is therefore probable that the *Mdewakantonwaṅ* was the original gens and that other gentes sprang from it in the manner above given, and that some of these gentes took possession of new territory and assumed an independence of the parent gens and were given names in accordance with the customs of the people, which generally are some characteristic of those named.

---

3. Divisions of the Lakotas. James R. Walker. (CHS)

When the Lakotas came from the middle of the world they were one as a people and made but one winter camp and kept but one council fire.[28] After a time some did not return to the winter camp and when they did associate with the original camp they maintained their council fire, so they were called *tonwan* [village] because they thought they had power sufficient to be independent. Then others did so until there were seven *tonwan,* or seven council fires, when the people all associated. While these people were independent of each other, they were friends, so they called themselves *Dakoda,* or friends *(Lakola* [*sic*] in the Teton dialect), and they were allies against all others of mankind.

When a formal camp is made it is circular with the entrance towards the rising sun and the place of honor at the opposite side facing the entrance. When all the Lakotas were associated in one camp, each *tonwan* placed its tipis together and built its camp fire. By common consent the original *tonwan* was given the place of honor and the others were arranged as agreed upon. But the Tetons became powerful and warlike and they usurped the place of honor which had been given to the *Blewakantonwan,* [*Mdewakantonwan*] and then the camp circle was arranged as follows, beginning at the north side of the entrance:[29]

Ihanktonwan	End detachment (Yanktons)
Sinsintonwan	Slimy detachment (Sissetons)
Blewakantonwan	Holy lake detachment (Spirit Lakers)
Tintatonwan	Plains detachment (Tetons)
Waȟpekutetonwan	Leaf shoot detachment (Santees)
Waȟpetonwan	Leaf detachment (Santees)
Ihanktonwanna	End little detachment (Yanktonais)

When two or more of these *tonwan* were associated in a camp each took the precedence in the following order:

1st: Tetons
2nd: Spirit Lakers
3rd: Santees; 1st: Leaf shooters; 2nd: Leaves
4th: Sissetons
5th: Yanktons

The Tetons were divided into seven bands, each of which when unassociated with another maintained its council fire. They were as follows:

Sicaṅgu	Thighs-scorched	Brulés
Oohenonpa	Boil-twice	Two Kettles
Minikanyewoźupi	Plant-near-water	Minikanźus
Oglala	Cast-on-own	Oglala
Itazipco	No-bow	Sans Arc
Sihasapa	Black-foot	Blackfeet
Hunkpapa	End-of-horn	Hunkpapa

The bands of the Tetons associated themselves in a formal camp circle in the order given, which always gave to the Oglalas the chief place in every formal camp of the Lakotas. When two or more of these bands were associated each took precedence in the following order:

1st: Oglalas
2nd: Minikanźus
3rd: Brulés
4th: Two Kettles
5th: Sans Arcs
6th: Blackfeet
7th: Hunkpapas

When the bands were thus associated, the one having the preceding order of precedence maintained its camp fire and assumed the place of honor, while all others held their camp fires in abeyance until they separated.

The Oglalas were divided into seven sub-bands, as follows:[30]

Pyabya Shove-aside
Tapiśleca Buffalo-spleen
Oiyuȟpe Unloads
Kiyuksa Disregards-own
Waźaźa Fringed
Iteśica Bad-face
Wagluȟe Improvident

When the Oglalas were alone in a formal camp circle, these sub-bands associated themselves in the order given and when two or more of them associated the precedence was as follows:

1st: *Kiyuksa*
2nd: *Oiyuȟpe*
3rd: *Waźaźa*
4th: *Tapiśleca*
5th: *Pyabya*
6th: *Iteśica*
7th: *Wagluȟe*

Thus the *Kiyuksa* of the Oglalas of the Tetons had the precedence in any formal camp of the Lakotas. (At the last sun dance practiced by this people, the Bad-face band usurped the place of honor in the camp circle.)[31]

There were many camps of the Oglalas which maintained a council fire; each was subordinate to the sub-band that it chose as its older camp.

---

4. Notes on Oglala bands. James R. Walker. (CHS and AMNH)[32]

The order of camping of the Indians of certain bands, beginning at the east:

Payabya (Below), Chief Young Man Afraid of His Horses
Oglala (Threw dust on), Chief Red Cloud
Oyuřpa (Pulled down), Chief Big Road
Śiśicala (Bad bad), Chief *Igmu wakuwa* [Chasing Cat], Silas Blind
Ḣokayuta (Eats badger), No Water
Unkpati (Stuffed in), Chief Crazy Horse

The Sun Dance was about the middle of June.

Red Cloud killed Little Wound's father, Bull Bear, near where Cheyenne City [Cheyenne, Wyoming] now is.[33]

Conquering Bear's band were the first attacked by the white soldiers fifty-five years ago, 1843, the year When They Brought In Captives.[34]

Little Wound's band, *Kiyaksa* (Bite in two)
Two Crow's band
Bull Bear's band, *Taśnahecayuta* (Gopher [ground squirrel] eaters)
Shedding Wolf's band, *Ḣokayuta* (Badger eaters)

Little Wound's bands take the precedence of other bands of the Tetons.[35] The Tetons agreed when breaking the camp in the spring on a place to camp the following winter. Little Wound was compelled to limit his rovings to such territory that he could arrive at the place of camping the first in the fall, and he must do so and camp there, whether any other bands came or not.

After Red Cloud killed Bull Bear, Little Wound's father, the bands that were loyal to Little Wound quarrelled with those who followed or upheld Red Cloud, and threw dust on them. Thus came the name of Oglala.[36]

---

5. Camps. Spotted Elk. (AMNH)

When a camp is made according to the customs of the Lakotas, the space surrounded by the tipis is called *hocoka*. The entrance to the *hocoka* should be towards the rising sun. All formal entry to the camp should be through this. A body of men entering the camp by any other entrance would be considered hostile.

A large tipi is erected in the *hocoka* next to the entrance, which is called the *tiyotipi.*[37] No one lives in the *tiyotipi.* The chiefs and headmen sit in the *tiyotipi* to council about the affairs of the camp and the people. They are called the *otiyotipi,* or those who sit in the council lodge. When the *otiyotipi* choose one to sit with them they send to him a wand marked with fire. He keeps this wand. It is made of ash wood.[38] If they ask one for his ash wood wand this means that they do not wish him to sit with them.

---

6. A Camp. James R. Walker. (CHS)

Otonwan (there-a-detachment) is a number of tipis belonging to associated Lakotas, placed in a circular form, having an opening on the eastern side called *oinapa* (there-enter), the entrance, surrounding a space called *hocoka* (there-middle), the area, and having on the area, at the side opposite the entrance, a *ti* with its door toward the entrance. This *ti* is called *tiyotipi (ti* for tipis), and it is the public tipi. All kinds of communal meetings are held in this *ti,* or lodge, and all communal business is transacted here. When a formal meeting is held a fire is lighted on the fireplace of the lodge and it is called *peta omniciye* or council fire. * * *

---

7. A Camp of the Oglala Lakotas. James R. Walker. (CHS)

In aboriginal times a Lakota camp was an assemblage of tipis belonging to a number of families who made a council fire as a symbol of their autonomy. In the winter camp or a formal camp the tipis were placed in a circular form known as the camp circle. A short space was unoccupied on the side towards the rising sun and this was known as the entrance. The space enclosed by the camp circle was the camp middle or area. The ends of the camp circle next to the entrance were known as the horns, and the place in the circle opposite the entrance was the chief place. A *ti* was placed on the area near the chief place, with its door towards the entrance, and this was the council lodge. It was the public lodge of the camp, where all communal gatherings were held, and all business of common interest to the camp was transacted. If business of importance was to be done, a fire was made on the fireplace of the council lodge, and this was known as the council fire. Business transacted about the council fire was of the nature of legislation and was binding upon all the members of the camp.

The societies in the camp placed their tipis or lodges upon the area at any place convenient, and if the camp supported a dance lodge, it was placed at the center of the area. The *ini tipi,* or vapor bath lodges, were placed outside the camp circle at any convenient place. An *ini ti* was not conical or of formal shape, and was rounded or dome shaped, and for this reason was not permitted in the camp circle. The chief place was the place of highest honor in the camp and the two horns the place of next honor.

The places most desirable in the circle were those nearest the chief place. A *ti* placed at the rear of another indicated subordination of its inhabitants to those of the *ti* in front of it. And a *ti* placed without the camp circle and in disregard of it indicated that the occupants were either in disgrace or that they did not recognize the authority of the camp council.

The most influential man of the camp was entitled to place his *ti* at the chief place; this was usually the chief of the camp, but might be any other powerful or influential person. The warriors of renown were entitled to place their tipis at the horns. All tipis had their doors so placed that they opened towards the center of the area, except the two at the horns, whose doors opened towards the rising sun.

A temporary camp was made without formality, tipis being placed according to the convenience of their occupants. * * *

---

8. Bands, Chiefs, and Laws. Charles Garnett. (CHS)

Among the Oglala Sioux Indians, a man in a camp was subject to the commonly accepted laws and customs, and to the regulations of that camp. If he desired to be free from these regulations he might set up his tipi alone, far away from the camp, where he would be chief of his own family and govern all within his own tipi. If others permanently placed their tipis near his, they formed a new camp, and a new band, of which he was the chief. If there were few who joined this new band, its chief was of little consequence and remained largely dependent on the band from which he came. But if a large number joined the new band, it became important in the affairs of the tribe, and its chief a person of corresponding importance.

If the affairs of the band were conducted in accordance with the desires of the people composing it, it maintained its prestige, but if the chief lost his authority or the respect of his people, his band was apt to desert him, and reduce him and his band to a minor place in the affairs of the tribe, or even extinguish the band altogether.

In a formal gathering of the bands, a band always took its place in the camp next below the band from which the chief or his predecessors came. A chief's authority depended on his personality and his ability to compel others to do his will, and if he were successful in his undertakings, followers were apt to flock to him and his authority be correspondingly great. If he were weak or cowardly, or unsuccessful, his people deserted him, and he became a person of little consequence, though he might be the head chief of the tribe.

A chief might choose the one who would succeed him. This was generally his oldest son, but it might be another son, or anyone else. If the choice pleased the people, they accepted it, and the one chosen became the chief. If the people were not pleased they might either join another band and leave the new chief with little or no following, or they might choose another chief, in which case the one first chosen was considered as deposed.

---

9. How New Bands and Chiefs Were Made. Bad Bear. (Antoine Herman and Nicholas Janis, interpreters.) (CHS)

When a man was not pleased with his camp or his people, he set up his tipi far away from the camp. He was the chief of his own tipi and all who lived in it. His friends would come to his place and set up their tipis there, and they would acknowledge him as their chief. If there were not many who went to his camp he did not amount to much. But if many joined him, then he became a chief of influence. He would choose two or three persons as his close friends and advisors. These would try to know all that went on in the camp and in the camps of other chiefs, and inform him, and counsel him in the matter.

When the camp grew, the old men would gather together and talk about the affairs of the people. The chief and his advisors were entitled to sit with the old men and discuss what was going on, and decide what should be done.

When the council of headmen wished, they appointed one or more men as *akicita.* The duties of the *akicita* were to see that all the people lived according to the customs of the camp, and to execute any command of the council, and if the chief was sufficiently powerful, to execute his commands also. The *akicita* painted a black streak down across the right cheek, from the eye to the lower edge of the jaw, as a badge of his office. The head man of the *akicita* painted three such stripes across his cheek. The number of *akicita* in a camp depended on the size of the camp. There might be one in a small camp, or there might be many in a large camp.

When there were several *akicita,* the head *akicita's* duties were like those of a herald or public crier. He cried out in a loud voice anything that was wanted to be made known to all.

A chief's authority depended on his wisdom and ability to carry out his wishes. If he was wise and the people found that his advice was good, then they obeyed him. Or if he was strong, and had many friends who would help him, then all obeyed him.

When a camp was small the chief commanded everything, the same as he did his own tipi. When the camp grew larger the councilors advised him in many things. If the chief was pleased to do as the councilors advised, he would do so. But if he wished to do different from that which the councilors advised him to do, then if he had many friends who would obey him, he would compel the people to do as he wished. If he were strong in this way he could make his wishes known in the council, and they would advise as he wished.

If a chief were a brave and a warrior, then his camp would be large. If he were a coward, then his people would leave him.

A chief could tell his people who he wished to succeed him as chief. If the people were pleased with this one he was accepted. If they were not pleased, then they left this camp and went to some other. One of the chief's sons usually succeeded him. Generally this was the oldest son, but if either son showed himself better fitted for the chieftainship than the others, he was accepted as the chief. If a chief had no son then he could choose someone to succeed him and unless the people wished someone else for their chief, he was accepted.

Some in a camp might oppose the chief, in which case the chief might punish such by killing their horses, taking their women, or even killing them. They might retaliate by killing the horses of the chief, by taking his women, or even by killing him. Such conditions did not last long, one side or the other succeeding quickly and the other submitting.

The chief was subject to the *akicita,* except where he was strong, when he directed them in all matters. The chief was entitled to the seat of honor in all meetings, and in every tipi.

When two or more camps came together, if one was formed by people from another, the chief of the camp from which the people went to form a camp took precedence over the chief of the other in all matters where the camps acted together. If the camps did not bear this relation to each other, then the chief of the older camp took the precedence. The chief of the oldest camp, that is, the one from which all directly or indirectly sprang, was acknowledged as the head chief of all. The head chief was entitled to the seat of honor at all gatherings and to speak on all subjects of general interest. But there might be other chiefs in the camp with a much greater following and influence than the head chief.

The councilors were the headmen, usually elderly, and shamans, braves, hunters, and medicine men. These were so by common consent, and anyone could join them and take part in their proceedings, but was not looked upon as one of them until he showed his ability in some accepted way.

Anyone might be invited or elected to become one of headmen or councilors, in which case they sent to such a one a wand ornamented with either bead, quill or pyrographic work. The councilors discussed all matters relative to the people, usually in an informal way, but all matters of much interest they discussed formally, and their decision on matters that were submitted to them for formal discussion was generally accepted as final. The matters that they formally discussed were such as the relations of their camp to others, war parties, hunting parties, winter camps, and the moving of the summer camps. Matters of controversy among their own people might be submitted to the councilors, in which case their decision was accepted, and if not it might be executed by the *akicita.* They had no authority in any matter except what was voluntarily given to them by the persons interested in a case, when their authority became absolute.

One became a warrior by going on the warpath and doing something which showed his bravery. Every able-bodied boy was taught that he should become a warrior, not only in order to defend himself and his people against hostile persons, but to get honor by doing something against an enemy which required cunning and bravery. When one had accomplished such things, he was entitled to certain decorations and privileges, and he could compose songs in honor of himself which the women would sing, and the more renowned he was the more often would the women sing his songs.

A warrior was entitled to a seat among the councilors, and his influence in the council was in proportion to his renown as a warrior. The warriors took the lead in all matters pertaining to war parties and raids. Anyone could get up a war party, but he must do it according to certain forms and customs, and the one getting up a war party was the leader of the party, but subject to certain rules and regulations.

Every boy was also taught that he should become a good hunter, not only in order to provide well for those depending on him, but because of the honor attached to the ability to hunt well.

The Oglalas were at all times hunters and necessarily became skillful in taking game of all kinds which was found on the plains, but they were especially hunters of the buffalo. The buffalo supplied them with a large part of the necessities of life, their skins being used for clothing, robes and tipis, and their flesh formed a large proportion of their food. Therefore the hunting of buffalo was the principal civil occupation of the Oglala men. The hunting of the buffalo was subject to strict laws and customs and a man who became unusually successful in such hunts was entitled to a seat in the council, and his voice was influential in all matters relative to the hunt.

The Oglalas were a nomadic people, roaming over the plains in the summertime, but gathering together in larger camps for the winter. A man might move his tipi as he desired, but for protection they usually moved in camps of a number of tipis. Such movements were in accordance with customs, rules and regulations. One who became acquainted with the country so as to know where wood and water could be found, or who became skillful in finding good camping places, was entitled to a seat in the council, and was influential in all matters relative to movements of the camp.

The Oglalas believed that by due form and ceremony they could get communications from the supernatural powers relative to any matter, and there were men among them who professed to be able to get such communications at their will, in which the supernatural powers would reveal matters for the benefit of the people. These men were the shamans and they were entitled to seats in the council. Their communications from the powers were listened to with respect upon any subject. Anyone having a dream or supernatural communication relative to anything was entitled to relate it in the council.

---

10. *Akicita.* Thomas Tyon. July 4, 1897. (AMNH)

The Lakota word *akicita* means many things. If I say *akicita,* this means that I am hunting for something that I know is there, or I am trying to find the right way to do a thing. If I speak of an Oglala in camp and say he is *akicita* I mean he is an officer appointed by the council of the camp. This kind of an *akicita* is the highest officer of a camp. Everyone in the camp is subordinate to the *akicita.* He is like a policeman and a judge and a jailer and an executioner. All must do as he says, and he can punish anyone, he may even destroy all the property of anyone, or strike anyone, and he may kill anyone. But if he does anything that is not according to the laws of the Oglalas the other *akicitapi* will punish him, and the council may depose him.

If I speak of a band moving, the *akicita* means officers that are appointed by the *wakiconze.* These *akicita* act only when the people are moving from one place to another. They are like the captains under the colonel when the white soldiers are moving. If I speak of a war party the *akicita* are the officers of the party who must see that the party conforms to the customs of war. If I speak of the *akicita* going from a camp to another band, or to a meeting of some kind, then they are the representatives of their band. If I speak of the *akicita* of the Lakota *Wakan,* these *akicitapi* are the representatives of the *Wakan.* The *Wakan akicita* cannot be of mankind, but may be anything else. This kind of *akicita* appears to mankind in a vision. When I speak of the *akicita* of the white people I mean the soldiers. But *akicita* never means a soldier of the Lakotas, except when a Lakota is in the army of the white people as a soldier.

---

11. Original Lakota Government. Thomas Tyon and John Blunt Horn. (CHS)

Before the Sioux Indians knew anything of the white people or their ways, it was their custom to choose four chiefs to be their councilors. These were chosen at times when the camps were large, usually in the winter. The men would gather at meetings and discuss various men for the place. Sometimes they would canvass the different candidates for many days before a choice could be made. At other times all would agree quickly.

Women never took part in these meetings, nor had anything

to say in the matter, except on rare occasions when an old woman would make a speech, which was always listened to with respect. But the women would talk to the men in their families about it and give their opinions as to the candidates.

No regular vote was taken. In the discussion of the candidates, when it appeared that some chief had the majority, he was accepted; or if a majority of the most influential men of the camp pronounced for any one, the others acquiesced, as a rule. But sometimes some chief and his followers would be dissatisfied with the choice and he and his followers would secede from the camp and start a camp of their own. But usually such secessions were only temporary.

The councilors made ordinances for governing the camp and advised in all matters of common interest, and they were the arbiters for those who wished to settle matters of dispute in this way. They decided when a camp should move and where it should move to, and the order of moving; when hunting parties should go and what territory such parties should hunt in; and advised as to the distribution of proceeds of a hunt. They governed in general feasts, ceremonies and games.

There were some rules and customs of long standing and recognized by all that they could not abrogate, but they could sit in judgment on cases of alleged violation of these customs and rules if they were submitted to them and their judgment was accepted.

A councilor, once chosen and accepted, continued to act as such until his death or deposition. A councilor could be deposed for cowardice or for repeated disregard of either the ordinances of the camp or for repeated disregard of the rules and customs recognized by all.

Each chief usually chose two trusted friends as his aides. These were generally braves. They were his advisers and detectives and kept him informed about the affairs of his band and all other matters that he would have an interest in. They were usually his messengers and envoys.

The councilors appointed marshals *(akicita)*. Anyone could be appointed a marshal except a chief. Even women were appointed marshals, but this was very rare. When one was appointed a marshal he was compelled to act as such, or if he refused he was treated by the other marshals as if he had violated an ordinance or rule or custom and his property was destroyed. It was the custom to appoint braves as marshals as a rule.

A marshal might be appointed for a specific time, as for the movement of the camp, a hunting party, a war party, or for the winter camp. Or a marshal might hold his position as such as long as he was not physically disabled. If a marshal disobeyed the rules or ordinances, or failed to do his duty or showed cowardice, the other marshals punished him by striking him or by destroying his property, and if he persisted in his wrongdoing they would even take his life.

The marshals wore as a mark of distinction a streak of black paint beginning on the forehead above the outer end of the right eyebrow and directly down across the outer edge of the right cheekbone to opposite the mouth. (A tradition among the Sioux is that once upon a time the people tried all the wood of every kind of a tree and they found that the wood of the ash was the most durable and strongest. So they made the ash the emblem of the marshals and the marshals made all their wooden utensils and implements of ash.)

The marshals took orders from the councilors and saw that all obeyed the ordinances and recognized rules and customs. They took the initiative at all councils, dances and ceremonies. The oldest marshal was usually the public crier for the camp *(eyanpaha)*. They supervised breaking camp, moving and setting up camp. They supervised a hunting or war party and the distribution of the spoils of the chase or of war.

If in their opinion anyone disobeyed the ordinances, rules, or customs they could summarily punish such a one. Such a one might want to appeal to the councilors or others, but the marshal might grant such appeal or not, just as he saw fit. Such a one might wish to give property in place of being punished, and the marshal might accept such payment or not, as he wished. If a marshal took payment in lieu of punishment it belonged to all the marshals alike. The punishment consisted in destroying the tipi, the robes, the implements, or in killing the dogs or horses, or in driving the person out of the camp, or in aggravated cases of killing the person of the offender. The offender was seldom killed except when he resisted the marshals, which was considered justifiable cause for killing.

Rules of the hunt, recognized by all: All must move together. No one must take advantage to get at the game before the others can profit by it. If anyone stampedes the game he must be punished. The meat gotten during a hunt must be fairly and equally divided among all members of the party. The marshals must direct the approach and attack on the game. Everyone in a hunting party must obey the directions of the marshals.

Rules of a war party, recognized by all: No one shall go on a warpath against friendly Indians. No one shall organize a war party without first getting the consent of the councilors. Anyone may organize a war party if he has the consent of the councilors. If a councilor is a member of a war party he shall direct the movements and acts of the party. If a marshal is a member of a war party he shall act the same as in camp. If anyone kills an enemy he shall have all the property the enemy has about his person. If a war party captures a camp all there is in the camp shall be divided fairly among the party. If the war party captures women they shall belong to the one who first lays hands on them. If the war party captures children they shall be given to any who shall be agreed upon. If a single warrior captures horses or women or children or dogs, they shall belong to him. The first one who strikes a dead enemy with something held in his hand is entitled to the scalp of that enemy. Every member of a war party is obliged to try to prevent the enemy from taking the scalp of any member of the party.

---

12. *Akicita.* Iron Tail. Recorded by Richard Nines.[39] 1911. (AMNH)

Akicita societies: Braves, *Tokala, Wicinska, Sotka yuha, Kanġi yuha,* Badgers. These two last are more used as *akicita* than the rest. That is in moving about, buffalo hunting, etc. The top four are used in the same way, but the last two are more noted as *akicita.*

He says that the *Miwatani* and other societies are under the list of societies like Big Bellies, not *akicita.* "No Flight" is merely a bunch of men in the Brave Society who pledged themselves to stand their ground. Going to war *(zuya)* and being *akicita* are two different things. The *Miwatani* go on war parties but do not do *akicita* service.

The chief or a chief is the one that chooses the *akicita*. He lets the herald know and the herald announces this publicly, that a certain society is called for *akicita* service. Then when they prepare to go the herald calls the *akicita* to assemble and then they do. Then they travel along to keep order in moving or buffalo hunting.

The *akicita* may serve about a year and when there is need for another bunch of *akicita* the chief may call on another society. This selection holds good for buffalo hunts and moving until another set of *akicita* is selected.

The organized *akicita* for the camp have four men they call *akicita itacan* (chief or head *akicita*). These four have a supervision of the *akicita* and they in turn will go to the chief on any question they cannot decide. The four head *akicita* can select any man or men from other societies if they choose, on account of needing more men or if any man looks to them capable of being a good *akicita*.

When the chief calls for the *akicita* through the herald, then the dance is made for the *akicita* and at the dance they call for other members if they want them, maybe two or three. It is a form of bestowing honor on any worthy young man; apparently it is at the dance that the extra two or three men are chosen.

They do not have *akicita* for the sun dance.[40]

In war parties the *blotaunka* * * * are the *akicita;* that is, they have charge of the maneuvers.

An *akicita* cannot quit but can be discharged on account of misconduct: murder, quarrelsomeness, stealing some other man's wife, or any unworthy act that may cause a fight or bloodshed.

He was a *Tokala* when they selected that society for *akicita*. The chief decided to move camp and selected the *akicita*. They had their dance. They selected two or three additional at the dance. Then they moved camp in a few days. (The chief selects the four head *akicita*.) They came to their place of camping and of course the buffalo hunts at different times were in the charge of the *akicita* until the set camp slowly dispersed. Then by natural conditions, as you see, the *akicita* lost their jobs, that is, on account of the camp gradually dispersing as they do in summer.

In the camp they look after quarrels or any lawlessness and adjust it. Any *akicita* adjusts these quarrels, not any particular ones for any special service. If a party goes out after buffalo and while gone some young men decide to join a war party they might come in contact with, the *akicita* try to keep them from going, but if they persist, the *akicita* go home and destroy the property of the men aforesaid. They started out to hunt buffalo and consequently disregarded the rules.

The idea of belonging to a society and the desire to belong is a matter of social distinction. The ambition of an Indian is principally to be high among his fellow men, to be superior to them in killing enemies, stealing horses, owning a fast horse, belonging to societies, having many wives. And on account of social eminence they belonged to societies. Then, too, a great attraction of the societies was the feasts and public gatherings.

Those young men of disreputable character were not desired for members, making a distinction socially. * * *

He says with reference to promotions within the different societies that they frequently select outsiders for officers if they deem it necessary. He did not belong to the *Tokala,* but was looking on when they were installing officers and they (the two men who were leaders) hunted him out of the crowd and presented him with a long knife. Generally it is customary to promote within the society. This office of long knife, or to get the correct meaning, *mi wakan,* sword, was introduced in the society when they later got these from white people. * * *

The boys' societies are independent from the regular societies. It is merely play, I suppose caused by their interest in the real societies.

---

13. Big Bellies Society. Anonymous. Recorded by Richard Nines.[41] 1911–12. (AMNH)

This society is also known (first name) as *Tatanka wapahun,* Buffalo headdress. This name is thus derived on account of one man dreaming of the buffalo and accordingly ten young men were rigged out with buffalo hair caps with horns on and also a strip of buffalo skin hanging down to the ground. The ten young men painted themselves white and wore this in their dances. Eventually they discarded this and were merely a society of the chiefs.

Pahin ptecela means Short hair. He thinks this name was applied on account of the short hair of the buffalo skin they wore.

The chiefs of *Naca* is another name for it.[42]

The lance they had was painted white and [tipped] with a spear. He does not remember the decorations on it. The members also painted their bodies white, that is, their paint that is near white (or light at least), in the dance.

They have the buffalo dance yet—that is their dance. They act like bunting buffalo hooking each other, etc. Originally they had ten lances, one for each man who dressed like a buffalo.

They have four chiefs in the society who each have a pipe and wear a scalp shirt. On being installed in the position they are instructed that they are given the entire tribe in their keeping. If they journey anywhere they must see that no old woman is lagging behind on account of not having a horse. They must not see that an orphan goes unnoticed. They must not fly to pieces when someone comes up and kills their horse. If something serious happens, that is, if someone steals their wife or if a death should happen, then he must take his pipe and smoke it and reason out the affair and not mind it.

Also he should get a large kettle for his wife and if strangers from other tribes come to visit this tribe he should receive them as guests.

They dance in their tents and feast but not out in the open air, going from place to place. An Indian by the name of Paints His Ear White dreamed of buffalo and started this society. In battle the ten men wear this bonnet and each has a spear. So it was a dream cult but eventually drifted into a lodge [society] and changed names.

The Big Belly society is given its name not because the members were usually old men and a general supposition would be that they were fleshy and large, but because of their great interest in the affairs of the society; the affairs of the society were the affairs of the tribe. They gave to the tribe all they had in wisdom and so were termed Big Bellies. If a quarrel arose in camp they went there with the pipe and made peace. If the enemy attacked the camp the Chiefs society's duty was to protect the children and women at the risk of their lives.

If a party comes to visit the camp they come to the center of the camp and one of the Chiefs society often gives a horse to some old woman in the party who apparently does not have anything. Or, if they should hold as captives some Indians of another tribe, and there is a child among them, one of the members of the Chiefs society will present a horse to the child; the same is true of a woman or a young man. He states that they never abused their captives in any way. It seems that the Cheyennes were very cruel to male captives, while women captives were forced to submit to sexual intercourse.[43]

The scalp shirts and official feathers are worn only at great public functions such as the sun dance, a meeting of the whole tribe when they publicly give presents to each other, or a war-party. At the ordinary feasts or gatherings they do not wear the shirt or feather. The hair on the scalp shirt is obtained from scalps of the enemy or they purchase it from other members of the tribe.

Any member of the Chiefs society is not supposed to care or pay attention to his wife if someone steals her. Of course, if she wants to come back she may, but this occurs very seldom.

---

14. Chiefs. Woman Dress. Recorded by Richard Nines.[44] February 16, 1912. (AMNH)

Concerning the scheme of government, the four chiefs of the Chiefs society were the chiefs of the tribe, but one of the four was the head chief. He is vested with the power of decision by the Chiefs society, that is, his word is final. He is the chief of the tribe. Of course, he counsels with the other three.

His father was one of the four chiefs who were at the head of the Chiefs society.

Woman Dress speaks about one head chief, Raking Bear,[45] who had several sons, but none were competent, so they were not chosen in his stead, although they were taken in the Chiefs society as ordinary members. Sometimes a son is chosen in place of his father. It is not hereditary as you will observe.

The Chiefs society was the council. It dealt with all questions concerning the tribe—moving, buffalo hunts, etc. They were selected in the following way. If a chief had a promising son, or if any other young man—middle aged, generally—was bright and smart he was called in and was given a lecture to give up fighting among themselves, to be in short a gentleman and take care of widows, orphans, etc., and was taken in the society.

The principal questions arising seem to be that of camp moving, provisions, etc., and the four chiefs assume authority to do as they please, also in matters of war. You see it is hardly possible to get the whole society to agree on a point and consequently it follows that the four chiefs take the matter in hand themselves.

I seem to gain the impression that generally the White Badge society is a step from which they enter the Chiefs society. The word White Badge is wrong. It is *Ska yuha* or White owner, that is, owner of a white horse. Of course there may be a White Badge society too [*Wicinska,* White-marked], but the society that Woman Dress entered previous to entering the Chiefs society was *Ska yuha.*

He states that Crow Owners [*Kaŋǧi yuha*] and *Iȟoka* [Badger] societies came from the northern tribes.

The meetings seem to be in the form of a feast. Tonight they will have a *Tokala* feast, a few days later they will have the Braves feast, later on the *Miwatani,* etc., and a person can belong to all and take them all in.

15. Chiefs. Red Feather. Recorded by Richard Nines.[46] 1912. (AMNH)

He states that the *Ska yuha* and Chiefs society had their songs in common but that the members of the *Ska yuha* were those who generally participated in war parties while the Chiefs society did not and were the chiefs of the tribe.

There were four or six head chiefs of the tribe who were chosen by the members of the Chiefs society. These four or six head chiefs spent most of their time in the lodge in the center of the camp. They, of course, cared for their horses, got tobacco, etc., but the greater part of their time [was spent] together sleeping and eating and discoursing on the general geography of the country, the most advantageous camping places, wars, buffalo hunts, and their affairs with white men.

The head chiefs (he calls them *wakiconza*) constituted the final authority. The Chiefs society may have a meeting and send a delegate to the head chiefs to see if they will sanction their view on any certain thing, and if they turn it down, that ends it. However, if the chiefs decide on any action and the people seem disinclined to accept, they call on the *akicita* to enforce the order.

The chiefs usually held offiice for about one year. They were the ones who chose the *akicita* and usually picked out some society that was agreeable to all. The *akicita* are also in office about one year. The chiefs then decide on who in the society will be chief *akicita*. The herald for the *akicita* is also chosen. The *akicita* chiefs are called to the chiefs' tent; they come with buffalo robes over their other clothing but carry no weapons. The candidates are then told that they are to be *akicita* chiefs; two black stripes are marked on their faces and war bonnets placed on their heads. They are addressed by one of the chiefs who says, "You are to help us in governing the tribe. You shall see that no prairie fires are started; that no one shall scare away the buffalo; that no one shall go away from camp to camp elsewhere; that no one, when on the buffalo chase, goes ahead and shoots buffalo; and that all offenders should be punished."

Then the chief *akicita* go around the circle and choose their *akicita* from among their society only and they also take the sticks kept by the chief of tribe according to the number of chiefs of tribe [*sic*]. While choosing the *akicita* they go to the tent of the wife of a chief who may be reinstated and notify her by placing one of the counting sticks in the tent (sticking it in the ground). The same day she takes the stick with what food she has prepared for the chief and they, with the *akicita* chiefs, have a feast. If a new chief is elected, he at once proceeds to get a good tobacco pouch and pipe with plenty of tobacco and takes his place in the tent.

Red Feather says that the *wakiconza* or head chiefs were not hereditary. The Chiefs society was somewhat hereditary but if anyone was extraordinarily brave he was admitted to the Chiefs society.

The sticks mentioned are made to suit the man they represent. Thus, if the Indians elected a chief, if he has been a *blotaunka* or a victorious *blotaunka,* the stick is striped. If the chief is a man who has been wounded in battle, the stick is red. If he has actually killed an enemy the stick is black.

---

16. Chiefs. Iron Tail. Recorded by Richard Nines. February 26, 1912. (AMNH)

Iron Tail says that sometimes there are two head chiefs and sometimes four; also that there is no one chief who is higher than another. They had power over the tribe in regard to the moving of camp, buffalo hunts, wars, etc. They chose the four *akicita* chiefs who in turn chose the remaining *akicita.* The head chiefs were chosen by the Chiefs society from among themselves.

The legislature or the council met in what is known as the *ti iyokihe* (the lodge adjoining). This tent is built in the middle of the circle and one of the members of the Chiefs society is given possession of it. He lives adjoining it and the tent is the council tent. The councilors were members of the Chiefs society.

The head chiefs were among the councilors and they dealt with all questions pertaining to the tribe. They had the power to force their decisions upon the tribe, but generally they referred it to the council, after which the orders and decisions were announced. The members of the council were members of the Chiefs society.

---

17. Men's and Women's Roles. No Ears. (AMNH)

When the men had killed many buffalo they returned to the camp singing the buffalo song. Then the women sang the song and hurried to the carcasses and skinned them. They skinned one half and cut the skin in two along the back. Then they turned the carcass over and skinned the other half. All the women went out to skin and cut up the carcasses, but the skin of a carcass belonged to the woman of the man who killed it. This could be known by the arrow. The meat was divided among all in the camp. The one who killed a carcass could claim the liver and the tongue and the brains. The women dried and tanned the skins and they belonged to them. They made tipis and robes of the skins and they made dresses and leggings and moccasins of the skins of the young animals. The women owned the tipis. They cut the poles and trimmed them. They put up and took down the tipis.

The place in the tipi opposite the door is the *catku*. This belongs to the man. He sits and sleeps here. The fireplace is in the center of the lodge. The woman sits at right of it looking from the door, or at the left of the man. If there are two women, then the favorite of the man sits at this place and the other on the opposite side of the fire, or if they are sisters they may sit side by side. The oldest son sits with the father on the *catku* until he is about six years old. One is honored in the tipi by being asked to sit on the *catku*.

---

18. Friendship. Anonymous. Recorded by Richard Nines. September 1912. (AMNH)

Speaking of friendship in the Indian sense this Indian speaks of his having a friend [*kola*] once who would continually ask him for favors and he always freely granted them, for whatever belonged to him was virtually the property of his friend, and that he slept with him in the same blanket when they happened to be out together, but that when he cast away his wife his friend married her and then acted bashful toward him.[47] He disregarded his friendship because he had taken up that woman which he no longer saw fit to keep. It was an insult to him that he should take her up after he had cast her away.

He says that sometimes it has been that a friendship ran in sort of a chain, my friend's friend, and his friend, etc., etc., but very seldom.

The practice of a friend allowing his friend to lay with his wife was not general but it has come under his experience and the privilege was reciprocated, that is, one marries and allows his friend to lay with his wife and then when the other marries he grants the same favor.

I can readily see that friendship was of no trivial consequence and it meant very much to them.[48]

I understand also that property was general in a family and my cousins or brothers could give away my property just as if it was their own or use it at their pleasure. If a young man should marry the eldest girl in a family it does not grant him the privilege of the rest.[49] However, if he is industrious, a good hunter, etc., and the old folks find favor with him, he can marry as many of the girls as he wants.

The practice of feeling the breast of a newly [wed] bride was limited to the younger brothers of the groom's household, which includes his cousins. However, those who do this are supposed to be children yet and a young man or older one never does it.

---

19. Marriage and Divorce. James R. Walker. (CHS)

In former times it appears that the social conditions and customs of the Oglalas were something as follows. A camp *(wicoti)* was a collection of tipis and persons associated by common consent for social purposes. Any member of a camp might withdraw from it at his will and either join another camp, make a camp of his own, or live alone. If he joined another camp he thereby became a member of that camp and subject to its rules and regulations. If he camped alone he was independent of all rules and regulations except such as he chose to make for himself. In his tipi he was lord and his will was law governing all the inmates.

His woman *(tawicu)* was his property, for which he either paid the customary price *(winyancin)*, stole her away *(wiinaȟma)*, or took her by capture *(wayaka)*. He might dispose of her at his will either by throwing her away *(iȟpeya)* or giving her away *(winyanku)*. He might keep her and treat her as a wife (for which there is no word in the Sioux language),[50] in which case she was consulted relative to the affairs of the family, or he might keep her simply to do the work incident to life in a tipi and to satisfy his sexual passions, or more often, to bear him children.

The animal instinct of preserving his female for his own use was strongly developed among the men of this people. If at any time a woman was found guilty of adultery *(wawiciȟaȟapi)* or of disgraceful and unbecoming conduct *(oȟanwahanhan)*,[51] her man *(hignaku)* might throw or give her away, or inflict such punishment on her as he saw fit, such punishment for this usually being to mutilate her in some way so as to show what she had been guilty of.

He might kill her for this transgression, when he would not incur the enmity of her friends, as he would if he should kill her without what, according to the customs of the Sioux, was considered a sufficient cause for doing so. Or he might mutilate her person by cutting off her nose or an ear. But the most usual manner of disfiguring her was to cut off one braid of her hair, leaving the other long for the first offense, and if it was repeated, then to mutilate her person in some way, and if she persisted in her conduct, then to kill her.

But if she was thrown or given away, then the man who did so had no more authority or control over her or her actions.

While the position of the woman in the family was subordinate to the man in almost every particular, she had certain rights which were recognized among the Sioux, as follows. She had the right to leave a man who had taken her, in which case her friends could take her part in the difference, and if they thought that she had not sufficient cause for her action they could restore her to her man, if he so wished it. Then the only way she could escape remaining his woman was to fly and remain in hiding from him, or to become the woman of someone who was the more powerful than her former man, and able to maintain his possession of the woman, by force if need be *(yazapi)*.[52]

Her rights while in the family *(wicowepi)* pertąin to the household *(tiwahe)*. It was her duty to skin the larger game, and the skins became her property, and she was expected to tan them or otherwise fit them for use. If she made them up into articles for the use of the man, they then became the personal property of the man, or if she made them up for the personal use of a grown up son or anyone not a member of the family, they became the personal property of the one for whom they were made. But if she made them up for any other person or use in the family they remained her own, which she had the right to dispose of in any manner she saw fit. But the men skinned the smaller furbearing animals, and while the women tanned and prepared these, they remained the property of the men, and when the buffalo skins became articles of commerce with the white people, the men took charge of the sale of them, and of the proceeds of such sales.

As the tipis were made of skins they were the property of the women, as were the clothing of herself and her children, until they were grown up, and she owned the robes used in the family, except those belonging to the man and grown sons, and all the domestic implements and utensils.

All the children that were the issue of her body belonged to her until they had arrived at puberty in the sense that her right to their possession took precedence over that of her man, their father. She is their mother *(hunkupi)* and they hold her as their ancestor *(hunkake)*. Her right to control her children took precedence over that of her husband until the sons became of an age when they could be instructed in the arts of the chase and of war, when the father took charge of them, but in the tipi they were still subordinate to the mother until they arrived at the age of manhood.

In the management of all ordinary domestic work the woman's authority was supreme. If she left a man her claim to her rights was unimpaired, but if her man disputed it she could maintain it only by the help of her friends whose aid depended on their ability to enforce their wishes because of numbers or influence. But if a woman was thrown away or given away for punishment, she lost all rights to all her property and her children, except babies, but the man could permit her to take such as she wished and he granted.

---

20. Oglala Kin Relationships. Thomas Tyon. 1911–12. Translated by the editor. (CHS)[53]

Among the Lakotas these are all the kin relationships *(wowahecon)* they recognize. In the first place, when a man is married, he addreses his wife as "my wife" *(mitawicu)*. And the woman addresses him as "my husband" *(mihingna)*. Now from this beginning relationships proceed. Now if they give birth to a boy and later they give birth to a girl, then the boy will address her as "my younger sister" *(mitankxila)*. And the girl will address him as "my older brother" *(tiblo)*. When again in time they have another, if he is a boy, then the first born ones, both the female and the male, will address him as "my younger brother" *(misunkala)*. And then for his part the youngest will address the one as "my older brother" *(ciye)* and the other as "my older sister" *(tanke)*. If the siblings *(wicowepi)* are both sisters, then the first born is addressed as "my older sister" (*cunwe*) and the younger child is addressed as "my younger sister" (*mitankala*). And if both siblings are male, then the first born is addressed as "my older brother" *(ciye)* and the younger child is addressed as "my younger brother" *(misunkala)*.

When a man and a woman are married, if the woman has an older brother or a younger sister or an older sister, then her husband will say "my sister-in-law" *(hanka)* to his wife's sister and to the males he will say "my brother-in-law" *(tanhan)* and the latter in return will say "my brother-in-law" *(tanhan)*. And in the case of a woman she will say to the male "my brother-in-law" (*sice* [sic, *xice*]). When two men are related as brothers-in-law, all their children, male or female, those who are female will address the male children of the fathers as "my male cousin" *(xicexi)*. And the males will address them as "my female cousin" *(hankaxi)*. When two men are related as brothers-in-law, the one will address the female child of his brother-in-law as "my niece" *(tonjan)* and the male as "my nephew" *(tonxka)*. On their part, when they address him they will say "my uncle" *(lekxi)*. Also his wife, when she addresses her brothers' children *(hakataku cinca)*, she will address the female as "my niece" *(tojan)* and the male as "my nephew" *(toxka)* and they themselves will both address her as "my aunt" *(tonwin)*.

Now when a man addresses his wife's father he will say "my father-in-law" *(tunkanxi)*. And when he himself addresses the husband of his daughter he will say "my son-in-law" *(mitakox)*. And also when a man addresses the mother of his wife he will say "my mother-in-law" *(oncixi)*. If she herself [addresses him] she will say "my son-in-law" (*mitakox*). Well, I am Thomas Tyon; I call the children of my child "my grandchild" (*takoja*). They call me "my grandfather" (*tunkaxila*).

So far this is right.

Now again, if I marry a woman who already has children then I will call them "my stepchildren" *(tawagan)*. And they will call me "my father" *(ate)*. And then I will call my son's wife's father "*omawaheton*." And he himself will call me "*omahetun*."

And I will call my uncle's *(lekxi)* male children "my male cousins" *(tanhanxi)*. And the females I will call "my female cousins" *(hankaxi)*. And they themselves, the males, will call me "my male cousin" *(tanhanxi)*. And the females will call me "my male cousin" *(xicexi)*.

Well, if I marry two women they will call each other "*teyaku*." But two sisters do not have that relationship; they address each other as "*miteyaku*."

Well now, I call my wife's father "my father-in-law" *(tunkan)*. And I call my wife's mother "my mother-in-law" *(oncixi)*. And they both call me "my son-in-law" *(takox)*. And my wife's father and mother together call [my father and mother] "*omahetun*." I call all my wife's sisters *(wicowepi)* "my sister-in-law" *(hanka)*. And they call me "my brother-in-law" *(xice)*. And all my wife's brothers *(hakataku)* I call "my brother-in-law" *(tanhan)*. And they themselves call me "my brother-in-law" *(tanhan)*.

Now when I address my female child I will call her "my daughter" *(cunkxi)*. And the males I will call "my son" *(cinkxi)*. And when my wife addresses her daughter she says "my daughter" *(cunkxi)*. And when she addresses the male child she will say "my son" *(cinkxi)*.

Now when someone else asks about my female child he will say this. He will say, "Who is his daughter?" *(cunwintku)*. And of he who is my male child he will say, "Who is his son?" *(cinhintku)*. And if he is not my child they say, "Who is his stepchild?" *(tanku)*. And also they say, "Who is his stepchild?" *(tawaganku)*.

Well, this much I know.

---

21. Oglala Kinship Terms *(wowahecon)*.[54] James R. Walker. 1913.

[*Relatives in generations older than ego*]

Hunkake	Ancestor
Tunkan	Grandfather (may be used by anyone)
Tunkanśi	Maternal grandfather (used in this sense only by grandchildren when addressing or speaking of their mother's father); Father-in-Law (when used by any other than the grandchildren)
Tunkanśila	Paternal grandfather (used in this sense only by grandchildren when addressing or speaking of their father's father); A term of respect used in addressing any very old man *(wicaȟca)*; a title of respect given to a high official, such as the President of the United States; it is also a title of address by the Oglala to their superior god *Wi*, the Sun.
Kun	Paternal grandmother (may be used by anyone)

Kunśi	Paternal grandmother (used only by grandchildren in addressing or speaking of their father's mother)
Onci	Maternal grandmother (may be used by anyone)
Onciśi	Maternal grandmother (used in this sense only by grandchildren when addressing or speaking of their mother's mother); Mother-in-law (when used by any other than the grandchildren); A term of respect used when addressing any very old woman *(winoȟca)*.
Atku	Father
Ate	Papa (used only by children when addressing their father or his brother)
Hun	Mother
Ina	Mama (used only by children when addressing their mother or her sister)
Lekśi	Uncle (the brother of the mother)
Tonwin	Aunt (the sister of the father)

[*Relatives in ego's own generation*]

Ciye	Eldest brother of a male
Tiblo	Eldest brother of a female
Sunka	Younger brother of a male or female
Cunwe	Eldest sister of a female
Tanke	Eldest sister of a male
Tanka	Younger sister of a female
Tankaśi	Younger sister of a male
Tahanśi	Male cousin of a male
Hankaśi	Female cousin of a male
Śiçeśi	Male cousin of a female
Śicepanśi	Female cousin of a female

Tahan	Brother-in-law of a male
Hanka	Sister-in-law of a male
Śiçe	Brother-in-law of a female
Śicepan	Sister-in-law of a female
Omaheton	The term used only by the parents of a married daughter when addressing her husband's parents
Omawaheton	The term used only by the parents of a married son when addressing his wife's parents.
Tawin	Wife of husband
Hingna	Husband of one wife, only wife
Teyak[55]	Plural wife of husband, not sister of other wife
Miteyak	Plural wife, if sister of other wife
Winu[56]	Wife captured from another people, or wife loaned temporarily
Tawicu	Wife of any kind, when connubial relation has been consummated.
Bluze	Husband of more than one wife

[*Relatives in generations younger than ego*]

Cin	Son
Cun	Daughter
Cinhan	Son, a definite person
Cunwin	Daughter, a definite person
Cinkśi	Son, so addressed by the father and his brothers, and by the mother and her sisters
Cunkśi	Daughter, so addressed by the father and his brothers, and by the mother and her sisters

Other terms for sons and daughters:[57]

Sons	Daughters	
Caske	*Witokape*	First born
Hepan	*Hapan*	Second born

Hepi	*Hepistanna*	Third born
Catan	*Wanska*	Fourth born
Hake	*Wihake*	Fifth born
Hakata	*Hakata*	Last born
Cekpa	*Cekpa*	One of twins
Tawaġan		Step-child
Takoś		Child-in-law
Tonśka		Nephew of a male
Tonźan		Niece of a male
Tośka		Nephew of a female
Tożan		Niece of a female
Takoża		Grandchild
Wicatakoża		Grandson
Winotakoża		Granddaughter
Hunka		Relative adopted with ceremony
Hunkawanźi		Brother in a fraternal manner
Winoħtin		Sister in a fraternal manner

[*Affixes used with kin terms*]

The suffixes *-ci, -kśi,* or *-śi* indicate that connubial relation should not be had with the one to whom the relationship is expressed.

The suffixes *-cu, -ku,* or *-tku* are the equivalent of the English preposition "of," as, for instance, *hunku* (mother-of). Sometimes this is duplicated, as in *atkuku,* from *atku* (father-of), the duplicated form being used in speaking of the father of a definite person.

The suffix *-la* gives to a term an endearing significance, and is equivalent to the English suffixes *-ie* or *-y* in such words as "auntie" and "sonny." This suffix may be added to most of the terms of relationship. It is habitually used with some of the terms, such as *hokśila* (boy), *tunkaśila* (grandfather), and many others.

The suffix *-ya* with terms of relationship expresses the concept of "considered" or "considered as."

The relationship to the first person is expressed by the possessive pronoun *mi* preceding the term, except in those cases where the term expresses this relationship. The relationship to the second person is expressed by the possessive pronoun *ni* (your) preceding the term. The relationship to the third person is expressed by the suffixes *-cu*, *-ku*, or *-tku*, the term being preceded by the name of the one to whom the relation is held.

The possessive pronoun *ta* (his or her) is habitually used with some of the terms of relationship, but does not alter the manner of expressing the relationship to the persons; for instance, *ta-wicu* (his-woman, wife) would thus be expressed in her relationship to persons:

mi-ta-wicu	my wife
ni-ta-wicu	your wife
ta-wicu-ku	his wife.

My father's brothers' children and my mother's sisters' children speak to and of my father and mother as if these were their own parents, while my father and mother speak to and of such children as if they were their own. The terms of relationship of the father's and mother's children, and of the father's brothers' children, and of the mother's sisters' children are the same as if they were all children of the same family.

To make the distinction between the actual father and mother and their children, and the father's brothers and mother's sisters and their children, possessive *ki* (own) is used, usually with a pronoun following the term of relationship, for instance: *tiblo* (her elder brother) may be the son of her father or of her father's brother, or of her mother's sister. *Tiblo wicaki* (her elder brother their own) would be the son of her [biological] father. The same conditions apply to step-relatives.

---

22. Oglala Social Customs.[58] James R. Walker. (CHS)

When the Oglala Sioux Indians were in their aboriginal state the family was the unit of their social organization and according to their customs it was established in this manner. A man secured a wife by either wooing her, abducting her, or, if she were an alien, capturing her.

If by purchase or abduction, as a preliminary, he courted the woman. If his attentions were acceptable to her and the one who had the disposition of her, the man donned his most fetching attire, painted his face with many gaudy colors, and wearing a courting robe, strode back and forth before the door of the tipi where the woman dwelt. She peeped coyly through the door at him, then came forth and stood before the door. He passed her, back and forth, feigning not to see her, but at each pass coming nearer to her until he came within reach of her, when he grabbed her. She feigned to struggle to free herself but the struggle was not frantic and usually was brief. Then they stood side by side before this tipi and he wrapped his robe so that it would enfold them together, thus facing the world, while he told her a story that is very, very old. This was equivalent to a public announcement of the engagement of this couple, and a warning that other men should not court this woman. As an acknowledgement of it, the people came from their tipis, but it was exceedingly bad form of anyone to gaze directly at the couple or speak to them while standing thus together.

If the guardians looked with favor on the wooing of a suitor they would, when he was parading before them, invite him to sit with them, and assign him a seat beside the woman wooed. According to the customs, if a woman looked in the face of a man and smiled, this signified that she was willing to accept his advances, or if she turned her back toward a man, this signified that she would repulse him. So, when a wooer was thus seated beside the wooed, she thus signified her inclination, and if it was very favorable to him, she brought water and gave him of it to drink and invited him to come wooing again. When he again came wooing, if she still favored his suit, she prepared food and gave him of it to eat. If she desired to become his wife she made and decorated a pair of moccasins and gave them to him. If he immediately in her presence put the moccasins on his feet, they two were considered as betrothed to each other.

After this the eldest nearest kin of the man visited the guardians of the woman and together they determined the price that should be paid for the woman. The standard price was six buffalo skins or their equivalent in value. But if the woman was very industrious and hospitable this price might be increased indefinitely.[59] These negotiations were of a festal character and might be prolonged to several sittings. Usually there was a feast at each such sitting and friends of the betrothed couple were invited guests at such feasts.

In the meantime, the young man courted the young woman. Usually at evening, near her tipi, he would play love music on the Oglala flute, and she would slyly go to him, while her female friends made little fires of the twigs of the cottonwood tree, for such fires exorcised the mythic Two Faced Woman, the fomenter of contention and strife.[60]

The conventional dowery of the fiancée was a tipi, a pair of robes, a bone awl and sinew thread, a cooking utensil, an ax, and a knife. This dowery was not essential to a wedding but was essential before a wedded pair would be considered as a family. The trousseau was according to the means of the woman and the generosity of her friends, the most desirable being a dress of soft tanned deer or antelope skin, the bodice ornamented with elk tusks [canines]; leggings from below the knee to around the ankle, made of soft tanned skins and ornamented with porcupine quills and feathers applied in conventional designs; and moccasins of soft tanned skins for uppers and rawhide soles, ornamented either with porcupine quills sewed in designs on the uppers, or with the uppers painted with bright designs. When so attired her hair should be parted in the middle, combed smooth with a comb made of the tail of a porcupine, oiled with marrow fat and plaited in two braids of three strands each, the braids to hang down her back until she was married, when they should hang over each shoulder and down across her chest. The wearing of the hair in these manners indicated their connubial state. If at puberty the woman had had the public ceremony [*Tatanka lowanpi,* Buffalo ceremony] performed for her benefit, she was entitled to (and should have) a red stripe painted from her forehead back across her head at the parting of the hair, and if the ceremony of adoption [*Hunka*] had been performed for her, she should have a red stripe painted across her forehead, from temple to temple.[61] If she had participated in some sacred ceremony she was entitled to have her hands painted red. If in deep or recent mourning, she was permitted to paint her face black. It was considered indecorous for a woman to paint on herself with any other colors or any kind of a design other than those mentioned.

At an appointed time the suitor carried the price of the woman agreed upon to the tipi where his fiancée dwelt and placed them before her guardian. He was usually accompanied by his kin and friends, both male and female, the females carrying provisions for a feast. It was expected that the fiancée and her friends would also have prepared food for a feast. When the price was thus delivered, the woman took the man by his right hand and led him through the door of her tipi and assigned to him a seat at the place of honor in the tipi, which was at the rear, opposite the door. When he was seated there, she should put a pair of moccasins on his feet, and then sit at the woman's place in the tipi, which was at the right side of the fireplace at the center of the tipi. When she had done this, that tipi was said to be husbanded, and the two were man and wife. They were considered as a family, and her tipi was counted according to the Oglala manner of census.

If the woman had no tipi of her own, she would lead her man through the door of the tipi where she dwelt and assign him a seat at one side of the tipi, place a pair of moccasins on his feet, and then sit beside him. In such cases they two were considered as man and wife but were not counted as a family. If so, the man was called a buried man[62] and he was obligated to dwell with his wife and not speak to any of her female blood relatives until they should dwell in a tipi of her own. If a child was born to them while dwelling in this tipi it was considered as the child of the one in whose tipi it was born. In such cases it was expected that both man and woman would erect a tipi of their own as soon as they were able to do so. But the tipi was always the property of the woman, unless she forfeited her rights as a wife.

When a man thus married a woman who had younger unmarried sisters, he was thereby endowed with authority to control their connubial affairs, and with the privilege of taking them as his plural wives, or he may give or withhold his consent to their marrying another man.

A man was permitted to have as many wives as he chose but he and all his wives were counted as only one family, though they might occupy a tipi for each wife, but only one tipi was counted for that family. In case there were plural wives, the first wife had the precedence of the others. In case the wives were sisters, the first wife was addressed by a term designating her as the superior sister wife, and the other sisters by terms that designated them as subordinate sister wives.

If a man desired a woman for his wife and her guardians objected to his suit, he could abduct her. Marriage by abduction most often occurred when a married man had claim to younger sisters of his wife and refused permission for another to take them for wives. The man who desired such a woman for his wife usually abducted her and carried her to the tipi where he dwelt, and then stood ready to defy any attempt to take her from him. Such attempts were seldom made for it was considered that when a woman was so abducted she acquiesced in the abduction. A woman so abducted was termed a buried woman until she had a tipi of her own and she was obligated to address no male blood relative of her man while she was a buried woman. Such man and woman were not considered a family, but as members of the family in whose tipi they dwelt. If the woman was satisfied, she made a pair of moccasins and put them on the feet of her man and led him through the door of the tipi and placed him on the seat of honor. It was expected that such persons would erect their own tipi as soon as they could do so, and then their tipi would be counted as one, and themselves as a family.

It will be perceived that a most important part of the trousseau of a Sioux woman was material for erecting a tipi. For this reason the one having control of the woman was expected to provide buffalo skins sufficient for a covering, and the mothers early taught their daughters the art of tanning. The prevailing ambition of the daughters was to possess sufficient tanned buffalo skins to cover a tipi so that they would not be buried women.

When a man secured a wife by abduction, he was empowered with no authority relative to her sisters. Usually such a wedding was accompanied by a feast given by the kindred of the man and it was good form to invite the guardians of the woman to the feast. If they accepted the invitation this indicated that they acquiesced to the affair.

It was esteemed an honor to have a wife who was captured from an alien people, especially if the people were hereditary enemies. A captured woman became the property of the one capturing her and he could dispose of her as he saw fit. It was commendable to take her as a wife, for one of the cardinal virtues of the Sioux was to have as many offspring as possible, and offspring by a captured woman had the same status as full blooded Sioux. No wedding ceremony of any kind was observed when taking a captured woman as a wife. After an indefinite time her status became the same as that of wedded Sioux women, the time usually gauged by the proficiency with which the woman spoke the Sioux language, and was defined by the Sioux women.

It was considered a mark of great esteem for one who had captured a woman to give her to another. Thus a captured woman might have been passed from the possession of one to another for a number of times, until one took her for his wife. If a captured woman bore a child to a man as her husband, she ceased to be property and her status became the same as that of an Oglala woman.

A man was permitted to have as many wives as he chose to take. It was expected that there should be no spinsters among the Sioux women. By far the larger number of families were monogamous because the supply of marriageable women was not sufficient to give plural wives to all the men. And further, some of the men thought that their troubles more than their pleasures would be increased by attempting to keep in harmony with more than one wife.

Polyandry was practiced to some extent among the Sioux but a woman could not take another husband without the consent of her man. But few were so obliging as to give such consent. In nearly every instance of plural husbands there was no offspring by the first husband, yet the couple were congenial and wished to live as man and wife. The second husband was taken that there might be children and such children were considered the children of the original pair. The plural husband was considered a buried man and treated as such.

A man could divorce his wife but if so he must be prepared to give to her kindred sufficient cause or to pay her nearest of kin such fine as her kindred deemed just. A man was permitted to dispose of his wife for intolerable contention, for laziness, for inhospitality, or for infidelity. He might dispose of her by sale or gift or abandonment, and if he so disposed of her, he could not reclaim her in any manner.

The customs permitted a man to divorce his wife by simply driving her from her tipi and publicly declaring that he had put her from him. She could appeal to the *akicita* or marshals of the camp, and if so, they adjudged the matter and their decision was final. If they decided that the man had just cause for divorcing his wife, she lost her claim to her tipi, its contents, and her children. If they decided that the cause was not sufficient, they were authorized to impose ammends upon the man, of any kind and to any extent that they deemed equitable.

A wife could banish a husband from her tipi by force or with the aid of her kindred, publicly declaring that she had cast him from her. From such divorce there was no appeal except to negotiation by friends, for she was permitted to annul such divorce by the simple practice of receiving the man in her tipi and offering him food. If such banishment appeared permanent, she was considered as widowed, and her tipi, unhusbanded, was not counted in the Oglala census. She was permitted to marry again, when all her children were considered the children of her second or last husband.

If a man divorced a woman because of infidelity, the customs permitted him to disfigure her by cutting off the tip of her nose, or one ear. But this was done only in extreme cases. If a woman divorced a man for such cause she was permitted to beat him with a club or wound him sufficiently to cause his blood to flow, but not so as to disfigure him. He was not permitted to resist such process on her part, but he could fly from her. To do so made him the butt of ridicule and contemptible to the women.

The property of a family all belonged to the woman except the personal apparel, implements, and insignia of the man, and the horses, which were common property of the family. The offspring belonged to the woman while they dwelt in the tipi with her. If a man disposed of his wife either by sale, gift, or abandonment, she retained all her property, and he took only that which she consented for him to take.

A woman was not permitted to dispose of her husband in any manner, but she could abandon him. If so, she forfeited all her property rights and it all became the property of the husband, including the children. She was permitted to return to him with his consent at any time, but such returning did not invest her with any property rights. A woman who abandoned her husband was called a lone woman and was not considered a member of any family.[63] She was free to wed anyone who chose to wed her.

In family affairs the mother's authority was greater than that of the father. The tipi and family belongings were considered her property. The relationship outside the immediate family was on the side of the father so that the family belonged to the band of which the father was a member.

The woman governed her children during their childhood and her daughters until they were wedded. When the voice of a boy began changing he passed from the authority of his mother to that of his father, or if the father could not act, to that of the nearest kin of the male relatives. This authority continued until the boy became a man and the head of a family.

An important distinction in a family was the birthright, which was hereditary, descending to the first born son of the male offspring of one holding such right, or in default of such a son, it was conferred by the oldest one holding the right on any male member of his blood relatives he chose. This right gave precedence of and parental authority over all blood relatives of this generation, or generations younger than that of the holder. For sufficient cause, anyone could be deprived of the birthright by either his blood relatives or the marshals of the camp. In such case the blood relatives chose another to exercise the functions pertaining to the birthright. The title of one holding a birthright was "My elder."

The Oglala terms designating kinship are very many and very complex and very exact. They give the order of birth and sex relative to parents, to brothers, and to sisters. Fathers speak *to* their children as sons and daughters, but *of* their children in terms that give the order of their birth and sex. Brothers address each other in terms that show order of birth, and sisters all alike, except when the first born in the family is a girl, when she has a distinctive title. Sisters address each other in the same manner. Children address the father's brothers and mother's sisters as parents, and the father's sisters and mother's brothers as aunts and uncles. Thus the children of the father's brothers and the mother's sisters are addressed as brothers and sisters while those of the aunts and uncles are cousins, but in different degrees. By the wedding of a man and a woman their parents are made relatives. The grandparents of the father's side have different titles to those on the mother's side. Terms of relationship do not extend beyond grandparents and grandchildren.[64] The relationship beyond these is reckoned by membership in the band.

An indefinite number of families who habitually placed their tipis near each other formed a band. Such bands were named and the name might be that of a prominent member of the band. If so, it was called his band. Or the name chosen might be that of some other thing, usually an animal. For instance, if the name so chosen was that of the badger, the band would be called the Badgers. The only officials of a band were the elders. These were the old men of good repute. Together they considered matters of common interest to the band, but they had no authority other than that of recommending. The officials of any camp could exercise their authority in such a band.

When there were a sufficient number of men in a band to fill the required offices they could organize a camp. The officials required in a camp were the council, composed of an indefinite number; a chief; an indefinite number of *akicitapi;* and a *wakiconza.* The council was the men of good repute who chose to take part in the proceedings, and who were given a hearing by the other councilors. It considered all matters of common interest to the camp. Its official acts were done by acclamation, the majority ruling, and from its edicts there was no appeal.

The chief was one who assumed that office at the beginning of the community or one who was chosen as chief by the majority of the camp. The tenure of this office was perpetual and hereditary. But a chief could be deposed by the majority of the camp. When a chief was deposed or died, the office descended to one of his offspring, either a male, or, unusually, a female, unless none of his offspring was esteemed of sufficient ability for the office. In such case a chief was chosen by the majority of the members of the camp, or some member of the camp usurped the place. The chief was entitled to precedence in all matters of common interest to the camp and his prestige was increased if he was the leader in matters of most importance. He was entitled to sit at the place of honor in the executive lodge and to preside at all assemblages to consider the common welfare of the camp. He was the representative of and spokesman for the camp.

When organizing a camp, the first act of the council was to erect a council tipi. This was similar to the tipis for habitation but larger. It was the place for public assemblages and especially for meetings of the council.The next act was to light a council fire by their designation.

The *akicitapi* of a camp were those of the civil organization. Their number was indefinite, depending on the number of people belonging to the camp. They were chosen by the council, the qualifications necessary being a knowledge of the traditions of the Sioux and a good reputation. One was chosen because he had a strong voice and he was nominated the herald. When chosen, a man was not permitted to refuse to serve, except when he could show a physical disability. The *akicitapi* were inducted into office with a ceremony conducted by a holy man. During the ceremony he instructed them relative to the duties of the office, which were to enforce compliance with the traditions, customs, and usages of the Sioux people and ordinances enacted by the council; to hear and adjudge all controversies relative to persons or property, either singly or in conjunction as they might choose; to enforce compliance with decisions of the *wakiconza*; to inflict punishment adequate to offenses, even to that of death; and to go as representatives of the camp in formal transactions with other camps. And they were admonished that if an *akicita* inflicted unmerited punishment he would be punished in kind of twice the severity of that which he had wantonly inflicted, and be deposed from office by his fellow *akicitapi*.

The duties of the herald, in addition of other *akicitapi,* were to proclaim aloud through the camp all matters of interest to the people and to be present at each formal meeting of the council and kindle the council fire.

When the ceremony of induction was complete the holy man painted on the face of each *akicita* the badge of his office. This was a black stripe on the right cheek from the outer corner of the eye to the lower edge of the lower jaw. The badge of the herald was two such stripes parallel on his right cheek. It was expected that the *akicitapi* would display this badge at all times. The term of the office of the *akicitapi* was indefinite. They could resign for sufficient reasons, or they might be deposed for sufficient offense, or they could hold the office as long as they discharged their duties in a satisfactory manner. The only appeal from the judgment of the *akicitapi* was to the council which could reverse their judgment or make it null. A long service as an *akicita* made one eligible to admission to the order of elders.

No English word expresses a correct concept of the office of the *wakiconza*. The *wakiconza* was such by common consent of the people. Usually he was an elder of reputed rectitude of life according to the Sioux standard of ethics. His duties were dual. When a camp was located he was the arbitrator of all disputed points relative to the traditions of the people, except those relative to the ceremonial; he was the umpire of all games or friendly contests; and he was the custodian of all wagers staked in gambling. When the camp moved, from the time when the tipis were taken down until they were again set up, the usual organization was in abeyance and the *wakiconza* was the supreme authority. Then he appointed his *akicitapi,* usually the *akicitapi* of the located camp, but he could appoint anyone he might choose. At such times his duties were to designate the route to be taken and the length of each day's journey; to divide each day's journey into four equal portions; to go at the head of the moving column and when he came to the points of the division of the journey to sit, fill and light his pipe, and smoke it to the Great Spirit, the patron god of moving. At the place where he sat and smoked for the fourth time the people encamped, either for a temporary pause or permanently, as the *wakiconza* commanded. When a permanent camp was erected the authority of the *wakiconza* was in abeyance and the ordinary organization of the camp was revived.

The duties of the *akicitapi* of a moving camp were to compel compliance with the customs governing such movements, such as that the column should move no faster than the slowest could travel, and all should remain sufficiently near each other so that help could be given to any who needed it. In time of war the *wakiconza* appointed scouts whose duty was to travel far ahead of and on either side of the moving column and if signs of an enemy near were discovered, to signal by smoke. These customs governed whether the distance moved was very short or long enough to require many days. The tenure of the office of *wakiconza* was until the incumbent resigned, was deposed, or died. He could resign at his pleasure. He could be deposed by the *akicitapi* for malfeasance of office. When the office was vacated the people immediately acclaimed one to fill it.

Two or more camps could associate, and usually a large number of camps associated to form the winter camp. When thus associated the organization of the camp first organized prevailed and the organization of all other associated camps was in abeyance during the association except that the council of each camp was recognized in the council of the associated camps.

Among the members of a camp were other important distinctions that were not relative to its organization. These were, in the order of the precedence they gave:

First, the shamans, who were men instructed in the lore of the Oglalas, qualified by proper ceremony and deemed to have imparted to them supernatural powers that made them mediums between the gods and mankind. When a shaman spoke authoritatively, his words were accepted as expressing the will of the gods, which none could gainsay. The authority of a shaman thus expressed was supreme, and in this manner they could suspend any custom or usage of the Oglalas, commend or condemn any person, command or prohibit any thing or act. But if it was found that he falsely spoke as the will of the gods, the marshals either disauthorized and banished him, or executed the death penalty upon him.

Second, the headman, who, because of his ability, was expected to lead in all matters of common interest to the camp. He might be either an official or not an official of the organization.

Third, the warrior, who was a man renowned for a deed of valor done in war and was entitled to wear an insignia indicating such deed. He might be or not be an official of the organization. There might be an indefinite number of warriors in a camp and their precedence relative to each other was shown by the insignia they wore.

Fourth, the hunter, who was one skilled in pursuing and taking big game. He might be or not be an official of the organization. Usually there was but one hunter in a camp, but there might be an indefinite number, and if so their status was equal.

Fifth, the story teller, who was one proficient in telling anecdotes, narratives, legends, and myths. It was expected that he would entertain the people with his stories and that he would be recompensed by donations. A story teller might be any member of a camp. Usually there were two or three in each camp. The shamans were most favored as story tellers, for they told for both entertainment and instruction.

Sixth, the medicine man, who was estimated according to his reputed ability to heal the sick or wounded. Any member of a camp could profess to be a medicine man and use remedies for the benefit of anyone who requested his services. It was expected that a shaman would be also a medicine man. Among the Oglalas there were several cults of medicine men. The Buffalo cult was the most reputable.

Seventh, wizards and witches, who were very old men or women that because of their age were deemed to have acquired occult powers which they could exercise to reward favors or vent their spleen.

For the Sioux the number four was a mystic number and when possible was applied to almost everything pertaining to their conduct and to all of their ceremonial and mythology. They were a very ceremonious people and quite all their repetitious action was in accord with specific rites.

There were among them a number of societies for men, some of which were purely militant and functioned only in time of war. The others were fraternal, most progressive, in that to be eligible for membership required membership in another society, and membership made eligible to still another society.[65] Thus one could be a member of many societies at the same time. The ultimate of these societies was membership in the order of the elders, which was called Big Eaters or Silent Eaters, because at feasts they ate together in silence or spoke only aphorisms. Each society had officers, variously designated, and conformed to certain rites. But no society did secret work or had a grip or sign or password. Each society had a song and dance peculiar to it.

There was an order, two societies, and a class for women. The order was composed of those women who had lost a father, brother, husband, or cousin in war. They were the only women who were permitted to wear on their heads the war eagle quills.

Each was permitted to wear only the quills that the lost one was entitled to wear. This order had precedence of all other women. The societies were of loyal, industrious, and hospitable women, and of virgins.[66] They were for distinction and sociability. Their badge was a plume from the eagle worn upright at the back of the head. When a girl arrived at puberty a certain ceremony [Buffalo ceremony] could be performed for her benefit. This ceremony was the equivalent of our parties for a debutante. It announced that the girl had become a woman and was eligible to wedlock, and it conferred upon her the right to wear a red stripe painted across her head at the parting of the hair. All who were entitled to wear this stripe formed a class.

When the voice of a boy changed, or soon thereafter, he could seek a vision according to the Sioux custom. If he received a vision a holy man would interpret it and devise and paint a design on the chest of the boy, who was then considered a man. This design was his totem and he was entitled to use it as his sign manual, and none other was permitted to use it. All who were entitled to wear or use such a design formed a class of men.

Any two individuals could, by a specific ceremony [*Hunka*], assume the relation of parent and child, or brothers, sisters, or brother and sister. This ceremony entitled those for whom it was performed to wear a red stripe painted horizontally across the forehead. All who were entitled to wear this stripe formed a class and considered each other as kindred.

The holy men formed a class and had songs and a dance peculiar to them.

The rounds of their lives were divided into two periods, the summer and the winter periods. During the warmer period they scattered and wandered afar in search of sustenance or adventure, but when the leaves began to turn yellow they traveled toward an appointed place where they came together and encamped for the winter. Here they indulged their social instincts to their fullest in gossiping, feasting, dancing, gaming, and listening to stories.

Their traditions held the female inferior to the male, and that she should serve him. For this reason the women did the drudgery pertaining to the camp, and they were more tenacious for this custom than were the men. If a man was found doing what was considered women's work, the women would ridicule him and attempt to dress him in women's clothing. The women brought wood and water and did the cooking and serving the food. The industrious assembled in groups to sew skin garments and supplies, using bone awls for needles and dried sinews for thread, gossiping as they wrought, as sewing circles do.

Others gathered to play games with a kind of dice made of plum stones; such usually gambled, the stakes being articles of use or ornament.[67]

The old men came together for no special purpose, smoked and talked in a casual manner. The younger men played games of skill somewhat like lacrosse and shinney, or of chance, played with dice made of the astragulus bones of the antelope or deer, or the more enticing and popular game of moccasins, which was a contest of wits and skill. In the two latter games the players gambled as desperately as their means would permit. The children romped and played with whip tops, horn-tipped javelins, bows and arrows, and a kind of miniature bowling, with two stone balls about the size of walnuts and two cylindrical blocks about two inches in diameter and two inches in length.

But the principle diversions in the communal camp for the winter were the feasts, the dances, and the stories.

Some feasts were given by all the members of a camp, the women preparing and serving the food and vying with each other to produce the most acceptable supply. At such feasts, if special honor is to be shown to one, he is served first, and with the choicest of the food. Then the chief and officials of the camp are served, and next after them the indigent and helpless. After these were supplied others were served as was most convenient. The food most highly prized was the flesh of the dog, and courtesy demanded that each adult feasting should have some of this, even if the supply was such that only a morsel could be given to each. Buffalo tongues and the flesh from the hump of the buffalo were esteemed choice delicacies, but there was no obligation to serve them to all the participants in the feast. If a shaman partook of the feast he was entitled to as much of the buffalo tongue and flesh of the hump as he desired.

Such feasts were jovial occasions and it was considered very bad form—in fact, a cause for action by the *akicita*—for one to show anger, petulance, or temper at such times. Feasts were given by members of the camp to celebrate any matter they considered of sufficient importance—ordinarily to celebrate some ceremony or cause for rejoicing, such as the *Hunka* ceremony wherein someone adopted another as a foster relative, or when one has recovered from serious illness.The guests to such feasts came by invitation, which was given by delivering an ornamented wand, usually a withe of the plum tree. The guests brought these wands of invitation to the feast and the one who delivered them was expected to redeem them with a present to each so invited. If one failed to redeem his wand of invitation, this was considered an equivalent to a declaration of social bankruptcy, and such a one was considered unworthy to receive a wand of invitation to a feast.

Generosity was, next to bravery, considered the highest virtue, so no visitor was permitted to go from a tipi hungry.[68] Courtesy demanded that when a visitor entered a tipi he should be invited to partake of food. If one refused such an invitation he was considered unfriendly, or possibly an enemy. Refusal to invite a visitor to partake of food, unless there was a lack of food to offer, was considered equivalent to a declaration of enmity. If one had sufficient supplies and failed to give feasts, such a one was ostracized until he redeemed his reputation by some notable deed or by giving a generous feast to many guests.

There were special ceremonial feasts which could be given by anyone, but at which a shaman must preside and conduct the ceremony. Such were the dog feast, given by one who was about to undertake some important matter, such as organizing a war party, and the buffalo tongue feast, given by a successful hunting party or by one who was eminently successful in some undertaking. These were not jovial, but were solemn occasions.

The dances of the Oglalas were either selective or social. The selective dances were either ceremonial or pertaining to certain social qualifications. The selective ceremonial dances were participated in only by those taking part in the ceremony and were conducted by the shamans. These were solemn occasions. There were many societies among the Oglalas and each society had a dance peculiar to itself. Only members of such society were permitted to participate in its dance. Such dances were jovial occasions and anyone was permitted to take part in the enjoyments other than actual dancing. The social dances were jovial occasions when all were permitted to take part in the festivities, though in some, such as the war dance and the scalp dance, only warriors were permitted to dance the step peculiar to such dances, though others were permitted to dance in unison with a different step.

Often social dances were adjunct to feasts, and when such, anyone who desired to do so was permitted to dance, but etiquette demanded that the women choose their partners for such dancing. It was good form to begin a social dance soon after noon and often they continued all night.

The most complicated dance practiced by the Oglalas was the Sun Dance that partook of the nature of both ceremonial and social. It was social because not only all members of the camp took part in it, but it was expected that all friendly camps would be invited to participate. It was ceremonial because it was conducted by a shaman according to certain rites and for the purpose of making certain persons eligible for places of distinction, or to requite a vow made under stress. It required much costly preparation and eight days for its full accomplishment. It could be done only at midsummer when vegetation was at a certain stage of growth, and the moon was at a certain phase. The period while going to, while at, and while returning from a Sun Dance was considered by the Oglalas as a time of universal peace, when no warlike demonstration should be made, except defending if attacked. At such times all of mankind should be treated as guests, even if known to be hereditary enemies.

Gambling was prevelant in the winter camps. The Oglalas, both men and women, are gamblers, for it pleases the god of games [*Yumni*] to wager on chance. They have a number of games for children and for adults. Some of those for adults require both skill and endurance, some require skill only, and some are of pure chance. Frequently the band pitted its most expert players against such players of another band, and when so, bets were freely made by such as wished to do so. One of the two games most frequently played in such contests was a kind of lacrosse, played with club-like rackets and a ball. The bands chose teams of equal number and these strove to put the ball from the center of a space to a goal opposite to the goal to which their opponents sought to put the ball. The play was strenuous, for no trick was barred, and bruises and broken bones often occurred.

The other popular game for gambling is called Moccasins. This requires skill of the highest order, for it is a purely psychological contest. It is played by four players sitting, two opposed to two, facing each other. The implements for the game are four moccasins; four pebbles of like size, but one differing from the other three so that it cannot be manipulated unknowingly; a drum; a rod; and sixteen counting sticks divided at the beginning of the game equally between the opponents. The play is to place the moccasins side by side between the opponents and then one of the players hides the pebbles, one under each of the moccasins, while his partner sings and beats on the drum. Then their opponents, having the rod, lift a moccasin. If the lifted moccasin covered the differing pebble they win a counting stick and take the drum and hide the pebbles. If it does not they lose a counting stick and must guess again.

In the telling this appears childishly simple and a play could be made in a moment, but as played by the Oglalas the play depends on reading the features, for the one who hides the pebbles knows which moccasin the differing pebble is under, and his opponents endeavor to have him betray his knowledge. A single play sometimes lasts a long time. Often the players of one band are pitted against those of another and the stakes wagered are large. In such cases the onlookers are apt to become uproariously vociferous in attempts to encourage or confuse the players.

II

Hunting, War, Ceremony, and Art

The documents in this part legitimately form a miscellany of topics on which Walker's studies touched but did not focus. They serve to flesh out our understanding of how the Lakotas lived their lives, supplementing the holy men's perspectives presented in *Lakota Belief and Ritual,* as well as the structural view of Lakota society presented in Part I of the present volume. Documents 23 and 27, which form the bulk of the material in Part II, were written as public lectures and as such are valuable for recording Walker's own imaginative reconstruction of traditional Lakota life.

Document 23, "Communal Chase of the Buffalo," presents information on scouting for buffalo, the organization of communal hunts, horses and horse gear, the extent of the Lakota hunting territory, and many other topics. Here Walker's materials supplement the already published record of Lakota ethnography, serving mostly as corroboration, but also providing additional detail.

The most significant published accounts of Lakota buffalo hunting begin with the fur trader Tabeau's "The Circle or Communal Hunt," written about 1804. Many contemporary accounts are available in the writings of other traders and travelers, with the writings of Edwin T. Denig, relating to the 1830s, being perhaps the most valuable. From an anthropological perspective, Frances Densmore's "The Buffalo Hunt (Wanasapi)," recorded between 1911 and 1914 on the Standing Rock Reservation, gives not only valuable personal reminiscences of hunting but good accounts of butchering as well. The summary account by Royal B. Hassrick in *The Sioux* includes some information collected on the Rosebud Reservation during the early 1940s. The standard work on Indian horses and horse gear is John C. Ewers's *The Horse in Blackfoot Culture* (1955), which includes comparative material on the Sioux and can be used as a general guide to the subject.[1]

Walker's reconstruction of the communal hunt is particularly important for providing a good sense of the actual organization and structure of the hunt as a tribal activity. Especially valuable is his discussion of the changeover in authority from the *wakiconza,* who directs the movement of the camp during the hunt, to the *akicita* leaders in case of attack or suspected attack by the enemy. His account gives a clear picture of Lakota political structure in action. Also interesting are the descriptions of the use of sign language for long-distance communication between two mutually suspicious scouts, the use of smoke signals to alert a moving camp of danger, and the use of blanket signals to indicate a scout's findings about buffalo herds. Although these are popular elements of folklore about plains Indians, there is relatively little about them in the literature.

Walker's technique of showing the extent of Lakota territory by recording the birthplaces of several old Oglalas of Bull Bear's camp provides incontestable data on the vastness of Lakota hunting territories. These birth records reveal that the Oglala hunting territory extended from the Grand River in North Dakota to the Smoky Hill River in Kansas and the South Platte River in Colorado, and from the Rocky Mountains east to the Minnesota River, and serve as documentary corroboration of Lakota oral tradition.

Documents 24–26 concern warfare and ritual. There is surprisingly little firsthand material on Lakota warfare in the literature. Wissler presented some important accounts from Oglalas in his "Societies and Ceremonial Associations." The reminiscences recorded by Densmore at Standing Rock are valuable, as are the materials collected by Stanley Vestal (Walter Campbell) in his work on biographies of Sitting Bull and White Bull. Lakota men recorded their perceptions of warfare in the form of drawings of brave deeds. Notable published examples include the pictorial autobiographies of Sitting Bull and White Bull, and the drawings of Amos Bad Heart Bull. There is also important unpublished material in the writings of George Sword.[2]

Documents 24 and 25 suggest a belief that sexual intercourse had a debilitating effect on the power of Lakota men—not because women were thought to be polluting, but because a conflict was seen between the female power that nurtures and gives birth and the male power that both creates and destroys. This belief accounts for the importance of cleansing by men before engaging in any ritual, including the purification lodge, and explains the sanctions in warrior societies against intercourse the night before society meetings. Very little has been recorded in the literature about Lakota sexual beliefs, giving even these brief accounts considerable significance.

Document 26 presents a warrior's point of view on the sun dance, which serves as a significant contrast to the holy men's points of view expressed in *Lakota Belief and Ritual* (documents 63–69). Here we see the warrior's vow to participate in the ceremony if he is granted success in war or raiding. The ritual of the sun dance is briefly described but without dwelling on its religious symbolism; from the pragmatist's viewpoint it is an ordeal as well as a prayer.

Documents 27 and 28 present information on Lakota art, including symbolism, war insignia, and discussion of clothing. The first is again a public lecture by Walker, consisting of a somewhat fanciful reconstruction of Lakota art in precontact times. He assumes that the porcupine quill and beadwork decorations characteristic of the late nineteenth century were, in earlier times, painted designs of basically similar patterns and usages. This is only guesswork and is unsubstantiated by Lakota artwork preserved in museum collections. The most important publications in this area are the various short monographs of Clark Wissler. Densmore also recorded relevant material, including a catalog of the objects she collected at Standing Rock. The standard and best general works on Lakota art are Carrie A. Lyford's *Quill and Beadwork of the Western Sioux* (1940) and John C. Ewers's *Plains Indian Painting* (1939). For parfleche (rawhide container) painting, Mable Morrow's *Indian Rawhide* (1975) is the best introduction. All of these accounts place primary emphasis on art as cultural tradition rather than on the role of individual artists. Walker's observation in document 27 that Lakota women mixed the various colors of glass beads together as a way of neutralizing their power before using them to make designs is a valuable bit of information that hints at the barely explored subject of the ritual connotations of Lakota art. In *Lakota Belief and Ritual,* Thomas Tyon's discussion of the Double Woman Dreamers, who are given supernatural power as artists, provides another perspective (document 54).[3] The value of Walker's miscellaneous materials—fragmentary though they are—for the interpretation of traditional Lakota life underscores the paucity of published accounts and emphasizes the continuing need to search out authoritative descriptions and make them available.

---

23. Communal Chase of the Buffalo.[4] James R. Walker. (CHS)

When the Oglalas lived according to their aboriginal customs the buffalo were an important source of supply to them for they used every part of these animals for some purpose: their hair for making ropes and pads and for ornamental and ceremonial purposes; the horns and hoofs for making implements and utensils; the bones for making soup and articles to be used in their various occupations and games; the sinews for making their sewing thread and their stronger cords such as bowstrings; the skins for making robes, tipis, clothing, regalia, thongs, and such other purposes as required a strong, flexible and tough material such as leather or like material is used for among the civilized peoples; the flesh and viscera for food; and the skull, as it was believed to be the place of abode of the spirit of the animal (which was intimately related to the supernatural being who presided over the chase and domestic affairs and which remained about the skull until it was swallowed by the earth), was regarded as *wakan* and was used to retain the spirit near at hand that it might act as an intermediary in invoking the aid of the supernatural being it was related to.

Some products of the buffalo were used in almost everything which the Oglalas did in their daily life, but the most important was the supply of food. They ate every part of the animal which could be masticated; for instance, they considered the testicles of the bulls a choice part and the fetus boiled in the water from the gravid uterus a great delicacy.

Because of the importance of these animals to these Indians, various forms, ceremonies and regulations were established relative to the buffalo among which was the chase in compliance with certain forms and regulations. If at any time, except during a communal chase, an Oglala had an opportunity he might kill a buffalo; then its carcass belonged to him and there were no formal proceedings unless some part of the animal had been tabooed to the one who killed it, or he had some supernatural communication directing him in the matter, in which case he would formally set aside the piece tabooed or comply with his supernatural instructions or with any vow he may have made relative to the matter.

At any time, if the people had little food, a hunt for buffalo might have been organized and if so was conducted in compliance with the regulations so far as they applied to the attack on the animals and the distribution of the products of the chase. But the communal chase was formally planned and organized when the grazing was good and the buffalo were likely to be fat for the purpose of getting a supply of meat and skins to last until the next communal chase. When the time approached for organizing the chase it became the subject of conversation among the people and they canvassed the matter from all their points of view, discussing every phase of it so that when the time for organization arrived each understood what the others thought about the matter.

Before organizing, someone, usually an old shaman, took a *wakan* vapor bath and sought a vision according to the customs governing in such matters and if he received a supernatural communication he explained it to the people and they governed themselves accordingly. If the vision was favorable to the chase they proceeded in the matter and if it required that any particular thing be done they complied with such requirements. But if the vision was unfavorable then the chase was abandoned for the time and the camp either awaited another vision that might be favorable or joined some other camp in the chase.

If there had been no vision or the vision had been favorable then a buffalo skull was decorated, usually with red paint, and it might have decorations of feathers and quillwork also. Attached to it were one or more small packages done up in tanned skin containing medicines that had been prepared by a shaman for the purpose of propitiating the supernatural powers and securing the aid of *Tatanka,* the supernatural being that presided over the chase and domestic affairs. This skull was placed in the *tiyoti* or council tipi, between the *oceti* and the *catku,* that is, the center of the tipi and the place of honor, opposite the door.

The council of the camp then met in formal session in the *tiyoti,* the principal personage, usually the chief of the camp, taking his seat on the *catku.* The others took their seats in the order in which they were esteemed in the matter to be discussed, to his right and left. The session was opened by smoking the pipe with willow bark in it during which someone, usually the shaman who had a vision relative to the chase (or if no vision had been had, then a shaman or *Mihunka*), held the lighted pipe with the stem pointing north, east, south and west and then towards the sun, the heavens, and the earth, pausing at each direction to invoke the four winds, the sun, the powers of the air and earth, calling on them for their favor. Then the pipe was smoked and offered to the skull of the buffalo and the Spirit of the Buffalo was called upon to give aid in the chase and to intercede with *Tatanka,* that he might bring the buffalo in plenty and make their chase successful.

After these ceremonies the council discussed the chase, deliberating upon the questions of when to start, what route to go, what territory to hunt over, how long the chase should continue, and where to make the next winter camp, and such other matters of common interest as might be brought before the council. The discussion of these questions might have been brief or they may have lasted over several days.

When the discussion was ended the women of the camp provided a feast at which they vied with each other to produce the best or most food, and all joined in making the occasion enjoyable. At these feasts the councilmen were first served in the order in which they sat in the *tiyoti,* after which all present were supplied with food, as it was considered bad form for any food to be carried away or left over from such a feast. And if any woman who provided food for such feasts carried food away from it, she became the subject of uncomplimentary remark, if not the butt of ridicule. Indigent persons might be permitted to take food from such feasts to their homes, but they seldom availed themselves of this privilege for fear that it might be thrown up to them in after times.

When the plans for the chase were determined upon it was organized by choosing the four marshals *(akicita),* investing them with the insignia of their office, administering to them the obligations, and placing them in charge of the camp to have control of all the movement and conduct of the people. This word, *akicita,* has been translated "soldiers" so often, and by so many authorities, that it will be here examined. The English speaking people call a man who is a warrior or who is skilled in military experience, or who is engaged to fight in a battle, a soldier. The

Dakotas call such a man *zuya wicaśa* [war man][5]. A man who is appointed to regulate marches and processions and to maintain order and conformity with recognized customs, and carry out the orders of a judicial body or executive power, is called a marshal by English speaking peoples, and *akicita* by the Dakotas.

The mistranslation probably came about in this way. The only duties of the *zuya wicaśa,* or Dakota soldiers, are to march and fight, and when not engaged in either of these they are not together as an organized body so that they are not under obligation to perform the ordinary duties of camp life. They considered such affairs as beneath their dignity, leaving it to the women to perform the manual labor, or to the *akicita* who were appointed to enforce compliance with regulations and execute the orders of the chiefs, headmen, and the council. When the Dakotas saw the soldiers of an organized army performing the labor about the camp and enforcing the execution of orders they called them *akicita,* or marshals, instead of *zuya wicaśa,* or soldiers. Then when they were asked for their word for our soldiers they gave *akicita,* and when asked for their word for their marshals they gave *akicita,* and the translators concluded that as our soldiers were called *akicita,* their *akicita* should be called soldiers, and so translated the word, which is correct when applied to our soldiers but incorrect when applied to the *akicita* of the Dakotas.

In the talk about the chase in the camp before the meeting of the council relative to it, the qualifications of the various persons who would likely be appointed as marshals were freely discussed, so that the councilmen understood the sentiment of the camp in this matter. But it was not the custom for anyone to avow a candidacy for the position. Friends desiring the appointment of one would try to influence the councilmen to do so and would even offer bribes for that purpose.

To make these appointments the council met in formal session in the *tiyoti* and after smoking formal smoke they would propose and canvass the names of young men suitable for the appointment. The qualifications necessary to secure such an appointment were that the appointee should be a young man of good repute and with some experience in the chase. The appointments were made by a majority of the councilmen agreeing on each of the four appointed. If after anyone was appointed a good reason was given to the council why such a one should not be marshal the appointment could be cancelled and another appointed to fill such vacancy. When the four young men were appointed marshals they were called into the *tiyoti* before the council and notified of their appointment. If either of them did not wish to serve as a marshal he would be excused from doing so upon paying a fine such as the council should impose, which fine was disposed of as the council saw fit. Young men rarely refused this appointment as it was considered an honor and a step towards becoming a leader of the people and a soldier, which was the highest honor among the Oglalas.

The young men having been notified of their appointment as marshals and having signified their acceptance of the appointment, the member of the council who sat on the *catku* invested each of them with a *wicapaha ogle,* or scalp shirt, and presented each with a *wapaha,* or feathered banner. These were the regalia and insignia of their office. The four young men then stood side by side between the door of the *tiyoti* and the *oceti*, or center of the lodge, facing the *catku,* and someone of the council, usually the one occupying the *catku,* or a *Mihunka,* that is, an elder in the camp, delivered to them the charge of their office, which in substance was as follows:

"We appoint you chief marshals and we authorize you to choose other young men to assist you as marshals. You must see that the rules and regulations of the chase are complied with. You must do your duty towards all of the people without fear or favor. You must at all times listen to the council, the chiefs, and the leaders of the people. If at any time you are in doubts as to what you should do, they will tell you what is right. You have accepted the appointment as chief marshals and I have explained your duties to you and you must do them or suffer the penalties for neglect of duty."[6]

After this charge was delivered, each of the marshals dipped his finger in black paint and drew it down across his right cheek from the eye to the lower jaw, making a black streak across his cheek. This black stripe on the right cheek signified that the wearer had accepted the appointment as marshal, understood the charge given him by the council, and would discharge the duties of his office without fear or favor, and it was considered as of the nature of an oath or obligation to this effect. It was also a badge of office and all the people were compelled to obey one who had such a badge. Or if a marshal attempted to command or direct anyone without this mark on his face, such a one could flout him with impunity.

The placing of the mark on themselves by the marshals closed the ceremonies of their appointment and soon after this they went about the camp, two and two, choosing young men to be assistant marshals, the number of assistants being in proportion to the size of the camp. They indicated their choice by putting a black stripe on the face of the young man similar to that on their own, or if the young man chosen was not in his *ti* when they came to it, they put a broad black stripe on the door of the *ti* and the young man was compelled to assume the badge unless he was excused by the council and paid the fine imposed.

When all were chosen the marshals and their assistants had entire control of the camp and governed every person in it, their power only limited by the recognized customs, rules, and regulations of the chase, and the only appeal from their action being to the council, which was chary of interfering with the authority of the marshals. A marshal or assistant was held more strictly to compliance with the customs and rules than any other member of the camp, and if he transgressed these, or was negligent of his duties, his punishment was more prompt and severe than that of any other member of the camp. The punishment administered by the marshals was given without a hearing of any kind other than by the marshals themselves. A single marshal or assistant could administer punishment at any time upon his own volition, and the only appeal from this was to the council, by charging that the marshal did not have sufficient grounds for his action. Such appeals were seldom taken, for the council would not entertain them unless the action of the marshal had been an extremely gross abuse of his power as an officer.

The punishment administered by the marshals might consist of anything, from the assessing of a trifling fine to the destruction of all the property of the one punished, and from the striking of the offender with a lash to killing him. Or they might debar him from taking part in anything done by the people, or control any of his domestic relations.

The appointment of the marshals was usually made only a short time before the day set for starting on the trip for the chase and from this time on everyone in the camp occupied him or herself with preparations for moving the camp and for the chase. The men prepared their weapons and horses and riding equipments. The favorite weapon was the bow and arrow because the wound of an arrow rightly shot either was immediately fatal or was so distressing that the animal would soon stop running. It was desirable to approach the buffalo from behind and shoot the arrow so that it would enter the body above the flank and range forward and downward passing through the viscera, and lodge there, or if at the animal's side, to have the arrow pass through the chest in the region of the heart and lodge there. Most of the men could shoot an arrow so that it would pass entirely through the body of a buffalo but this was not desirable as an animal so wounded, unless some vital part was injured, would run a long distance before stopping, whereas if the arrow was lodged in the body it would cause so much distress that the animal would soon stop and stand or lie down when it could be killed at leisure. In later times the gun was used in the chase, but it was never as effective as the bow and arrow. The spear or lance was used but seldom in the active chase as it was more cumbersome than the bow and arrow, but it was frequently used to kill the wounded.

It was the desire of each man to have a horse trained to the chase of the buffalo, and if so, such a horse was little used for other purposes except in a war party or horse racing. In the preparation for the chase, such horses were groomed and favored and gotten ready for use. Those who had no horses trained for the chase would train a horse by riding him at a run alongside of and into herds of running horses, and by rubbing buffalo robes over and about them, to accustom them to the smell of the animals.

The headgear with which the horse was ridden in the chase was made of buffalo hide with the hair scraped off, and consisted of a band passing over the head behind the ears, down to and supporting another band passing around its jaws just above the corners of the mouth. To this a long strap was fastened so that it would conveniently pass back to and beyond the rider, the whole something like the common leather halter sold in harness shops but fitting snugger to the horse's head. The men most expert in the chase used no other gear on their horses while running the buffalo but older men and boys would use the Indian saddle for men. This was made by shaping two pieces of wood about twenty inches long so that they would be about an inch and a half thick and fit on the back of a horse just behind the withers. These were held in place by two pieces of elk horn taken from that part where a prong and the shaft would form a suitable arch, which was suitably shaped and scraped smooth and fitted to the two wooden pads, one forming the front and the other the rear of the saddle. The whole was covered with green buffalo hide which was sewed in place with sinew thread and then dried. This formed a strong saddle tree and was the prototype of the McClellan saddle tree used by the U.S. Cavalry. After the tree was made, a girth and stirrup straps of buffalo hide were placed on it and stirrups of either rawhide or wood attached, and the whole completed without the use of metal in any part of it. Such a saddle if well made was comfortable to both horse and rider and was of such strength that it would last for generations with all the hard usage incidental to the property of an Indian.

The women used a saddle of entirely different form and construction, but which was better adapted for their use than the man's saddle. They rode astride, as did the men, but packed more on their saddles.

The men prepared their weapons, overhauled their riding gear, and packed away their war equipments, for it was the custom that no one should go on a war party during the time of the communal chase except to drive an enemy from the territory claimed as hunting grounds. The shamans made medicines and performed ceremonies to secure good luck in the chase, and many of the men took the mysterious vapor bath to purify their bodies and drive away evil influences that might operate against their success in the chase.

If it was desired that any other camp should join in the chase, this was settled on in the council, and the chief of the camp got from a shaman (if he were not a shaman himself) a package of good medicine, that is, something which the shaman had prepared by ceremony and incantation so that it would influence to friendship, and added to it a quantity of tobacco or willow bark and invitation wands. He then called for volunteers to go to the camp to be invited and carry the medicine, tobacco and wand to the chief of that camp. Usually one or two young men volunteered to do this service, and dressing themselves in their best attire, carried the articles to the camp, entering no tipi until they came to the *ti* of the chief of the camp invited. They entered, bearing exposed in their hands the medicine, willow bark, and invitation wand, and before speaking, presented them to the chief. The invitation was recognized by the articles presented and they were received in silence, after which the young men were made welcome and feasted and then questioned as to the proposed chase.

The young men reposed for one day in the camp of those invited, during which the council of that camp met in the *tiyoti* and discussed the invitation, the young men remaining away from the meeting of the council and hearing nothing of their discussion or decision in the matter. The following morning they prepared to start on their return to their own camp and the chief of the camp invited gave them to carry to the chief of their camp a package of medicine, some willow bark, and if the invitation was declined, the invitation wand which had been sent to him. But if the invitation was accepted the wand was not given to these couriers. If they returned without it, it was understood that the camp invited would join in the chase, bringing with them the invitation wand. On the return of the couriers they went direct to the *ti* of the chief and, before speaking to anyone, handed to him the articles sent by the chief who had been invited, and then were at liberty.

In the preparations for the chase the women took the most laborious part. They did all the work incidental to moving the camp and making the trip, overhauling wardrobes, tipis, travois and harness, and putting all in good repair, and prepared everything for packing and conveyance. At break of day on the day set for starting, all were astir in the camp, the men grouped discussing the plans, the young men and boys rounding up the horses, and the women getting things into shape to pack on the horses, travois, or on their own backs. Their travois were made by bending a sapling into an oblong hoop about four or five feet long by about three or four feet wide, and webbing the enclosed space with rawhide thongs, with interstices about four to six inches across. This webbed hoop was fastened to two tipi poles so that the smaller ends of the poles would fit along side a horse or dog, with the larger ends farther apart projecting beyond the hoop. The smaller ends of the poles were attached to a horse or dog by a suitable harness made of buffalo hide, and the larger ends dragged on the ground. This lifted the webbed hoop behind the horse or dog, and the things to be conveyed were placed on it and fastened there. The travois hoop was an important part of the paraphernalia of an Oglala woman and a large part of the estimation of her was in proportion to her dexterity in arranging and packing a travois. Those for horses were proportionately larger than those for dogs.

When the morning meal was eaten, the marshals donned their reglia, took their banners in their hands, and mounting their horses, assembled on a nearby hill. This was the signal for breaking camp and it disappeared almost like a puff of smoke, the women quickly removing the covers and taking down the poles and packing everything ready to load for the move. The men mounted their horses and assembled near and below the marshals. The boys and young women mounted horses and took charge of the drove of spare horses. The women busied themselves in packing their goods and children on horses, travois, and dogs, and in arranging their own mounts. The indigent and the old pottered about with the women, trying to keep a place in the community. The assistant marshals were busy quieting wrangles and giving directions, and when all were ready, they so reported to the marshals, who led the way, and all started on the route for the communal chase.

The plan of the march was usually to arrive at a place where there was wood and water each night. This made a day's journey from the camp from ten to twenty five miles ordinarily. But under stress it might be greater or less than these distances. When on the march the intention was to keep all in a compact body, and usually they were in about the order they started, the men in front, boys and young women in charge of the extra horses next, followed by the women, children, old and decrepit, with the entire camp equipage, some riding, some walking, and some, especially small children or very sick, carried on the travois.

After starting, two of the marshals were expected to be at all times in the lead and the other two mingled with the people as they saw fit, in order to supervise matters. The assistant marshals were directed to go far ahead of the marching people and far on either side, to watch the country for game or enemies. One or two of them were detailed to follow at some distance to act as rear guard and see that none lagged so far behind as to be endangered from lurking enemies. Men could hunt for game along the line of march, but only by permission of marshals, and game killed by such men was considered common property and divided as far as it would go among such persons as the marshals designated. Such hunters also acted as scouts along the line, watching for signs of bufalo in numbers, and for enemies.

The Dakotas were at all times watchful for enemies. They were a warlike people and were often at war with other tribes, or at any time a Dakota might go on a warlike expedition against another tribe for merely personal reasons. And other tribes observed the same hostile customs towards the Dakotas. So they were never assured at any time that someone was not seeking an opportunity to do them some injury in a hostile way, such as killing the men or stealing their women, children or horses, or trespassing on the territory they claimed as their hunting grounds. So at all times they were alert for such marauders and were especially vigilant when moving camp or on a march.

The Oglalas were plains Indians and usually avoided a wooded country in making their camp, which they ordinarily placed where it could not be seen from long distances away, but with open country about it so that it could not be located by an enemy from a distance and could not be approached closely under cover that would hide an enemy. The scouts would ride far ahead of the moving column and far to either side of it. They would carefully approach the top of a hill and dismount and without exposing themselves, closely search everything visible, watching for game or enemies. Having satisfied themselves that neither was in sight, they would mount and ride rapidly to the next eminence and survey the surrounding country as before.

If at any time a scout discovered signs of persons he first examined them to learn whether they were made recently or not. If he saw someone he would, while screening himself closely, observe such a one and if he concluded that it was a friend he would show himself and raise his right hand high above his head, with the palm forward, and then wave it from side to side, which in the sign language of the plains meant that he wished to speak to the one signaled.[7] If the one signaled was friendly, he extended his right arm in front and made a downward hooking motion with his extended index finger, moving the whole hand. Then they approached each other and conversed, after which the scout returned to the marshals and reported what he had learned. If there was a friendly camp on its way for a chase, a meeting was arranged and an agreement made either to chase together or to hunt in different territories.

If the scout was in doubts about the one observed, whether he was a friend or an enemy, he would watch him long and closely, and if he could not satisfy himself in this way, he would then show himself, and signal as given above. If the one signaled was in doubts about the friendliness of the one signaling he would either not answer the signal or would raise his extended right arm to about half way between horizontal and perpendicular and wave his right hand from side to side, which in the sign language of the plains meant "Who are you and what do you want?" The scout would then draw his right hand across his throat from left to right, then raise his closed hand in front of his face and bring it suddenly towards his face, extending his fingers while doing so, as if throwing something into his face. This in the sign language of the plains meant that he was an Oglala Dakota. He would then make the sign that the other had made, which would mean "Who are you and what are you doing?"

If the one signaled was friendly to the scout he would give the sign for his tribe and they approached and conversed. If he was an enemy he would refuse to answer and the two would warily watch each other, each trying to learn as much of the other as possible, and, if the opportunity offered, to take the other's horse or his scalp. Having learned all he could of the other, the scout would withdraw to a hill at a safe distance and scoop a small hole in the ground at the top of the hill. Then he would build a fire in the hole of dry material that would give little smoke, and when the fire was burning well he would throw on it a bunch of green stuff that would make a dense smoke. When the smoke began to rise he would throw his robe over it and hold it there for a few moments and then withdraw it, thus making an interrupted column of smoke. This he would repeat four times. After waiting a short time he would repeat this operation, and do so for several times. This was the signal among the Oglalas that an enemy was discovered, for which they at all times were watching, and when seen by the other scouts they hurried towards it, moving cautiously when near the place where it had been seen. When such a smoke is seen by the moving column, the men at once get their war equipments and hasten towards the place where it was seen.

Two marshals remained with the people but the others and the assistants went quickly to the place where the signal was given, and as they were at all times prepared for such emergencies, they would arrive on the ground before the others. It was their duty to examine well into the affair and if in their opinion a sufficient number of the enemy was dangerously near so as to be a menace to the people, or were trespassing on the hunting grounds, then they so informed the headmen of the camp, and the *zuya wicaśa,* or warriors, took charge of all affairs, and the marshals were without authority. The people were hurried into a camp at some place that offered more or less security and all who could bear arms went in pursuit of the enemy. Or if the enemy were too powerful to be attacked, the people were hurried away in search of another camp of Lakotas, while the warriors tried to keep within striking distance of the enemy until they were reinforced by friends, or until the enemy had left the territory claimed as hunting grounds.

If at any time the Lakotas considered themselves sufficiently strong to attack the enemy with hopes of defeating them, they did so, or if they thought the enemy too strong to attack openly they sought opportunity to lead them into ambush, or to strike straggling parties of small numbers, or to stampede or steal their horses, and to harass them in every way they could until they were out of the territory claimed as hunting grounds by the Lakotas.

When the enemy was disposed of the warriors laid aside their war equipments and washed off their war paint. Then the marshals put the black stripe on their faces and resumed control of the camp. On the march they led the way and all were compelled to follow, and if anyone attempted to go away from the route taken by the marshals, a marshal would come upon such a one and lash him with a whip until he agreed to return to the track of the people. The marshals located the camp each day and might specify where each or any one tipi should be placed. They could order anyone to use or release any horse, to tie up, muzzle, or kill any dog, to ride or walk in a certain place in the marching column, or to aid others in any manner and compel obedience with their orders of this kind. No person in the camp was exempt from their authority.

At one time Red Cloud, the head chief of the Oglalas, who was of a turbulent disposition, refused to obey the orders of a marshal to break camp. When the marshal lashed him repeatedly and severely across the face, he quietly submitted.

The people moved in this manner until they came to the territory where they proposed to hunt for herds of buffalo large enough to chase in the communal manner. The territory claimed as hunting grounds by the Oglalas, in common with the other Tetons, was of vast extent, the boundaries being made by agreement with other tribes, or such as they could establish and maintain by force of arms. An idea of the extent of this territory may be gotten by locating their camps while on hunting expeditions, and this can be done by the following method.

The older Oglalas can rarely tell their age in years but almost without exception they can tell without hesitation the year of their birth according to the Oglala winter count, and give the camp they were born in and where it was located at the time. The Dakota winter counts are calendars by which they fix dates of past events and were made as follows. The Dakotas have kept a record of the years from before the beginning of the nineteenth century A.D. by making a pictograph of something which occurred during each year and naming the year for the thing which the pictograph represented, and this was called a winter count.

The larger divisions of the Dakotas such as the Sissetons and the Tetons kept winter counts of their own, differing for some years, and some of the subdivisions, such as the Brulés and Oglalas of the Tetons, each kept a winter count that differed for some years from that of the other. But the greater number of the years were named for something that was known to all the Dakotas, and the pictographs on all the winter counts represented the same thing. They come as near perfect agreement as would histories written by different authors independent of each other, their differences being internal evidences that they are not merely copies of each other. Their authenticity is established by the fact that they agree in the succession of the years, and by counting them backwards from a known year, and giving to each the Anno Domini, if the thing pictographed is a matter of historical knowledge, the winter count is found correct in every instance. Therefore when a Dakota, without hesitation, gives a date according to his winter count, it may be accepted as reliable until proven otherwise.

The Oglala winter counts are Bull Bear's, Red Cloud's, and American Horse's. Bull Bear's winter count is the oldest and probably is the original winter count. Some unknown Oglala began it at some unknown time, but it was old in the year "When they performed the ceremony with horse's tails," A.D. 1805. Soon after this time it was bequeathed to Bull Bear, who turned it over to a member of his camp, whose son sold it to a collector. But before it was sold a copy was made and this copy has been interpreted and written in the Lakota dialect, and this translated into English. This is now known as the No Ears Winter Count. The older Oglalas, almost without exception, in fixing the date of past events do so by the Bull Bear or No Ears winter count, and the Dakota names for years given in this paper are those found on this count [document no. 30].

During the earlier part of the 19th century A.D., Bull Bear was the head chief of the Oglalas. His was probably the largest camp of the Tetons, which roamed over all the territory claimed by them as hunting grounds, and its location at certain times is established as follows. According to the information they gave, the following named Oglalas were born in Bull Bear's camp during the years, at the places, and when the camp was engaged as given.

White Hawk, born the year "They built a house of rotting logs" (A.D. 1819), when in winter camp at the big bend of the Minnesota River in Minnesota.

Red Cloud, born the year "A star sounded going" (A.D. 1821), when on a buffalo chase on the Smoky Hill River in Kansas.

Little Wound (Bull Bear's son), born the year "They killed many Mandans" (A.D. 1828), when on a buffalo chase near the headwaters of the south fork of the Cheyenne River in Wyoming.

Wolf Ears, born the year "The stars fell" (A.D. 1833) when on a buffalo chase near the mountains on the south fork of the Platte River in Colorado.

American Horse, born the year "Little Thunder killed his brothers"[8] (A.D. 1840), when in winter camp near the mouth of Grand River in North Dakota.

From a large amount of information like the above, it appears that the Tetons usually made their winter camps near or east of the Missouri River, and in the summertime roamed as far north as well up in North Dakota, as far west as the Rocky Mountains, and as far south as well down into Kansas, claiming all this territory as their hunting grounds, and ready to make war upon Indians of any other tribe they found trespassing on it. Thus, if they chose to make their chase on territory well to the south or west of their hunting grounds, the trip from their winter camp to the place they had chosen would last for many days.

While going, the camp moved each day by easy marches so as to arrive with their horses in good condition, and all looked forward to the sport with good humor. On arriving at a place chosen for the camp at night the men gathered in groups for talk and smoke and the women immediately put up the tipis. The horses were herded together with a watchful guard of boys and girls during daylight, and of young men after nightfall, and if near an enemy they were hobbled and kept near the camp. Older men scouted about at frequent intervals each night, searching for possible raiders.

The shamans often performed ceremonies and made incantations and medicines to bring good luck to the camp and success in the chase. At any time from the first to the last a shaman could seek a vision, and if it pertained to the chase, upon his word everything would be done as the vision prescribed, even to an abandonment of the chase altogether.

Certain games were frequently played, and these were believed to have an influence upon the success of the chase by the players, as for instance if the games were played quickly and with little struggle between the players this meant success to all the camp, but if the game lingered then the chase would be slow, or if someone lost continually he would have poor success or some misfortune would come upon him. If the games presaged ill fortune, then a shaman was called upon to exercise his mystical powers to overcome the evil influence that threatened poor success to the chase, and he performed ceremonies, strong incantations, and made medicines, and prescribed the manner of proceeding with the view of propitiating the supernatural beings and securing their aid in the chase.

When the camp arrived at the territory it was proposed to hunt over, it was placed where water was handy, preferably where it would be screened from observation at a distance. Then all but those who scouted the regions about for buffalo remained quietly in camp, avoiding all loud noises, and using fuels that made little smoke. The herald would go about the camp admonishing the people in a low tone to neither sing or shout, or make any loud noise, and to keep their dogs quiet. If anyone made a loud noise the marshals would go to his tipi and destroy that which he made the noise with, and if the provocation were great they would strike the offender with a club or tomahawk, or if he should show resentment or resistence they would destroy his tipi or even kill him. If a dog barked or made a noise that would probably alarm the buffalo, the marshals would kill that dog, or they might kill dogs that had made no disturbance so as to be sure that they would not do so.

While waiting in the camp for the report of the scouts, the women made preparations for curing the meat and skins, the old men sat in conference, the younger men played *heȟaka* or the hunters' game [hoop and pole],[9] and the little children played about in a subdued manner.

When a scout discovered buffalo in numbers he returned to the camp and as soon as he came in sight of it he dismounted from his horse and waved his robe, waving it in the direction he had seen the game. If he waved it in this manner continuously he had discovered a number of buffalo; if he waved it and folded it and then waved it again, he had discovered as many as the number of times he waved his blanket; if he waved his blanket for a time and then spread it on the ground he had discovered countless numbers of buffalo. He continued to signal in this manner until he saw that his signals were observed in the camp, when he came into the camp. As he approached the camp, and old man who had been chosen for this office met him and said to him nearly as follows:

"Come straightway here. I have been sitting watching for you." This he repeated four times when the scout entered the camp, and then the people gathered about him and greeted him with thanks. The old man would conduct him to within the camp where he had placed buffalo chips ready to burn, and would sit with him there. Then he would fill a pipe and light it and smoke four whiffs while holding the pipe on a buffalo chip. Then holding the bowl of the pipe on the chip he would with his other hand turn the stem to the scout who would smoke four wiffs in the same manner. The buffalo chip signified the presence of *Tatanka,* a supernatural being who, according to the mythology of the Tetons, presided over the chase, and the four whiffs from the pipe on the chip were a ceremonial offering to this being for propitiation made by this old man as a token of his authority to ask for reliable information, and by the scout as a token that he would truly tell what he had discovered.

The old man would then address the *Taku Wakan* as follows:

"Ruler of all living things on the earth, thou knowest every part of the earth. Reveal to me from what hill good things have been seen. Do not deceive me, but tell me truly. Be gracious and do not deceive me." He then said to the scout:

"Have you seen anything within my reach? You are not a baby."

The scout then pointed with his thumb in the direction he had seen the buffalo and minutely described the hill he had seen them from. This ended the ceremony of receiving the successful scout, and then the people hurriedly began preparations for the chase.[10]

The herald went about the camp saying in a low voice, "To-o-o. To-o-o," which signified that the buffalo had been discovered and all should make haste in a quiet manner to get ready for the chase when the marshals should give the signal to go. In the meantime someone went to the top of a nearby hill and made a smoke, which, when the other scouts saw, they would return to the camp. If the buffalo had been discovered near the camp, then all prepared for the chase leaving the camp as it was, but if the buffalo were at a long distance away, then the women prepared to move the camp near where the chase would occur.

It was usually arranged to make the chase on the morning following the report of the scout, and other scouts were sent to keep watch of the herd while the others got ready. When all were prepared the marshals assembled them and if there was time on the evening before the chase, led them to some locality near the herd where they stayed for that night. The regulations were very strict in regard to all going together and if anyone went alone he was subject to severe penalties such as having his horse killed, or his property destroyed, and being debared from the chase, and if he should kill an animal its carcass was taken from him. All were careful to keep to the windward of the herd during the night before the chase, fearing that their scent would alarm the animals.

As soon as it was light enough to see the next morning, the scouts who were watching the herd came to the hunters and reported the location and surroundings of the buffalo. Then as silently as possible all mounted and keeping close together moved to that place closest to the herd where they would be hidden from it. Then the marshals examined the grounds and chose a point where they thought the nearest approach to the herd could be made without exposing the hunters to it, and then led the hunters there, keeping all close together. When all were as near as it was thought they could be without the buffalo seeing them, the marshals disposed of all so that each should be as near as every other and all have a fair start in the chase, or if they thought better results might be had by dispersing the hunters, they did so. But no one could begin the chase until the marshals gave the signal.

When the marshals had arranged the hunters, then one of them rode in view of the hunters and buffalo and waved his hand above his head. Immediately on seeing this signal all rode as fast as their horses could run straight towards the herd, keeping silent and bending as low on their horses as they could ride, so as to hide their bodies as much as possible. Usually the buffalo paid little attention to them when they first appeared in sight, and then stared at them as if they were other buffalo that were stampeded, waiting to see the cause of the stampede. Often the hunters would be close upon or even among the herd before it would take fright.

After the first of the rush upon the herd every hunter acted independently of all others and aimed to wound as many of the animals as he could. Each one chose the animal he wished to get and rode after it at full speed, and just as he came alongside of it, shot an arrow aimed to enter above the flank and range forward and downward. Or he might attempt to ride alongside the animal and shoot an arrow through its chest, aiming to pierce the heart, but this was a much more dangerous method of shooting than the former, for if the animal was hit and not fatally wounded, it would almost certainly charge the horse at its side, and there was danger to both horse and rider. If the arrow hit as desired, the hunter immediately started after another animal. Each hunter continued to do this until either all the buffalo were killed or those not killed had escaped, or until his horse was exhausted. When the active part of the chase ended, then the hunters went over the ground and killed the wounded. This was by no means the least dangerous part of the chase as probably the larger part of the buffalo had not been killed outright and their arrow wounds made them angry and dangerous. Many more horses and hunters were hurt at this time than during the active part of the chase.

If there were a white buffalo in the herd everyone made an effort to secure it, as such animals were considered *wakan.* A robe made from the skin of a white buffalo was a highly valued possession, making a fit offering for the supernatural beings or a present of the highest value to mankind.[11]

In the meantime, those who had remained at the camp when the hunters started, the women and children and the old and decrepit, came to the scene of the chase with horses and travois and other means for carrying away the meat and skins. As soon as the chase had ended, a shaman chose one of the carcasses as an offering to the *Taku Wakan,* of which *Tatanka* was believed to take charge. If there had been a white buffalo killed, its carcass was always chosen for this purpose. The skin was removed from this carcass, but otherwise it was left entire where it had died, and the spirit of the buffalo took up its abode there, pleased with the generosity of the people.

Then each hunter picked out the animals he had killed, and if there was a dispute in any case the marshals viewed the carcassess and usually by the arrow found in it decided to whom it belonged. The women began at once to skin the animals and cut up the meat and as soon as the livers could be delivered to them the men feasted on raw liver dipped in gall, which they believed gave them strength and courage. If fuel could be gotten, fires were built at once and parts of the viscera were cooked as soon as possible, and all ate their fill.

The meat was cut into convenient sizes for carrying to the camp, and as soon as it could be done all was carried there. Here the hides were stretched and pegged on the ground to dry and the meat cut into thin slices and hung up on poles until it was completely dried, and then packed into bundles suitable for carrying. The women did all the work of caring for the carcasses and drying the skins and meat, and while they were doing this the men took their leisure.

After a successful chase a shaman usually sought a vision, and if he received one, revealed it to the people. This generally called upon them for some action or sacrifice to repay the supernatural beings for the aid they had given in the chase. It generally took the form of presents or a feast to be given to the shaman, or an offering to be placed at some particular place.

When the meat was dried an estimate was made of whether there was sufficient for the year's supply or not, and if not the chase was repeated. When it was thought that enough had been secured to last until the next formal chase, then the chase was ended. The marshals' authority ceased and the chiefs and leaders assumed the ordinary control of the camp. Then each one was free to go and come as he chose, and to occupy himself as he saw fit, and anyone could organize and lead a war party or join one if organized, provided he was otherwise qualified.

The most of the camp usually remained together and moved from place to place for such purposes as they chose. The chief announced early in the spring where the next winter camp would be made so that however far any members of his camp wandered they could return to it in the winter time.

---

24. War Pipe. Anonymous.[12] Recorded by Richard Nines. 1911–12. (AMNH)

A shaman who has dreamed of the wolf will make a sweat house *(Inikaġapi)* and whoever wishes to may join. Anyone who has had sexual intercourse during the previous night may not enter the sweat house as he will be blinded.

The shaman chooses four men who are instructed to go out and each kill a wolf and have it tanned by some virgin. When this is done they bring them to the tipi. The back end is strewn with wild sage while the front end is just scraped off. He sings. Whistles make a noise without being blown, the wolf hides move about, and tracks can be seen. When the ceremony is over he announces that they are to go out on the warpath. Some of his medicines are fastened on the whistle and some on the back, also four crow feathers and one eagle feather. Below the eyes it is painted red and the ends of each foot have a piece of buckskin painted red attached. The black pipe *(ozuye canunpa* [war pipe]) is wrapped in buckskin and placed in [the] charge of a young man, making five in all.

When they go on a warparty the wolf hide bearers carry the wolf hides on their backs and wear the whistle on their necks. The slit between the shoulders goes over the head leaving the head piece on the chest and the rest on the back. They paint their arms from the elbows down and their legs from the knees down with red paint. The four go away from the rest of the party in pairs and only return when they locate the enemy and report. They are very fleet of foot (like a wolf).

Then the war party moves forward to the enemy's camp and as they draw near the shaman takes the black pipe and the medicine on the back of the wolf hide and holding the pipe chews some of the medicine and blowing it out into the air, makes it misty and dense—a wolf's day. Thus they approach the enemy unseen and take the horses away. The enemy goes out to look for the horses and will be killed. The shaman and the wolf hide bearers each get a horse as a reward. The shaman does this quite often and acquires considerable wealth.

---

25. Ritual Cleansing. Anonymous.[13] Recorded by Richard Nines. 1911–12. (AMNH)

He says that the Indians have a great fear of the morning after sexual intercourse, especially those who are official pipe carriers or lance bearers or who hold any other office [in the *akicita* societies]. They fear to smoke a pipe because it may blind them or hurt them otherwise. In the summer they bathe in the creek to cleanse themselves and thus be at liberty to smoke, and in the winter they wash their privates.

---

26. The Sun Dance. High Bear.[14] Recorded by Richard Nines. 1911. (AMNH)

This is a form of prayer to the Great Spirit. A warparty will go out and upon nearing the enemy, one who happens to be more zealous and I presume religiously bent will say, "*Wakan Tanka,* help me. I want to kill an enemy and I want to get some horses and if you help me, when I return I will make a sun dance. Also that the tribe will grow up without dying, also that there will be lots of buffalo to keep us alive."

Now if he succeeds in killing an enemy and stealing some horses he comes back and of course they have the victory dance. After a few days some evening about sundown the herald announces that there is a big feast in the center of the camp circle made for the occasion. "All those who want to attend, come." Usually about thirty or forty come, some among those who attended the war party and some otherwise. Then they dance till morning, blowing a whistle, jumping up and down—no special form of dress or regalia at this preliminary, as I may call it. They have a drum and singers (any number). After the night dance they go home.

The next morning the herald announces that they must all come to the center—a large crowd. Then ten or twelve older men wearing scalp shirts, bonnets—those not having bonnets wearing eagle feathers—walk around the camp circle singing and as they pass the tent of some good young brave man, they bring him out until they have about fourteen or sixteen and then take them to the center. In the meantime they are dancing various dances in the middle.

Then the young men are told to go home and put on their regalia, bonnets, etc., and get their horse, tie up his tail, and paint him up as they must go out as spies. They go to their tents and prepare to go. The herald shouts for them to hurry and they appear in the center, the young men appearing in line in the order that they were chosen. They sing a song for them to leave and they ride around the crowd four times and they go off in a row. They go to a large hill and descend to ride around the hill and come back, the last man making a noise like a wolf continuously as they start to return.

Then when they are about a mile from the camp, the members from camp on horseback (a large crowd) charge for them and circle around them and they all come charging for a small bunch of most any kind of brush or branches they have placed in the center. The first one in hits the brush and says, "I have killed an enemy." Then the spies are asked what they have seen and they reply, "On the other side of the hill we saw lots of Crows slaughtering buffalo. We killed the nearest one and brought back the scalp. On this side of the hill there are lots of buffalo."

Then they all go to the creek where they have previously selected a cottonwood tree—straight and rather small and tall with a fork at the top. Then four men—brave ones—are selected and each cuts at the tree telling their deeds before cutting at the tree. Then they select two women who fell the tree. As the tree falls everybody shouts. Then the lower and small branches are cut off; the men get poles, one man at each end, and together they pack the tree to the center of the camp circle. They tie some cherry bushes to the fork and paint the tree red from the fork downward. Then they hoist the tree up with ropes and as it falls in the designated hole they all shout again and they fill in the dirt so it will be solid. Then they tie on an image of a buffalo made out of rawhide, also one of a man with an eagle feather on his head. Then they place around the pole in a circle some smaller stakes with forked tops and place poles in the forks making a sort of fence. No, not a fence, but a circular shade the same as they make for the Fourth of July shades.

Then they bring a dry (staked) buffalo hide and four drums; a good many men bring long sticks with portions of buffalo tails tied on. The buffalo hide is drummed while the rest beat the drums. In the meantime the sun dancers are coming, each with a buffalo robe and an eagle feather in his hair, also, each one with a pipe filled and the stem pointed forward. They come crying. Then they all assemble and sit down. When they cast away their robes they have on a buckskin skirt and G string. Then the shamans paint their bodies for them, some red and some yellow, some blue-black, but always with a different color for a circle on the stomach, representing the sun. Some wear bonnets, some wear a wreath of sage grass with a black feather on each side representing horns. Each has an eagle bone whistle. Each has an eagle feather wrapped in sage grass.

Then the one who is thinking of piercing his sides and fastening the rope to it walks around crying and with his pipe in his hand. Then some outsiders lay him on the ground face up and his head resting on sage grass. Then one pulls out his skin and taking a sharp knife cuts it and puts a stick in the opening (two openings) near the breasts. Then they fasten two ropes in each place (buffalo braided ropes). When he is fastened he stands up. He prays, "*Wakan Tanka,* have mercy on me, let the tribe live long and let us have lots of buffalo. Let no one get sick so the tribe will increase." Then the singers start up and he pulls hard at the ropes, dancing. Then some outsider comes up and grabs him around the waist and gives away a horse, that is, turns it loose for anyone. Then he helps pull at the rope; holding him around the waist and giving him a throw, he swings around, but the skin holds him. As he swings around he grabs him and cuts into the skin a little and gives him a throw and this time the rope breaks loose from him and he falls to the ground. (He gives away another horse.) When he starts crying, he gives his pipe to anyone, then he is laid on the ground.

Then another way of tying them to the rope is to fasten the ropes in the same place on the breast and also on top of each shoulder with other ropes. These ropes are tied to two stakes back of him; he dances and breaks the two on his shoulders loose from his flesh as these are fastened thinly. Then he dances around, pulling, and breaks himself away from the two on his breast on account of being fastened thinly. Then his relatives (any of them) throw away three or four horses.

Next they take one man and lay him down and cut four places on his shoulders and back and fasten four buffalo heads to them. Then he gets up and the singers singing and beating the drum, he dances with a stick to hold himself. Then one might tear loose and as he keeps on dancing another might tear loose and as he keeps on dancing the other two will break loose. Then his relatives come up and throw away horses.

When any of these dance, the rest join in and dance, too. Sometimes four or five go through the ordeal. The dance lasts one and one-half days and a night. The men usually get faint on account of fasting and see all sorts of animals and birds.

In painting their bodies they also make a mark on their chest thus: \ | / . This is *wakan*. I believe it indicates the rays of the sun, as the sun is painted on the stomach, and of course all the decorations are *wakan*.

---

27. Arts of the Sioux Indians.[15] James R. Walker. (CHS)

In all their arts, certain features made Sioux designs peculiar to the Sioux Indians. * * * The colors recognized in their arts were red, blue, green, yellow, black, and white. Each of these was symbolic: red of the chief of their Gods, the Sun, and of all things held sacred according to their traditions; blue of the most potent of their Gods, the Sky [*Škan*]; green of the most beneficent of their Gods, the Earth; and yellow of the most constructive and destructive of their Gods, the Rock. Black and white were symbolic of human passions, black of anger, grief or determination, white of pleasure.[16]

The coloring material of their paints were shales and clays ground to powders in crude stone mortars or on smooth stone surfaces. These powders were kept in soft skin receptacles and when to be used were mixed with the medium. The mixing was done by grinding as the powders were ground. The media were water and animal fats, preferably the fat rendered from marrow. The mixed paints were kept in receptacles made of dried bladders or dried intestines. When to be used they were extruded into small cuplike utensils made of the hoofs of deer or antelope.

The implements for applying paints were made of the porous portions of horns of deer or elk, chipped and whetted to the desired shapes. They are from two and one-half to four inches in length, one-half to an inch and one-quarter in width, and about a quarter of an inch thick. Either end was used in applying paints and the shape of an end was pointed, knife edged, or blunt. A pointed end was used to draw curved lines, the knife edge to draw straight lines, and the blunt end for applying solid coats. There was also a wooden straight edge used in drawing straight lines. All other lines and designs were applied freehand.

In applying the paints, the article to be painted was outspread, usually on the ground. The paints, made of the desired consistency in the cups, were placed at hand. The painter dipped the implement in the paint until it had taken up the desired quantity. He or she then squatted or stooped over the article and rubbed the paint on it, usually chanting a formula while so doing, because the formula imparted to the paint more lasting and effective qualities. A brush was never used in painting.[17]

The materials painted were skins, implements, utensils, quills, and persons. The skins were either rawhide or tanned. The rawhides were skins of the adult buffalo soaked in water until the hair slipped easily from them. Then the hair was scraped off and the skin stretched and pegged on the ground where it dried with a smooth, even surface that was little flexible. They were used to make soles for moccasins, receptacles of various kinds, and shields for warriors. The soles were not painted, except by a holy man to impart to the moccasins mystic properties, when the design was always occult, and never conventional. The painting on the receptacles was always conventional designs and usually mnemonic and legendary or gnomic. The best examples of the geometric designs were placed on such receptacles. The paintings on shields were usually both imitative [naturalistic] and mnemonic, and were legendary. Such painting was individual and none other than the possessor of the shield was permitted to reproduce it. Often the shield was painted by a holy man, who, by his incantations, imparted to the shield mystic properties.

The soft-tanned skins that were painted were those of the buffalo, moose, elk, deer, antelope, mountain sheep, and sometimes of fur-bearing animals. The skins of buffalos were tanned either with the hair off or on. The adult buffalo skins tanned with the hair off were used exclusively for tipi coverings. These were often painted, the designs being either or both imitative and mnemonic, and were always heraldic, usually suggesting a characteristic of the occupant of the tipi, or a renowned deed he had done.

The buffalo skins tanned with the hair on were always used as robes. These were often painted on the flesh side, the paintings being like those on the tipi coverings, or more often special pictographs of a legendary nature, or individual designs devised in compliance with a vision or by a holy man. The best examples of esoteric painting were on such robes. The skins of buffalo calves were used for making receptacles used by women and holy men, and for pictographic work to record events, and for wraps for babies. These receptacles for women were often highly ornamented, but seldom painted. Those for the holy men were always painted with individual designs of an esoteric character. The wraps for babies were elaborately ornamented, seldom with any signification. The art on the records was always imitative and suggestive as are the illustrations in our works of fiction.

The skins of the moose, elk, deer, antelope and mountain sheep were always soft tanned with the hair removed and were used to make garments, the more choice receptacles, saddle skirts and covers for shields. The garments for men were moccasins, leggings, breech clouts, wamuses [shirts] and bonnets. Those for women were moccasins, leglets and gowns. A ceremonial garment worn by holy men and either men or women who took part in certain ceremonies was a skirt. Belts were important adjuncts to the clothing of both men and women.

The uppers of moccasins for both men and women were usually painted and, sometimes, the soles of those for unmarried women.[18] The designs were mnemonic, usually as mascots, or they might be talismanic with magic potencies. The leggings were garments covering the lower limbs from the hips to the ankles, made of one piece, sewed on the outer side, with the edges forming a wide, flapping border. The entire garment might be painted a solid color with water paints. The conventional place for painting designs was on the front flapping border. The designs were similar to those painted on the moccasins. Leggings were suspended from the belt. The breech clout was a rectangular garment about twelve inches wide and a yard long. It was worn by passing it under the belt behind, between the lower limbs, and under the belt before, so that it hung as wide flaps behind and before the hips. These flaps were embellished with designs both mnemonic and imitative, usually legendary or heraldic. The wamus was a shirt-like garment that covered the body from the neck to below the waist and was donned by passing the head through the opening for the neck. It covered only the upper arms. The entire garment might be colored either red, green or yellow, and if so colored it was an insignia: if red, that the wearer was a sanctified person; if green, that he was noted for his generosity and hospitality; and if yellow, that he was a noted warrior. The garment was never colored blue, for this is the symbolic color of the Great Spirit, the Sky, and blue should indicate only things of the spirit.[19]

The conventional location on a wamus for mnemonic designs was a strip from each shoulder to the lower border, both before and behind. The designs painted here were mnemonic and similar to the paintings on the moccasins and leggings. The entire body of the wamus might be painted with imitative designs, these usually depicting deeds done by the wearer. Wamuses were usually embellished by cutting their edges into fringe-like strips. If deeds done in war entitled one to wear it, his wamus might be embellished with tapering flaps attached at the neck opening so as to hang over the upper part of the chest before and behind. These were usually painted with mnemonic designs. If one had scalped an enemy he was entitled to embellish his wamus with tuft-like fringes made of human hair. This hair was that cut from the heads of women who mourned for their dead. The scalp taken might be added, but usually it was attached to a staff of peculiar shape. Such wamuses and staves were insignia of the highest honors confered by the Sioux.

The bonnet was a close-fitting cap without a brim. The conventional location for painting on it was its border where mnemonic designs were painted, usually as mascots or mottoes. They might be embellished by quills and feathers of any birds, or furs of any animal, and by pendants that might be embellished as were the bonnets. But the quills from the tail of the young golden eagle, the horns of the buffalo, and the hair from the tail of the horse or the buffalo were symbolic and could be worn only by those entitled by deeds done. None but warriors were permitted to embellish their bonnets with the white, black-tipped eagle quills. The manner of embellishing with these was conventional, governing the number of quills that could be attached, and only warriors of great renown were permitted to wear a bonnet so embellished and with a pendant embellished with such quills. Bonnets so embellished were called warbonnets. An eagle plume attached to a warbonnet signified that the wearer had lived a life of rectitude according to the ethics of the Sioux. The pendant of a warbonnet might be embellished with the hair from the tail of the horse for it is a symbol of desperate bravery, because the horse is an *akicita* of the Destructive God. Holy men could embellish their bonnets in any manner they chose, but only they could use buffalo horns on their headdresses or have buffalo skin with the hair on for a pendant. This is because the potency of the Buffalo God is in the skull and horns of dead buffalo and in their skins when used for merely decorative purposes. Such bonnets were insignia of holy men.[20]

Leglets were garments of women covering the lower limbs from below the knees to the ankles. They were cylindrical and closefitting, and were usually painted with mnemonic designs, either mottoes or mascots. The gown was a bag-shaped garment reaching from the neck to the leglets before and behind, and to the ankles on the sides. Flap-like projections from the shoulders lay over the upper arms. Belts worn by women drew their gowns about their waists. These belts were made of elk or moose skin, and were about two inches wide—long enough to go around the waist and leave a dangling end that dragged on the ground. They were ornamented with trinkets of various kinds that had no signification. The borders of the gown were often cut into fringes. The conventional place to be decorated is that portion covering the upper part of the chest. This might be painted, usually in stripes of solid colors without signification, but mnemonic or pictographic designs might be painted there. The more usual method of ornamenting a gown was by attaching trinkets to its upper portion or even to the entire garment. The trinket most desired for this purpose was the tusk [canine] of the elk.[21]

An article that was always a work of art was an effigy of a lizard made of soft-tanned skin, and stuffed. It was painted in conventional manners, usually with mnemonic designs that were supposed to be potent against the malevolence of the Woman of Two Faces, a mythic character who delighted with pains and frightful dreams. The effigy was worn by babies because the lizard is one of the *akicita* of the Winged God [*Wakinyan*] (often mistranslated the Thunderbird), who is the enemy of the Woman of Two Faces and the patron of increase, nourishment and growth.[22]

Choicer receptacles were ornamented, some very elaborately. The best examples of these were tobacco pouches and the smaller receptacles for the implements and materials used by the women. These ornaments might be conventional or merely embellishments without signification.

Men painted their implements, either to adorn them or most often to mark them for ownership. When a man adopted a design as such a mark, all others were prohibited from using that design.

Ownership of an ornamented saddle blanket was a mark of distinction similar to the ownership of a high-priced automobile among the citizens of Denver. Such blankets were made of soft-tanned skins, preferably of the moose or elk, but might be of the deer. They were rectangular, large enough so that all their borders would be beyond the saddle when on horseback. That part of a blanket under the saddle was plain but all the borders beyond the saddle were ornamented, often in a very elaborate manner, either conventional or arbitrary.

The only quills that were painted were the white, black-tipped quills from the tail of the golden eagle. These were worn always as insignia and might be painted with conventional designs, each signifying that which entitled the wearer to wear the quill.[23]

The only parts of the person of a woman that were painted

were her hands and feet that might be painted red to signify that she was entitled to take part in sacred ceremonies, or a red stripe across her forehead horizontally as an insignia that she belonged to the class of ceremonially adopted persons [*Hunka*], or a red stripe across the head at the parting of the hair as a badge signifying that she belonged to the class of women for whom the Buffalo ceremony had been performed. The intent of this ceremony was similar to that of our coming out party for a debutante. The prestige of a woman was according to the profuseness of the feast and the prodigality of the gifts at the Buffalo ceremony performed for her benefit. Or any woman might paint her cheeks red for mere embellishment. But it was considered ridiculous for wrinkled cheeks to be so painted.

Men might paint any portion of their persons above or below their hips. All such paintings were either insignia, badges, or symbolic, except such as were placed on the face for mere embellishment. Each of the conventional designs had a conventional signification, the most of them referring to deeds done in war or chase. The badges were insignia of office and were painted on the face. The symbolic were solid colors without figuration. The colors were red and blue. The entire person painted red was symbolic of holiness. Ordinarily only holy men were thus painted, though one who had danced the Sun Dance and lived a life of rectitude according to the ethics of the Sioux was entitled to so paint his body, the scars incurred while dancing the Sun Dance differentiating him from a holy man. A holy man might add the symbolic blue, placed as broad stripes around the head or around the upper part of the chest, which signified that he had communicated with the Great Spirit, the Sky. A red stripe painted across the forehead horizontally was an insignia that a man belonged to the class of ceremonially adopted persons [*Hunka*], the same as the class of women so decorated.[24]

When the voice of a boy was changing, or soon thereafter, if he had a vision, a holy man would interpret this vision and devise a design. This he painted on the chest of the boy who was then considered a man, and this was his design that he could use on his person, property, or products, or as a sign manual. All those entitled to such designs formed a class of men.

The dyes of the Sioux were vegetable, extracted by boiling

water, and their mordants were earths containing salts, probably of alum. The things dyed were porcupine quills, feathers, quills and hair. The porcupine quills were attached as colors were painted, the designs being the same as those for paintings. Feathers and quills were dyed for embellishment and most used for mere ornamentation. Hair from the tail of the horse or the buffalo was dyed red and was attached to various things as symbols of the Winged God and the Buffalo God, thus securing their patronage.[25]

The long hair from the roach of the moose was woven into a roach and dyed red as a symbol of the Winged God who is the patron of desperate courage. A warrior wearing such a roach had his courage sustained by the Winged God so that he could do desperate deeds of valor such as would entitle him to wear distinguishing insignia.[26]

Women were not permitted to wear quill insignia [i.e., eagle feathers] except those who had lost near kindred in war. Such were permitted to wear the insignia that the lost ones were entitled to wear. The eagle plume was an emblem of purity of life and the green feathers from the head of the mallard drake were emblematic of generosity and hospitality, and these might be worn by either men or women. The red feathers from the head of the redheaded woodpecker were symbolic of holiness and sincerity. They were worn only by holy men but might be attached to any implement that was used in social intercourse.

Sioux pyrographic work was done by burning the end of a small stick until it was a live coal until the design was scorched on. The designs were the same as those of painting and were applied to anything not injured by scorching.[27]

The Sioux did little carving, the men mostly on pipestems and pipe stokers, the women on domestic utensils, such as the wooden and horn spoons and ladles and on the handles of their hide-scraping implements. Ceremonial pipestems were carved with symbolic figures emblematic of the purposes for which they were to be used.[28] Domestic utensils were ordinarily carved with figures of game animals for the purpose of increasing the culinary ability of their users.

The only sculptural work by the Sioux was done by the men in intaglio on smooth rocky walls, usually pictographic of communal deeds done. The implements for sculpture were pointed or edged flints.

Since their contact with the white people, the Sioux have added to their art material beads, shell and metal trinkets, aniline dyes, and textiles. Because beads give more brilliant colors the Sioux preferred them to paints in applying their arts. The Sioux designs for beadwork are the same as those for painting.[29]

The Sioux technique for attaching beads is peculiar in that the beads are strung on threads of sinew, and these threads stitched not through, but into, the article to be beaded, and each stitch is knotted to the adjoining stitches. An introduced method of applying beadwork is practiced by the Sioux women. This is by weaving the beads into a band of the desired length and width and attaching this band to the article to be beaded. A peculiarity of the Sioux technique of this weaving is that each thread of the woof is knotted to each adjacent thread of woof and to the outside threads of the warp. The weaving is done on a rectangular frame around which the warp is wound, the shuttle being a needle threaded with the woof thread.[30]

Another peculiarity of the Sioux women's technique for beadwork of any kind is that they first mix the beads of all colors and then pick out each bead as it is to be used. This is because glass beads are made by white men who do not know how to control their potencies and by mixing the beads their potencies are equalized so that no bead may have the power to overcome other beads, and the potency of the design will not be disturbed.

---

28. Symbols. Seven Rabbits. (CHS)

The Lakotas did not write. They remembered things by figures and symbols. A circle meant a camp, and the sun, and the world. A circle with marks across it meant the spider and a whirlwind. A square meant the four winds, and the country of the Lakotas. A triangle meant a tipi; triangles side by side meant mountains. A triangle with its base up meant the people. A trident meant going against. A straight line meant a trail. A straight line with a head and points meant a journey, a war party or hunting party. A diamond meant water. There are many other figures which meant much.

III

Time and History

Conceptions of time vary dramatically from one culture to another. In Western culture, time is conceived of as an invariant aspect of nature, ceaselessly progressing from the beginning toward eternity. Precisely quantifiable, time is valued as a commodity to be measured, saved, wasted, or used wisely. For the Lakotas, such a concept of time is quite foreign. Although we do not have the kinds of information that would allow for a complex understanding, it is clear that the Lakota traditional concepts relating to time lacked the invariant and quantifiable nature of Western time concepts. Anthropologists have suggested that time can be understood as the measure of significant intervals in social life. In industrialized society, microseconds become significant units, but in the Lakota society of the buffalo-hunting days, the significant time units were based on natural phenomena: the sun, moon, seasons. In Western society, time is thoroughly objectified; for the Lakotas, time more fundamentally expresses qualities and relationships, not quantities.

In document 29 Walker outlines his understanding of Lakota time categories and classifications as he came to develop them from talking with the Oglalas. Many of his attempts at etymological interpretations are strained and must be rejected on linguistic grounds. Whether they represent Lakota folk etymologies is unknown. In any case, they vividly reveal Walker's overwhelming drive to systematize data. Significantly, Walker's own Western notions of time led him to focus on classifying measures of time instead of attempting to understand Lakota time concepts in more fundamental ways. Perhaps the point is this: Walker was able to conceive of the importance of *wakan* and the neccessity for complex, discursive definitions of it precisely because he did not categorize it as a real phenomenon. Time, on the other hand, seemed to him a real and constant aspect of nature; the problem was not how the Lakotas conceived of time but merely how they measured it. We once again see Walker trapped within his own cultural conventions.

Like time, the definition of history varies entirely from one culture to the next. History may be conceived of as the organization of past time. For Western culture, history has all past time firmly under control, imagined as a geometric grid of seconds, minutes, hours, days, weeks, months, years, decades, centuries, eons. In this conception of history, the ultimate test of historical fact is its truthfulness: can it be placed precisely in the time grid, in relation to other historical facts? Chronology is rigid, locked into the monolithic concept of invariant time. The Lakota concept of history is vastly different. Only two significant units of historical time appear: the year (called *omaka*, "year," or *waniyetu*, "winter") and the generation (*wicoicaġe*, understood as seventy years, the life span of an old man). The winter counts *(waniyetu iyawapi)* literally counted back the winters from the present as far back as memory would allow. During the late nineteenth century, if not before, these counts were objectified as pictographs on hide or paper, one pictograph representing each winter. These served their keepers as mnemonic devices to recall the event for which each winter was named. Some count keepers also had a series of generation pictographs that preceded the yearly portions of the count, taking Lakota history back to the days before the horse and the time when the Beautiful Woman brought the sacred pipe and founded the traditional Lakota way of life. Unfortunately, we know little about the significance of these generation counts.[1]

Within the Lakota conception of history, which lacked the objectification of Western concepts of history, winter counts had two main functions. The first was to serve as a calendar by which past events could be located in time. Thus Walker recorded that all Oglalas could identify on the winter count the pictograph representing the year in which they were born, and in this way individuals were able to figure their age. Individual Lakotas did not keep an active memory of their age; it was not a relevant variable and could be easily established by counting back the pictographs on a winter count.

The second function of winter counts was to teach and instruct. In addition to recalling the names of the winters, the keepers integrated stories of all kinds into their oral repertories, and when telling the names of winters, they could also provide related stories of battles, natural catastrophes, encounters with the spirits, and every kind of entertaining tale. There is no doubt that the content of such stories changed over time as the counts passed from one keeper to the next: we have evidence that they did just in the few counts that have been preserved and interpreted in writing. In this way history was kept current and relevant. Historical fact was valued not according to its chronological accuracy but according to its relevance to the people. That events actually happened in a certain way, to certain individuals, at certain times and places, instead of being the focus of Lakota history as it is for us, was rather the background. The message of the anecdote was more significant than the details.

It is, of course, a Western tradition as well that history should be used to inform the present. Yet in contemporary academia, history has come to be valued for its objectivity, which allows us to judge the past and make relevant statements for the present. The discipline of history rejects information that comes from sources which cannot be evaluated, or from mythological or religious realms. Its self-image is as a discipline that is secular and objectively evaluative. Lakota history, on the other hand, is at foremost a moral endeavor. History is never simply the past, but the past as it relates to the present. This past is preceded, accompanied, and followed by an ever present, sacred dimension which is outside the realm of human time. Here the gods and spirits are the relevant participants, who sometimes intrude into the flow of human history but are not dependent on it. The integration of these aspects of history into the telling of the winters was an important duty of the count keeper. Without it, mere human history would lack the larger relevance that is essential to the Lakota concept. For them, history is sacred history.

In many cases interpretations of winter counts vary because the actual memory of a specific event has been lost. While the counts were recorded as pictographs, the memorized phrases that served to name each winter and the pictographs themselves were mutually reinforcing, helping to preserve the meanings. When the counts were shifted over to written form, with only the names of the winters recorded in Lakota, the potential for confusion became greater. The orthography used was not precise enough to differentiate between words that differed only in minor phonetic ways. Without the visual image, alternate interpretations became equally plausible unless the count keeper had memorized the events, as told by the previous keeper. But much of the purpose of transposing the counts to writing seems to have been to relieve the keepers from the necessity of memorizing the whole count. Some keepers merely copied someone else's count and then began to add their own events to designate subsequent years. As a result, they would frequently be unclear about the meanings of the earlier years. This kind of confusion, as well as jumblings of sequences, may be attributed to the problems of transferring the winter counts from pictographic to written form.

A good example of such confusion in interpretation is provided by the event for 1874 in the No Ears and Short Man winter counts printed in document 30. The text reads: *Ehake kowakantan ai,* "For the last time / across the river / they went." Walker misread it as *Ehake ko Wakan Tan ai,* "At last / quickly / God / great / comes with," which he freely translated as "The Great God at last comes quickly with (others)." The problems were that the orthography was not precise enough to distinguish whether the *t* of *kowakantan* was aspirated or not, the handwriting did not allow a precise definition of word boundary, and the keeper evidently did not recall the event. In the copy of the winter count kept by Ben Kindle, the meaning of the phrase was correctly remembered but not the event. Kindle's count gives "The Sioux cross the Missouri for the last time."[2] This interpretation is deduced from the fact that the Lakotas had originated across the Missouri. The actual event was remembered by John Colhoff in his copy of the winter count: "For the last time, a trip across. This means that the Oglalas made their last trip on the south side of the North Platte River."[3] These kinds of confusions mar the interpretations of winter counts; the best corrective is comparison of many winter counts and corroboration, when possible, from historical documents.

Most of the translations of winter counts available to us now give only names for winters in a calendric sense, with little remembrance of the events memorialized. Each winter's event is presented more or less distinct from anything that went before or came after. In other words, for most winter counts, there is absolutely no sense of narrative history linking events together through time. However, in the three Oglala winter counts recorded in 1879 and 1880 by Dr. William H. Corbusier at Pine Ridge, there is a considerable amount of narrative in the translations that link the events of successive years together. Frequently, one winter's event is interpreted as occurring in retaliation for the previous winter's event. Whether this was the way in which the counts were originally understood—as seems likely—or whether it was a peculiarity of Corbusier's manner of recording the translations of the events, is not known.[4] At least the strong possibility exists that at earlier periods the winter counts were somewhat more like narrative history, but by the time Walker collected them they had lost this dimension and become more strictly calendars.

Oglala Winter Counts

Winter counts were, in a symbolic sense, an important part of social life. It seems that there was at least one keeper in every Lakota camp. We have no way of knowing how many Oglala winter counts existed during the nineteenth century, but among those available in published form and preserved in archives, seven distinct traditions may be identified. Each winter count shares a percentage of yearly designations with others. These likenesses may be attributed to the count keepers' living in the same or closely related bands, to extraordinary occurrences (for example, a meteorite shower or the murder of a prominent chief), and possibly to borrowing. Each of these seven traditions seems to be an original winter count, representing a unique historical tradition of counting the winters. Ultimately, each probably reflects a family group.

The following list of the seven Oglala winter count traditions begins with that of No Ears, which, according to Walker, was the count used for standard reference at Pine Ridge. The others are listed in order of their similarity to the No Ears count.

1. NO EARS. Walker's copy for the years 1759–1912 is printed in document 30. According to Walker, John No Ears stated that this winter count was first written down in Lakota from a pictographic record by his father, Walking Eagle. The pictographs ended in 1888, later years being recorded only by Lakota texts. No Ears died in 1918. Subsequently, other keepers continued the count, at least until 1925. I have located ten versions of this count, each of which is discussed below.[5]

2. SHORT MAN. Only one version of this count is known, covering the years 1821–1912. The original was drawn in a blank book; the water-color drawings reproduced here were copied by Short Man in 1913 from his original winter count, each drawing

on a separate sheet of typing paper. The names of the winters were dictated by Short Man and written down in Lakota by Walker, who typed them with translations and dates on the bottom of each sheet. (This typewritten information has been cropped from the photographs reproduced in this book.) Inadvertently, Walker began numbering the winters with 1822, only later discovering that he should have begun with 1821. This transposition has been made in the text of the count as printed in document 30. There is about a 69 percent overlap in the events selected in the Short Man winter count to designate the winters with the events as given in the No Ears count. The differences are scattered throughout the count, suggesting that the two counts were kept by members of the same or very closely related bands.[6]

3. WHITE COW KILLER. Dr. William H. Corbusier saw this winter count at Pine Ridge about 1879. Although he was unable to obtain a copy of the pictographs, he recorded the names of most of the winters from 1775 to 1878, as translated into English. For the years recorded, there is almost a 69 percent overlap with that of No Ears, although the differences do not match those of Short Man. Again, this count seems to represent another by a keeper in the same band, or a closely related one to that of No Ears.[7]

4. IRON CROW. Two versions of this count are known. The one printed in document 30 was collected by Clark Wissler on Pine Ridge Reservation in 1902 and covers the years 1785–1902. The names of the winters were written out in Lakota by Iron Crow. Wissler recorded English translations and brief commentary by Iron Crow as interpreted by Charles and Richard Nines and Walker. This count overlaps with that of No Ears by about 39 percent.[8]

The second version was recorded in pictographic form and in Lakota by Wounded Bear for the years 1815–96. This count differs from that of Iron Crow in only fifteen of the eighty-one designations for winters, mostly after the beginning of the reservation period.[9]

5. RED HORSE OWNER OR FIRE THUNDER. This count is owned by the Fire Thunder family of Pine Ridge Reservation. Three basic versions are known. The first consists only of pictographs in a small book, begun by Moses Red Horse Owner, the original keeper. He kept the count by memory, only late in life

drawing a pictographic version. This count began in 1786; Red Horse Owner died in 1908. It was maintained by his wife, Louisa, until her death in 1922 and was continued, mainly by Angelique Fire Thunder, until 1947. For 1786–1912 there is about a 34 percent overlap with the No Ears count.

The second version is a copy of the pictographs made by Angelique Fire Thunder in a school copy book, with Lakota captions dictated by Louisa Red Horse Owner. Angelique Fire Thunder maintained this version of the count, with some lapses, at least until 1968.[10]

The third version was recorded by Ella Deloria in the mid-1930s. She traced Angelique Fire Thunder's pictographs for 1786–1906 and recorded a phonetic transcription of the Lakota text, with interlinear and free translations in English. The translation and commentary were evidently prepared with the help of the Fire Thunder family.[11]

This winter count has also been the subject of several artistic renderings on animal hides and canvas.

6. Cloud Shield. Corbusier obtained a pictographic copy for the years 1777–1878 from Cloud Shield, evidently at Pine Ridge, about 1879. He also recorded the names of the winters, in English translation only. This count has about a 34 percent overlap with that of No Ears.

7. American Horse. Corbusier obtained a pictographic copy and English translation for the years 1775–1878 at the same time and place as he had procured Cloud Shield's. Of the Oglala counts, this one shares the least with that of No Ears, there being only a 26 percent overlap.[12]

The No Ears Winter Count

The No Ears winter count is probably the most widely known of the Oglala winter counts. The interrelationships among the ten copies that I have located are complex, but the copies may be classified in three groups.

The first group (I) is represented by three versions. The first version (IA) is the Deloria No Ears winter count, which covers the years 1759–1906. Ella Deloria designated it as an Oglala count, but she recorded it on the Rosebud Reservation about 1937. She did not copy the actual Lakota text as it was written, but rather made a phonetic transcription, either from the dictation of the person who owned the count or possibly from her own reading of it. This procedure resulted in some errors in interpreting the sense of the Lakota text. Nonetheless, her interlinear and free translations and notes are invaluable, and I have been guided by her work in making the translation that appears in this volume. The Deloria count differs from Walker's No Ears count in two particulars. In the first place, Walker's copy makes an error in the transcription of the event for 1831 (see p. 137). Second, Deloria's count records a different event for 1906, the final year of her copy. This suggests that Walker's and Deloria's counts may both have been copied from an earlier one (or Deloria's may have been a copy of Walker's) and maintained independently thereafter—Deloria's for only one year, Walker's until 1912.[13]

The second version (IB) was obtained from Flying Hawk on the Pine Ridge Reservation, evidently during the 1920s, by M. L. McCreight, who published it in *Firewater and Forked Tongues* (1947). This count consists of both Lakota text and English translation and in content is identical to Deloria's.[14]

The third version (IC) was made by Frank White-buffalo-man on the Cheyenne River Reservation about 1953. It covers only the years 1850–1906, consists of both Lakota and English texts, and was evidently copied directly from McCreight's book. This copy was given to James H. Howard, who published it in "Two Teton Dakota Winter Count Texts" (1960).[15]

The second group of No Ears counts (II) is also represented by three versions. Each begins with a brief paragraph about winter counts and the Lakota concept of the year *(omaka)*.

The first version (IIA) covers the years 1759–1908; the contents are identical to Walker's, except that the 1831 error is lacking. This count consists of both Lakota text and English translation, recorded in a notebook that was owned by John B. Garnier, son of Baptiste ("Little Bat") Garnier, the famous scout at Fort Robinson, Nebraska. Judging from the evenness of the handwriting, this count was copied into the record book at a single time. The published version of this count incorporates many mistranscriptions in the Lakota text.[16]

The second version (IIB) is a typed manuscript in the Bureau of American Ethnology collections. Its history is unknown. This count is identical to Garnier's but continues until 1919.[17]

The third version (IIC) was published in mimeographed form by Fred B. Hackett of Chicago under the title "Calendar for Oglala Sioux Names for Years from A.D. 1759 to A.D. 1908" (ca. 1960). It is identical to the previous two, and may have been copied from the one in the Bureau of American Ethnology collections, ending in 1908 because of space limitations.[18]

The third group of No Ears counts (III) is represented by four versions, all of which incorporate the 1831 error. The first version (IIIA) is Walker's copy, published here, covering the years 1759–1912. The manuscript in Walker's papers consists of the Lakota text with various interlinear and free translations by Walker. These translations were made at a time when Walker was attempting to create syllable-by-syllable etymological translations. I have consulted them in making the translation presented here, although they are in many respects inaccurate.

The second version (IIIB) is from a typescript manuscript in the North Dakota Historical Society entitled "History of the Oglala Sioux from Original in Possession of Maj. Gen. Hugh L. Scott." It is possible that Scott was the collector mentioned by Walker to whom No Ears sold his original count. The typescript consists of Lakota text and English translation and was published in Howard's "Two Teton Dakota Winter Count Texts" (1960). It is identical to Walker's except that 1765 and 1766 are inverted and the years from 1907 to 1918 are unique. Another copy, made by Eugene Buechel, S.J., is identical to Scott's version for the years 1759–1914 and bears the notation "Dr. Walker's work." It is in the files of Holy Rosary Mission, Bureau of Catholic Indian Missions Records, Marquette University, Milwaukee, Wisconsin.

The third version (IIIC) is the count of Ben Kindle, 1759–1925, collected by Martha Beckwith at Pine Ridge in 1926. Kindle stated that he had obtained the count from his grandfather, Afraid of Soldier. Kindle made a copy of the Lakota text for Beckwith and dictated many brief explanations of the events. The contents of the count are identical to Walker's copy except that 1765 and 1766 are inverted (suggesting a relationship to Scott's copy); the event for 1860 is given for 1861 and the 1861 event is missing; 1872 is unique; 1909 and 1910 are inverted; and the events for 1912–25 are unique. A phonetic transcription of Kindle's text by Ella Deloria, interlinear and free translations by Deloria, and Kindle's explanatory comments were published in Beckwith's "Mythology of the Oglala Dakota" (1930). Kindle's commentary provides considerable detail, much of which is historically inaccurate. It is unclear whether Kindle's information came from oral tradition or whether it was simply invented to please Beckwith.[19]

The fourth version (IIID) was recorded by John Colhoff (Whiteman Stands in Sight) and was given to William K. Powers in 1949. It consists of Lakota text with English translations and extensive commentary by Colhoff combining oral tradition and information taken from published sources. The count begins in 1759 and ends in 1896 and is identical to Walker's except that a unique interpretation is given for 1872. This count is published in Powers's "A Winter Count of the Oglala" (1963).[20]

Other Winter Counts

In addition to the Oglala winter counts, there are many others recorded from different Sioux groups. Winter count traditions have been identified at Standing Rock, Cheyenne River, Rosebud, and Crow Creek reservations. Some of these counts are closely related to the Oglala ones, especially for the earlier years. These counts are all from the Tetons and Yanktonais; none from the Santees or Assiniboins have been located. Other tribes known to have kept winter counts are the Mandans, Blackfeet, Poncas, and Kiowas.[21]

The Winter Count Texts

Document 30 presents the texts of three Oglala winter counts in Lakota and English: those of No Ears, Short Man, and Iron Crow. In addition, the drawings depicting each winter's event are reproduced for Short Man's count. Pictographic versions of the No Ears and Iron Crow counts have not been located. The Lakota texts of No Ears's and Short Man's counts are reproduced from typewritten copies made by Walker; typographical errors have been corrected, diacritical marks added, and hyphens between words in personal names eliminated. The Lakota text of Iron Crow's count is reproduced from his own handwritten copy, retaining all orthographic inconsistencies. One peculiarity of this document is the occasional use of *d* where *l* is expected, usually in the diminutive suffix *-da* attached to personal names. This is complicated by the similarity of Iron Crow's method of writing *d* and *l;* the determination of which was intended is in some cases very subjective. For notes on orthographies, see Appendix II.

I have used No Ears's count as the basis. When the same events are recorded in the same words in the other counts, I have not reproduced them but simply referred the reader to the No Ears count, eliminating unnecessary repetition when two versions are identical or vary only in the orthography. If there is a difference of even a single word, however, I have reproduced both texts.

The translation of tribal names in winter count texts provides some problems because one term may be used in some cases to refer to different groups. For consistency, I have translated tribal names as follows: *Palani,* "Arikaras"; *Scili* (or *Sicili*) "Pawnees"; *Kangi wicaša* or *Psa,* "Crows"; *Miwatani,* "Mandans"; *Škutani,* "Gros Ventres (Atsinas)"; *Šahiyela* (or *Šanhiyela*), "Cheyennes"; *Witapahatu,* "Kiowas"; *Sapa wicaša,* "Utes"; *Susuni,* "Shoshones."[22]

In making the translations of the Lakota texts, I have relied heavily on Ella Deloria's work and have incorporated her comments whenever they provided additional information. In quoting from her writings I use an *n* in place of a subscript hook to indicate nasalization of vowels. In preparing my translations I have also carefully consulted the work of James H. Howard and have benefited from it greatly.

The purpose of presenting these winter counts here is to make them available for further study. I have not made exhaustive winter-by-winter comparisons with other counts; that is beyond the scope of this volume. I have given brief historical annotations to provide the reader access to historical references on identifiable events and persons. These citations are given in the text for the reader's convenience. Much study remains to be done in working out a fuller understanding of specific events, although solid groundwork has been laid in the various studies of winter counts by James H. Howard.

In order to minimize confusion I give only one calendar year for each winter, although the reader must remember that the Lakota "winter" was defined as the period from the first snowfall of one year to to the first snowfall of the next year and hence overlaps two of our calendar years.

Document 31 presents an eyewitness account by Beard of the ghost dance and Wounded Knee massacre. It was recorded by Walker and gives a vivid picture of the horror and confusion of that tragic event. Beard—later known as Dewey Beard (also as Dewey Horn Cloud and Iron Hail)—dictated a number of similar accounts throughout his long life, the fullest of which was recorded by Judge Eli Ricker in 1907. A shorter account by Beard is printed in James H. McGregor's *The Wounded Knee Massacre from Viewpoint of the Sioux.*[23]

---

29. Divisions of Time. James R. Walker. (CHS)

The Oglalas have no name for time alone but their word *etu* expresses the concept of a time, as, for instance, the term *anpetu* means daytime. They reckon their time by *anpetu,* daytime; *hanyetu,* nighttime; *wiyetu,* moon time (month); *makoncaǧayetu,* earth-changing-time (season); and *omakayetu,* world-time (year).

The day is divided into *anpao,* before sunrise; *anpa,* sunshines; and *ȟtayetu,* fading-time (evening). From sunrise until sunset is divided into *wicokayaśni,* sun-middle-made-not (forenoon); *anpecokaya,* sun-shines-middle-made (midday); and *wicokayasanpa,* sun-middle-made-beyond (afternoon).

The night is when the stars shine. Midnight is when the first stars seen in the east are in the middle of the sky, *hancokaya,* night-middle-made.

Days and nights were not given permanent names or numbers nor recorded in any way.

A moon was the time from the first appearance of the new

moon in the west after the sun had set until the last appearance of the old moon in the east before the sun rose. The name of the moon was *hanwi,* night-sun, which was commonly abbreviated to *wi,* sun. The old and the new moon were called *yaśpapi,* bitten-off, and the time during the dark of the moon *yaśpayetu,* bitten-off-time. The full moon was called *mibe wi,* circular moon, and the time of the full moon *mibeyetu.*

There were thirteen moons and four seasons. The four seasons were: *wietu,* sun-time (spring); *bloketu,* male-time, or potato-time (summer); *ptanyetu,* changeable-time (autumn); and *waniyetu,* snow-existing-time (winter).

There were two moons in the spring season which were: *Magaksica agli wi,* Ducks together-come moon; and *Canwape ton wi,* Tree-leaves potent moon. There were four moons in the summer season which were: *Tipsinla wi,* Prairie-rice-like (Wild turnip) moon; *Canpa sapa wi,* Tree-head (Choke cherry) black moon; *Kanta śa wi,* Plums red moon; and *Canwape ġi wi,* Tree-leaves yellow moon.

There were two moons in the autumn season which were: *Canwape kasna wi,* Tree-leaves shaken-off moon; and *Waniyetu wi,* Snow-exists-time moon. There were either four or five moons in the winter season, which were *Wani cokan wi,* Snow-exists midst moon; *Teḣi wi,* Hardship moon; *Wicata wi,* Racoon moon [*Wicaṭa wi,* "Dead moon"]; *Iśta wicayazan wi,* Eyes them-suffer moon; and *Tanin śni wi,* Discernible—not moon. The Discernible not moon sometimes appeared and sometimes did not, and no one could tell for certain whether it had appeared or not until the seasons showed that it had appeared. The year began with the first moon of the first season which ordinarily was when the ducks return together in flocks, but if there was an Indiscernible moon then the year began with it.

The winter season completed the year, and in speaking of the past, a winter meant a completed year. For this reason the Oglalas designated the past by winters instead of years. And the nearest that they could specify a particular time was of a moon of a season of a winter. They recorded these winters by pictography of some notable event occurring during that year that was a matter of common knowledge to the people, which designations were maintained in their order of sequence. This made a calendar.

30. The No Ears, Short Man, and Iron Crow Winter Counts. Translated by the editor. (CHS and AMNH)

1759 NO EARS: *Wicableca hehan waniyetu.* The people scattered during the winter.

When the count entry ends with the word *waniyetu,* I translate "during the winter," although it should be kept in mind that the Lakota concept *waniyetu* refers both to the winter season and to the year as a unit of time. In a general sense, every entry may be considered to end with the word *waniyetu:* "In the winter that . . ." Iron Crow indicates this on his copy of his winter count; hence some of his entries end with *waniyetu waniyetu,* "In the winter that . . . during the winter" (e.g., see Iron Crow 1797).

1760 NO EARS: *Ho kuwa wicaktepi.* Fishermen were killed.

1761 NO EARS: *Wambli kuwa wicaktepi.* Eagle trappers were killed.

1762 NO EARS: *Pte anu wanpi.* They swam after buffalo.

Deloria commented: "They swim, with buffalo as their objective. (The idea here is different from 'They swim towards some buffaloes.' Specifically intended, the plural object *wica* would have been necessary.)"

1763 NO EARS: *Mila wanica.* No knives.

Deloria commented that *wanica,* as an idiom, implies not an absolute lack, but a scarcity.

According to Walker, an alternate name for this winter is *Toka mila yuke.* If the first word is *toká,* the entry means "They had knives for the first time"; if the first word is *tóka,* the entry means "They had enemy knives." Deloria, translating Kindle's version of the count, suggested *toka* might be intended for *t'ukí*, "shells," "They used shells for knives" (Beckwith 1930:351).

1764 NO EARS: *Tajuśkala ktepi.* Ant was killed.

The diminutive suffix *-la* added to a personal name indicates it is a nickname, according to Deloria. Hence, where it appears, I do not translate it as part of the name (e.g., "Little Ant"), since it does not convey the meaning of small, but rather of familiarity.

1765 No Ears: *Waleġala ktepi.* Bladder Pouch was killed.

1766 No Ears: *Waze* [*Wazi*] *kutela ahi ktepi.* Pine Shooter was killed by the enemy.

Deloria comments that *ahiktepi,* literally, "arriving they kill him," is an idiom meaning "to be killed in battle, killed by the enemy."

1767 No Ears: *Anub ob iyeyipi.* They divided themselves into two sides.

Deloria commented: "*Kic'i iyé,* with him he is, is idiomatic for, To side with him"; *ob iye* is evidently equivalent in meaning.

1768 No Ears: *Iyeska kicizapi.* Those who speak the same language fought with one another.

Deloria commented: "There is civil war; or war within Dakota-speaking groups. (This seems to be a natural development of what began in 1767, wherein all took sides.)" The word *iyeska* can also connote "interpreter" or "mixed-blood."

1769 No Ears: *Itehan kiton ktepi.* Mask Wearer was killed.

Deloria commented: "Itéha, referring to horses, means halter or hackamore. With reference to man, it is a mask."

1770 No Ears: *Wakan Tanka gnaśkiya. Wakan Tanka* was enraged.

Kindle's copy has *Wak'ánt'anka ihánb.la winyan wan g.naśkínyan,* "A woman has a vision of *Wakantanka* and goes insane" (Beckwith 1930:352). Deloria commented, "I have no explanation for this, neither has anyone. It is lost, whatever the meaning might have been." White Bull commented: "There was a man who claimed he was a shaman. He kept talking about it all the time until he went crazy" (Vestal 1934b:260).

1771 No Ears: *Miwatani oġuwicayapi.* They burned the Mandans.

1772 No Ears: *Can qin yamini wicaktepi.* Three wood carriers were killed.

1773 NO EARS: *Śunka ko iśta niyapi.* Even dogs had sore eyes.

Deloria notes that March is called the Moon of Sore Eyes; this may indicate a late, snowy winter.

1774 NO EARS: *Heyoka kaġala ktepi.* They killed *Heyoka* Impersonator.

Heyoka kaġa means "to impersonate *Heyoka*," to perform a ceremony acting out a *Heyoka* dream, that is, a dream of Thunder which commands the dreamer to act out the role of ceremonial clown. See Deloria (1944:53–55) and Walker (1980:155–57).

1775 NO EARS: *Pahata i nonp wicaktepi.* Two scouts were killed.

Deloria commented that *Pahata i,* "to go to the hill," is idiomatic for "to scout."

1776 NO EARS: *Kiglela hi.* Goes Home arrived.

Deloria commented that the man's nickname is literally "He starts for home."

1777 NO EARS: *Hohe ahi.* Assiniboines arrived.

1778 NO EARS: *Can naksa yuha ktepi.* War Club Owner was killed.

1779 NO EARS: *Tukte el wanitipi tanin śni.* The location of the winter camp was not discernable.

Deloria suggested that this indicated that the camp had moved continually throughout the winter. Mallery (1893:306) commented on this event in Battiste Good's count (1777–78): "They made no permanent camp, but wandered about from place to place."

1780 NO EARS: *Slukela raka iwoṭo. Slukela* bumped into *ḣaka.*

The text is unclear. *Slukela* is said to mean "Skinned Penis" (Mallery 1893:308) or "Circumcised" (Denig 1930:434, Assiniboin form "Sndo-kah"), but Wissler recorded the translation (from the Nines brothers, evidently) of the name *Slukeraka* as "Masturbator" (Iron Crow 1788).

Deloria commented on this event in the Fire Thunder count for 1787: "The explanation of this says that a certain man gambled in this particular variety of hoop and stick game [*ḣaka*], staking more and more until he lost absolutely everything, including his wife and home, and went forth stark-naked and alone." Both the Fire Thunder or Red Horse Owner (Karol 1969:22) and Battiste Good (Mallery 1893:308) count pictographs clearly show a *ȟaka* stick. For further discussion see Mallery (1886:131) and Culin (1907:505–6).

Concerning the name, Deloria commented: "The name has all the indications of vulgarity, as if bestowed by a hermaphrodite [*winkte*]." The *winkte,* transvestites, frequently bestowed on people obscene or scatalogical nicknames which became commonly used.

1781 NO EARS: *Śunka wakan natan ahi.* Horses arrived stampeding.

1782 NO EARS: *Nawicaśli.* Measles.

According to Deloria the word means "rash" and was the usual designation for measles.

1783 NO EARS: *Śina luta in wan ktepi.* One wearing a red blanket was killed.

1784 NO EARS: *Akicita cuwita ṭa. Akicita* froze to death.

Deloria commented that *Akicita* was the man's name. Kindle's winter count has *Akíc'ita óta c'uwítat'api,* "Many soldiers froze to death" (Beckwith 1930:353).

1785. NO EARS: *Oglala kin rante wan icupi.* The Oglalas took a cedar (juniper).

American Horse's count gives this event for 1775–76: "Standing-Bull, the great-grandfather of the present Standing-Bull, discovered the Black Hills. He carried home with him a pine tree of a species he had never seen before" (Mallery 1886:130). However, Battiste Good's count, which gives the event for 1784–85, traces the name of this winter to a medicine man's trick of pretending to draw a cedar tree out of the ground and then making it disappear again (Mallery 1893:309).

IRON CROW: *Mato nakpa ahi ktepi.* Bear Ears was killed by the enemy. (First year of the Iron Crow winter count.)

1786 NO EARS: *Peici maza zuya ti.* Metal Hair Ornament entered a camp while away at war.

Deloria's copy has *ti-i,* "camp he-enters." The translation of the man's name is by Walker.

IRON CROW: *Zintkada huwegahan ahi ktepi.* Broken Leg Bird was killed by the enemy.

1787 NO EARS: *Ohanzi atkuku ktepi.* Shade's father was killed.

IRON CROW: *Miwatani om wanitipi.* They made winter camp with the Mandans.

1788 NO EARS: *Heyoka kaġa nonp wicaktepi.* Two *Heyoka* impersonators were killed.

IRON CROW: *Sluke raka ahi ktepi. Sluke raka* was killed by the enemy.

See No Ears 1780.

1789 NO EARS: *Kanġi ota ṭapi.* Many crows (birds) died.

Mallery (1886:132) commented on this event in the American Horse count: "The cold was so intense that crows froze in the air and dropped dead near the lodges."

1790 NO EARS: *Miwatani nonp caṙ cokan wicaktepi.* They killed two Mandans on the middle of the ice.

IRON CROW: *Pangi iwani tipi.* They made their winter camp with the wild artichokes.

Wissler translated: "Lived on nothing but artichokes."

1791 NO EARS: *Wowapi wan mako kawinṙ yuha hiyaya yapi.* They went around the country carrying a flag.

The Flame's winter count interprets this event as the bringing of the first U.S. flag by military troops (Mallery 1886:101), but no historical verification seems possible. A Spanish document for 1791 mentions that English traders were going as far as the Missouri River to trade with the Indians (Nasatir 1952, vol. 1:80, 145).

IRON CROW: *Conpeškada cuwitaṭa.* Glue froze to death.

The Fire Thunder winter count, which gives this event for 1804, shows a glue stick in the pictograph (see Karol 1969:25). Deloria commented: "A stick similar to illustration was dipped repeatedly into a kettle of boiling hoofs, each time causing some of the gelatinous substance to adhere to it. This was done from time to time, and the dried stick was kept for rubbing on sinew in flinting and winging arrows, to make it stick."

1792 No Ears: *Winyan wan ska wanyakapi.* They saw a white woman (i.e., white in color, not necessarily a European).

Mallery (1893:311) comments on the drawing representing this event in Battiste Good's count: "The dress of the woman indicates that she was not an Indian," and suggests that it was the first white woman seen by the Dakotas.

Iron Crow: *Wiglušaka ota ṭapi.* Many pregnant women died.

See No Ears 1799.

1793 No Ears: *Miwatani awicatipi.* They camped with the Mandans.

Iron Crow: *Wašicun winyan wan hanṭeyapi.* A white (European) woman was killed at night.

Wissler translated: "Unknown Indian shot a white woman with an arrow." Since the term *wašicun* refers either to a type of spirit or a European, this and other early events might refer to spirits rather than Europeans.

1794 No Ears: *Ite ciqa wan ktepi.* One with a small face was killed.

Iron Crow: *Wašicun wan tokiyata hi ca wanyakapi.* They saw a white man who came from some unknown place.

1795 No Ears: *Pehin hanskaska wan ktepi.* One with very long hair was killed.

Iron Crow: *Ṡiyotanka yuhala ahi ktepi.* Flute Owner was killed by the enemy.

1796 No Ears: *Mini yaye yuha wan ktepi.* One carrying a water bag was killed.

Iron Crow: *Pehin hanskaska wan iwakte glipi.* They came home victorious with a long-haired scalp.

See No Ears 1795.

1797 No Ears: *Wapaha kiton wan ktepi.* One wearing a warbonnet was killed.

Iron Crow: *Capa ciqa hi waniyetu.* Little Beaver arrived during the winter.

American Horse's winter count identifies Little Beaver

as a white trader (Mallery 1886:133). Howard (1968:14) suggested that this was the Dakotas' name for the trader Régis Loisel. Iron Crow's count for 1808 suggests that Little Beaver died that winter. Loisel, however, died in 1804 (Nasatir 1952, vol. 2:757). See No Ears 1802.

1798 NO EARS: *Wakan Tanka winyan wan iyeyapi.* They found a female *Wakan Tanka.*

Mallery (1886:102) suggests that the event given by The Flame for this year, "A Ree [Arikara] woman is killed by a Dakota while gathering 'pomme-blanche,' a root used for food," refers to the same event, "changed by other recorders or interpreters into one of a mythical character."

IRON CROW: *Hupeka śahiyela iwaktegli.* Picket Pin came home victorious from the Cheyennes.

Wissler translated: "Picket Pin killed a Cheyenne and the people danced."

1799 NO EARS: *Winyan iglúśake ota ṭapi.* Many pregnant women died.

IRON CROW: *Toka mazawakan kpamnipi.* First distribution of guns.

American Horse's count comments that the guns were brought by "The Good-White-Man" (Mallery 1886:134), evidently a trader. See No Ears 1802.

1800 NO EARS: *Tacante yute śni wan waecon.* Eats No Heart performed a ceremony.

Deloria commented that the name is literally "ruminant heart he eats not." Battiste Good identifies the ceremony as a commemoration of the dead (Mallery 1893:313); see Walker (1980:141–42).

IRON CROW: *Waśicun napciyunk hipi.* Nine white men came.

This may refer to a trading party headed by Régis Loisel that is supposed to have visited the Sioux on the upper Missouri during 1800 (Abel 1968:24).

1801 NO EARS: *Nawicaśli.* Measles.

IRON CROW: *Titom iwakte agli.* Came home victorious from four lodges.

An alternate interpretation is, "Four lodges came home victorious."

1802 No Ears: *Waśicu wan waśte hi.* A good white man came.

Probably a reference to Régis Loisel, who built a trading post in 1802 on Cedar Island, near the mouth of the Cheyenne River (Abel 1968:27).

Iron Crow: Same as No Ears 1804.

1803 No Ears: *Śake maza awicaglipi.* They brought home iron shod (horses).

The Flame identifies these as the first shod horses they had ever seen (Mallery 1886:103); Battiste Good's count indicates that these horses were stolen from the Pawnees (Mallery 1893:313).

Iron Crow: *Si maza eya awicaglipi.* They brought home some iron feet (shod horses).

1804 No Ears: *Śunġuġula awicaglipi.* They brought home curley-haired horses.

Deloria commented: "*Ġuġula,* referring to hair, means woollike."

Iron Crow: *Omaha winyan wan hanṭeyapi.* They killed an Omaha woman at night.

1805 No Ears: *Tasinte on akicilowanpi.* They sang over each other using animal tails.

Walker identified them as horse tails, as did Deloria in her translation of Kindle's winter count (Beckwith 1930:356). However, in commenting on the No Ears count, Deloria wrote: "Refers to the change from brushwood, or plain sticks, to sticks somehow ornamented with hangings of buffalo tail hair, used in the *Hunka* ceremony."

Iron Crow: *Wowapi ota oyate okiju.* The people came together with many flags.

The Lakotas met the Lewis and Clark expedition at the mouth of Bad River September 25, 1804. The next day they had a council at which the Indians displayed their Spanish flags and the explorers presented them with an American flag (Thwaites 1959, vol. 1:164–74).

1806 NO EARS: *Śagloġan ahi wicaktepi.* Eight were killed by the enemy.

IRON CROW: *Inyan sapa ahi ktepi.* Black Rock was killed by the enemy.

1807 NO EARS: *Wambli kuwa eya wicaktepi.* Some eagle trappers were killed.

IRON CROW: *Huwegahan wan ahi ktepi.* One with a broken leg was killed by the enemy.

1808 NO EARS: *Ogle luta on wan itkop ahi ktepi.* A man wearing a red shirt was killed by the enemy face to face.

An alternate translation might be "was followed back to camp and killed." Kindle's winter count has *Óg.leluta un wan itkóp heyók'a ahíktepi,* "A *heyoka* wearing a red shirt was killed by the enemy."

IRON CROW: *Capa ciqa gu kin.* Little Beaver burned.

Wissler commented, "A trader and all his goods."

See No Ears 1810, Iron Crow 1797.

1809 NO EARS: *Śina to atkuku Palani ahi ktepi.* Blue Blanket's father was killed by Arikaras.

IRON CROW: *Inyan sapa wakicage waniyetu.* Black Rock held a ceremony during the winter.

Wissler translated: "Black Rock makes Four Pipe Dance."

1810 NO EARS: *Capa ciqa ti ile.* Little Beaver's lodge burned.

IRON CROW: *Ogle luta un wan ahi ktepi.* One wearing a red shirt was killed by the enemy.

See No Ears 1808.

1811 NO EARS: *Sinte wakśupi awicaglipi.* They brought home decorated tails.

Deloria commented: "Horses taken from the enemy and brought home had ornamental feathers etc. tied to their tails."

IRON CROW: *Oglala śung kuwapi.* The Oglalas chased horses.

American Horse's count states: "They caught many wild horses south of the Platte River" (Mallery 1886: 135).

1812 NO EARS: *Palani top wicaktepi.* Four Arikaras were killed.

IRON CROW: *Okšanige cinca wan aktepi.* A child of Round Stomach was killed.

1813 NO EARS: *Canku tanka atkuku Palani ktepi.* Big Road's father was killed by Arikaras.

IRON CROW: *Ṡkutani ṡakpe wicaktepi.* They killed six Gros Ventres (Atsinas).

1814 NO EARS: *Witapahatu wan kaṙuġapi.* They crushed a Kiowa's skull.

American Horse's count records that this event occurred when the Lakotas went to the Kiowa village near the head of Horse Creek (six miles from Scott's Bluff) with the purpose of making peace (Mallery 1886:135).

IRON CROW: Same as No Ears.

1815 NO EARS: *Itazi cola ti tanka otipi.* The Sans Arcs (No Bows) lived in big houses.

Deloria commented: "Sometimes log houses are called *ti-tanka* in contrast to tipis; but more often it means the Ree [Arikara] style of log house, the circular ones."

The Lone Dog count reads: "The Sans Arcs made the first attempt at a dirt lodge. This was at Peoria Bottom, Dakota Territory [near present Pierre, South Dakota]" (Mallery 1886:109).

IRON CROW: *Otonweheta eṭapi.* They died at the city.

In July 1815, representatives of all the Sioux met with officials headed by William Clark at Portage des Sioux (near the confluence of the Missouri and the Mississippi) and signed treaties of allegiance with the United States. Black Buffalo, a Minneconjou chief, died there while the council was assembling (Robinson 1904:96).

1816 NO EARS: *Ake okitipi.* Again they lived there.

IRON CROW: *Išinkcin nape okiciyuspapi.* Angrily they took hold of each other's hands.

Wissler translated: "Shake hands hard. (The settlement of trouble with Crows.)" According to American

Horse, "They made peace with the Crows at Pine Bluff" (Mallery 1886:136).

1817 NO EARS: *Can šeca on ti cağapi.* They made lodges of dead wood.

According to The Flame, "Trading store built at Fort Pierre" (Mallery 1886:109).

IRON CROW: *Tatarpa ota iwanitipi.* They made winter camp with much buffalo breast meat.

Deloria commented on this event in the Fire Thunder winter count for 1816: "*T'at'áȟpa* is the large meat over the breast of the buffalo; breast and front. I cannot say what it is really called, but it is very extensive and lies over the ribs and down, and is the uppermost, after the hide is removed, they tell me."

1818 NO EARS: *Nawicašli.* Measles.

IRON CROW: *Nawicašli waniyetu.* Measles during the winter.

1819 NO EARS: *Can zi can punpun ti cağapi.* They made lodges of rotted sumac ("yellow wood").

Kindle's winter count has *Sic'áŋğu c'anpúnpun un t'icágapi,* "The Brules made lodges with rotted wood" (Beckwith 1930:358). According to Walker, this structure was built at the big bend of the Minnesota River (see document 23, page 88). The Lone Dog count has: "Another trading store was built, this time by Louis La Conte, at Fort Pierre, Dakota" (Mallery 1886:110). Battiste Good gives the trader's name as Choze (Mallery 1886:110).

IRON CROW: *Kanği wicaša ota iwakte agli.* They came home from killing many Crow Indians.

1820 NO EARS: *Wan nunblala wicicaške cağapi.* They made sashes for Only Two Arrows.

Possibly a reference to the making of warrior society sashes (cf. Mallery 1886:110–11). According to John Colhoff, this man was Red Cloud's grandfather (Powers 1963:29).

IRON CROW: *Wan noumlala adowanpi.* They sang over Only Two Arrows.

Wissler translated the name as "Carries Two Arrows."

1821 NO EARS: *Wicarpe wan hoton hiyayeci.* A star passed over making a noise.

SHORT MAN: Same as No Ears. (First year of the Short Man winter count.)

IRON CROW: Same as No Ears.

1822 NO EARS: *Waskula hu śpan.* Cuts Off froze his leg.

SHORT MAN: Same as No Ears.

IRON CROW: *Waskuda hu špan waniyetu.* Cuts Off froze his leg during the winter.

Wissler translated: "Whittling Stick burns his feet." *Špan* is litterally "burned," but the implication is that the burn is caused by the cold.

1823 NO EARS: *Wagmeza ota śica* [i.e., *śeca*], Much dried-up corn.

Deloria commented: "Corn that is dead, dry from lack of water, not dried corn, which would be *puza.*" This contradicts Iron Crow's explanation.

The event referred to is undoubtedly the Lakotas' participation in Colonel Henry Leavenworth's attack on the Arikara villages in June 1823, during which the Lakotas looted the Arikara corn fields. See Mallery (1886:111–12, 137).

SHORT MAN: Same as No Ears 1824.

IRON CROW: *Wagmeza šeca iwanitipi.* They made winter camp with dried corn.

Wissler translated: "Lived on hard corn."

1824 NO EARS: *Yeyela rmunġa ktepi.* Sender was killed by witchcraft.

This is Deloria's translation. Walker translated the same event in Short Man's count for 1823, "They killed Throws-Magic."

SHORT MAN: Same as No Ears 1825.

IRON CROW: *Marpiya mato rmanr wicakte.* Bear Cloud killed people by witchcraft.

1825 NO EARS: *Mini wicaṭe.* People drowned.

Deloria commented on this event in the Fire Thunder winter count for 1825: "*M.ni t'a,* idiom, to drown; to have a great flood, and suffer from its causes." For an attempt to locate the site of this flood, see Howard (1976:45–46).

SHORT MAN: Same as No Ears 1826.

IRON CROW: *Mni wicaṭa waniyetu.* People drowned during the winter

1826 NO EARS: *Kaiwa gli ṭa. Kaiwa* came home and died.

The meaning of the man's name is unclear. Deloria commented on this event in the Fire Thunder winter count for 1826: "*Kaíwa żó g.lí ca* (1826) Man named Kaíwa / whistling / he returns. This refers to an event. Warriors were lying in wait of the enemy at the confluence of two rivers at what is now Alliance, Nebraska. There they were stranded, food gone, and so they shot a buffalo; but it had an enlarged pancreas, and so thought they ought not to eat it as it must be either diseased or '*wakan.*' But when their hunger got the best of them they all ate it and were dying when their scout, 'Kaíwa' by name, returned from the hills. 'Come quickly,' they called, 'for you have news to bear home.' And they sent their messages and died; after urging him to leave that meat alone. He traveled home in agony, and arrived there whistling, because he had news of ghosts." (Cf. Mallery 1886:114; 1893:318.) The Short Man winter count for 1825 shows *Kaíwa* holding a whistle.

SHORT MAN: *Kanġi ti akla.* Crows flew around the lodges.

IRON CROW: *Kaiwa jo gli waniyetu. Kaiwa* returned whistling during the winter.

1827 NO EARS: *Psa ohanpi.* They used snowshoes.

SHORT MAN: *Toka tarca kuwa ai.* Enemies went there hunting deer.

The drawing shows that the game was antelope.

IRON CROW: *Waniyetu waśma.* Winter of deep snow.

1828 NO EARS: *Miwatani ota wicaktepi.* They killed many Mandans.

SHORT MAN: Same as No Ears 1829.

IRON CROW: *Tarca kuwapi waniyetu.* Hunted deer during the winter.

1829 NO EARS: *Ite gleġa waakšija.* Striped Face retained them.

Deloria commented on this event in the Fire Thunder winter count for 1829: "Striped Face retained some captives and would not give them up." The word *waakšija* means "to hold back" or "to take or retain something claimed by another." According to Battiste Good, "Old-Speckled-Face" murdered his son-in-law, then clung to the body, begging to be killed himself (Mallery 1893:319).

SHORT MAN: Same as No Ears 1830.

IRON CROW: Same as No Ears.

1830 NO EARS: *Pte san ota wicaopi.* They shot many white buffalo cows.

SHORT MAN: Same as No Ears 1831.

IRON CROW: *Cantipi toka kagapi.* They made the first wood houses.

American Horse gives, "They saw wagons for the first time. Red-Lake, a white trader, brought his goods in them" (Mallery 1886:138).

1831 NO EARS: *Ble stan ġu kaweġa.* Dark Red Lake burned.

Kaweġa, "break," is an obvious scriptographic error copied by mistake from the entry for 1832. American Horse gives, "Red-Lake's house, which he had recently built, was destroyed by fire, and he was killed by the accidental explosion of some powder" (Mallery 1886:138).

SHORT MAN: Same as No Ears 1832.

IRON CROW: *Ble stan gu waniyetu.* Dark Red Lake burned during the winter.

1832 NO EARS: *He wanjica hu kaweġa.* One Horn broke his leg.

Mallery (1886:115–16) identifies this event with the suicide of One Horn, the Minneconjou chief, as related by George Catlin. Grieving over the death of his son, One Horn was gored when he attempted to kill a buffalo bull using only a knife. (See Catlin 1926, vol. 1:249–50.)

SHORT MAN: Same as No Ears 1833.

IRON CROW: *Ṡkutani wicaktepi.* They killed some Gros Ventres (Atsinas).

1833 NO EARS: *Wicaṙpe o kicamna.* Meteorite showers.

Mallery (1886:116) notes that the meteorite shower of November 12, 1833, was observed throughout the United States.

SHORT MAN: Same as No Ears 1834.

IRON CROW: Same as No Ears.

1834 NO EARS: *Śanhiyela tigle* [i.e., *tigli*] *wan ktepi.* A Cheyenne was killed as he arrived home.

Deloria commented: "*T'i-g.lí* indicates that the Cheyenne's home was here, where the count was made." However, according to both American Horse and Battiste Good, the Sioux were at war with the Cheyennes (Mallery 1886:139; 1893:320).

SHORT MAN: Same as No Ears 1835.

IRON CROW: *Ṡahiyeda tigli wan ktepi.* A Cheyenne was killed as he arrived home.

Wissler translated: "A wandering Cheyenne killed (he strayed into a Sioux village)."

1835 NO EARS: *Tatanka wan capa* [i.e., *cepa*] *opi.* They shot a fat buffalo bull.

SHORT MAN: Same as No Ears 1836.

IRON CROW: *Tatanka wan cepa opi.* They shot a fat buffalo bull.

1836 NO EARS: *Caǧa akiçiipi.* They fought across ice.

Both American Horse and Battiste Good identify this as a fight with the Pawnees (Mallery 1886:139; 1893:320).

SHORT MAN: Same as No Ears 1837.

IRON CROW: *Car akicininpi.* They fought across ice.

1837 NO EARS: *Ite hepi śa kiya tiapa ktepi.* Paints the Lower Half of His Face Red was murdered in his lodge.

SHORT MAN: *Ota aki wicaktepi.* Many were killed.

Iron Crow: Same as No Ears.

1838 No Ears: *Śunk gnaśkinya cinca wan ktepi.* A child of Mad Wolf was killed.

Short Man: *Kanġi bloka śung gleśka ota awicagli.* He Crow brought home many spotted horses.

Iron Crow: *Sungnaśkinyan wacekiya.* Mad Wolf prayed.

1839 No Ears: *Wicakiran watakpe ai.* Starving, they went out to fight.

Deloria translated *wic'áakiȟ'an* as "famine-stricken." Battiste Good indicated that the Dakotas united in an expedition against the Pawnees, killed one hundred, but nearly died of starvation on the expedition (Mallery 1893:321).

Short Man: *Oglala śunka wakan manu awicaglipi.* They brought home stolen Oglala horses.

Iron Crow: Same as No Ears.

Wissler commented that the expedition was to revenge the death of Paints the Lower Half of His Face Red two years earlier.

1840 No Ears: *Wakinyan ciqa sunkaku nonp wicakte.* Two of Little Thunder's younger brothers were killed.

Short Man: *Itomni kicizapi.* Drunken fight.

See Iron Crow 1841.

Iron Crow: *Ṡunka wakan opawinge awicaglipi.* They brought home one hundred horses.

1841 No Ears: *Śunk gnakpa ġi ota ṭewicayapi.* They caused many brown-eared horses to die.

Deloria's copy has *iyéwicayapi,* they found many brown-eared horses. "Horses, white background with brown spots, are prized highly, and are called Brown-inside-the-ears." Most Oglala counts record the stealing of horses from other tribes for this year (Mallery 1886:118, 140).

Short Man: Same as No Ears 1842.

IRON CROW: *Itomni kici ktepi.* While drunk, they killed each other.

Probably a reference to the murder of Bull Bear by Red Cloud during a fight in which other Oglalas were also killed. See Mallery (1886:140–41), Hyde (1957:53–54), Walker (1980:195).

1842 NO EARS: *Wiyaka owin śunk yuha najin kte.* Feather Earring killed a horse herder.

SHORT MAN: Same as No Ears 1843.

IRON CROW: *Titom iwakte agli.* Came home victorious from four lodges.

See Iron Crow 1801.

1843 NO EARS: *Wayaka aglipi.* They brought a captive home.

In a fight with the Pawnees, the Lakotas rescued one of the Cheyenne sacred arrows. See Mallery (1886:141).

SHORT MAN: Same as No Ears 1844.

IRON CROW: *Wan wakan wan aglipi.* They brought home a *wakan* arrow.

1844 NO EARS: *Kanġi bloke ahi ktepi.* He Crow was killed by the enemy.

SHORT MAN: Same as No Ears 1845.

IRON CROW: *Oglala wikcemna yamni ahiwicaktepi.* Thirty Oglalas were killed by the enemy.

1845 NO EARS: *Nawicaśli.* Measles.

SHORT MAN: *Hoka waśte sunkaku eipiyapi.* They abandoned Good Heron's younger brother.

IRON CROW: *Nawicaśli waniyetu.* Measles during the winter.

1846 NO EARS: *Susu ska wan ktepi.* One with white testicles was killed.

SHORT MAN: Same as No Ears 1847.

IRON CROW: *Wazi hanska ti ktepi.* Tall Pine was murdered.

1847 NO EARS: *Kanġi wambli capapi.* Crow Eagle was stabbed.

SHORT MAN: Same as No Ears 1848.

IRON CROW: *Huwicakawega ota.* Many broken legs.

Wissler commented: "Indians injured chasing buffalo." American Horse explained that the ground had been covered with ice (Mallery 1886:142).

1848 NO EARS: *Winkte wan ktepi.* A transvestite was killed.

SHORT MAN: Same as No Ears 1849.

IRON CROW: Same as No Ears.

1849 NO EARS: *Nawicatipa.* Cramps.

Deloria commented: "Epidemic of cramps, or spasms, some sort of contracting of the ligaments or muscles, causing great discomfort." An epidemic of Asiatic cholera, brought by white emigrants on the Overland Trail (see Hyde 1957:63–64).

SHORT MAN: *Sicili wan śunka ha qin ca ktepi.* They killed a Pawnee carrying a wolf (or dog) skin.

IRON CROW: *Nawicakśeca.* Convulsions.

1850 NO EARS: *Wicaṙanṙan.* Smallpox.

SHORT MAN: Same as No Ears.

IRON CROW: Same as No Ears.

1851 NO EARS: *Wakapamni tanka.* Big distribution.

A reference to the goods given away at the great treaty council on Horse Creek, near Fort Laramie, during September 1851. See Hyde (1957:65–66).

SHORT MAN: Same as No Ears.

IRON CROW: Same as No Ears.

1852 NO EARS: *Wa śma waniyetu.* Deep snow during the winter.

SHORT MAN: Same as No Ears.

IRON CROW: Same as No Ears.

1853 NO EARS: *Mato wan winsan manu.* A bear stole a virgin.

John Colhoff's winter count gives *Mato wan ti hi,* "A bear arrived in the camp," and Colhoff commented: "A prowling bear was killed" (Powers 1963:31). A bear that entered the camp is said to be prowling like a young man who attempts to sneak into a lodge at night and touch the privates of a girl while she sleeps, thereby obliging her to marry him. Deloria commented: "The bear in the 'count' is jestingly said to have entered the tent for the same purpose" (in Beckwith 1930:361). That it was an animal and not a man named Bear is made clear in Short Man's drawing.

SHORT MAN: Same as No Ears.

IRON CROW: *Tarca cesli tahu pawega.* Defecating Deer broke his neck.

1854 NO EARS: *Mato wayuhi ktepi.* Conquering Bear was killed.

Appointed chief of the Sioux at the 1851 treaty council, Conquering Bear, a Brulé, was killed by Lieutenant J. L. Grattan's command August 19, 1854. In retaliation, the outraged Lakotas killed Grattan and his twenty-nine soldiers, the event which triggered the Sioux war of 1855. See Hyde (1957:72–75). Deloria translated the chief's name as "Scattering-bear (Bear creating confusion)."

SHORT MAN: *Akicita wikcemna yamini wicaktepi.* Thirty soldiers were killed.

IRON CROW: *Waśicun wikcemna yamni wicaktepi.* Thirty white men were killed.

1855 NO EARS: *Wicayajipa waakśija.* Wasp retained them.

Wasp was one Lakota name for Brigadier General William S. Harney, who led his troops against Little Thunder's Brulé village on September 2, 1855, in retaliation for the Grattan affair of the previous year. Eighty-six Lakotas were killed, and seventy women and children were taken captive and held at Fort Pierre throughout the winter. See Hyde (1957:79).

SHORT MAN: *Ite glega waakśija.* Striped Face retained them.

Identical with the No Ears 1829 count; obviously an error, since the pictograph shows a military officer.

IRON CROW: *Si wicaśpan wakte agli.* Frozen Foot returned victorious from the enemy.

1856 NO EARS: *Kangi wicaśa okiźu.* Crow Indians came together.

SHORT MAN: *He topa waolowan.* Four Horns sang over someone (the *Hunka* ceremony).

IRON CROW: *Wakpamni waakšija.* Distribution was withheld.

"Distribution" may be used here in a metaphorical sense to refer to captive women and children. Wissler translates: "Agent refuses to give up a woman (held by agent as hostage)." This undoubtedly refers to the imprisonment of the women and children captured by Brigadier General William S. Harney from Little Thunder's village at the battle of Ash Hollow in 1855. They were held at Fort Pierre and returned to their people the following May when Harney signed a treaty with the Sioux (see Hyde 1957:79–81).

1857 NO EARS: *Kanġi wicaša wikcemna wicaktepi.* Ten Crow Indians were killed.

SHORT MAN: *Hunka wašte wicinca ton.* Good *Hunka* gave birth to a girl.

Deloria recorded the following concerning this event, given in the Fire Thunder winter count for 1857: "This was memorable because *Hunká-waštewin* was, as her name indicates, a daughter-beloved, respected and loved by the tribe because of countless benefactions in her name. She was a paragon of good behavior and mothers set her up as a model for their daughters. . . . But suddenly she shocked and rocked the whole tribe by giving birth to a child when she was nearing forty, and still a virgin, to all appearances."

IRON CROW: *Winyan wan cinca ton.* A woman gave birth.

Wissler commented: "Occurrence of an illegitimate birth."

1858 NO EARS: *Tašina ġi ktepi.* Brown Robe was killed.

SHORT MAN: Same as No Ears.

IRON CROW: *Hewotoka ahi ktepi.* Blunt Horn was killed by the enemy.

1859 NO EARS: *Kanġi tanka ktepi.* Big Crow was killed.

SHORT MAN: Same as No Ears.

IRON CROW: *Mina yuha wan ktepi.* A knife carrier was killed.

Wissler commented: "A Pawnee carrying a knife was killed."

1860 NO EARS: *Hokšila ota ṭapi.* Many children died.

SHORT MAN: Same as No Ears.

IRON CROW: *Hokšicada sotapi.* Babies died off.

1861 NO EARS: *Śunk gleška ktepi.* Spotted Horse was killed.

SHORT MAN: Same as No Ears.

IRON CROW: *Iktomika ahi ktepi.* Spider-like was killed by the enemy.

1862 NO EARS: *Hokšila wan waśpapi.* A boy was scalped.

SHORT MAN: Same as No Ears.

IRON CROW: *Pecokan aglipi.* They brought home a scalp lock.

Wissler commented: "Some Sioux found a scalp of Pawnee and claimed the honor of killing the enemy."

1863 NO EARS: *Śaglogan ahi wicaktepi.* Eight were killed by the enemy.

SHORT MAN: Same as No Ears.

IRON CROW: *Tawicu ogna iwakte agli.* Towards His Wife returned victorious.

The text is ambiguous. Wissler translated: "Husband and wife die. (Both were killed on successive days.)"

1864 NO EARS: *Psa top wicaktepi.* Four Crow Indians were killed.

SHORT MAN: Same as No Ears.

IRON CROW: *Ite nonpada panakseyapi.* Two Faces was hanged.

Two Faces was unjustly hanged by the U.S. army when he returned a captive white woman he had rescued from his own people. See Hyde (1957:119–20).

1865 NO EARS: *Śunk sotapi.* Horses died off.

SHORT MAN: Same as No Ears.

IRON CROW: *Tarca ota olakotakaga waniyetu.* Many Deer made peace during the winter.

This refers to the treaty of 1865 which some of the Lakotas signed at Fort Laramie in January 1866. Colonel

1821
A star passed over making a noise.

1822
Cuts Off froze his leg.

1823
Sender was killed by witchcraft.

1824
People drowned.

1825
Kaiwa came home and died.

1826
Crows flew around the lodges.

1827
Enemies went there
hunting deer.

1828
Striped Face retained them.

1829
They shot many
white buffalo cows.

1830
Dark Red Lake
burned.

1831
One Horn broke his leg.

1832
Meteorite showers.

1833
A Cheyenne was killed as he arrived home.

1834
They shot a fat buffalo bull.

1835
They fought across ice.

1836
Paints the Lower
Half of His Face Red
was murdered in his lodge.

1837
Many were killed.

1838
He Crow brought
home many spotted
horses.

1839
They brought home stolen Oglala horses.

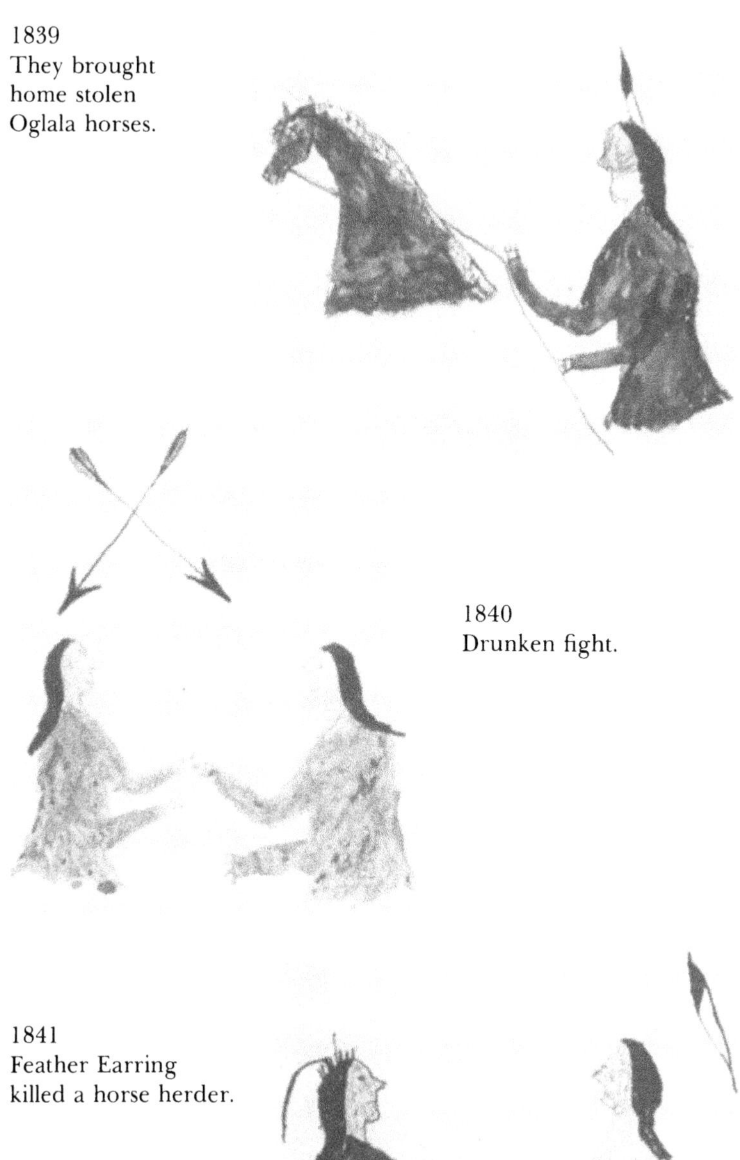

1840
Drunken fight.

1841
Feather Earring killed a horse herder.

1842
They brought
a captive home.

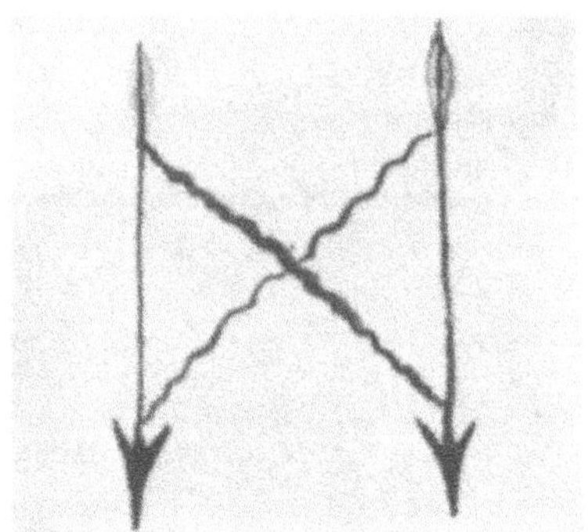

1843
He Crow was killed
by the enemy.

1844
Measles.

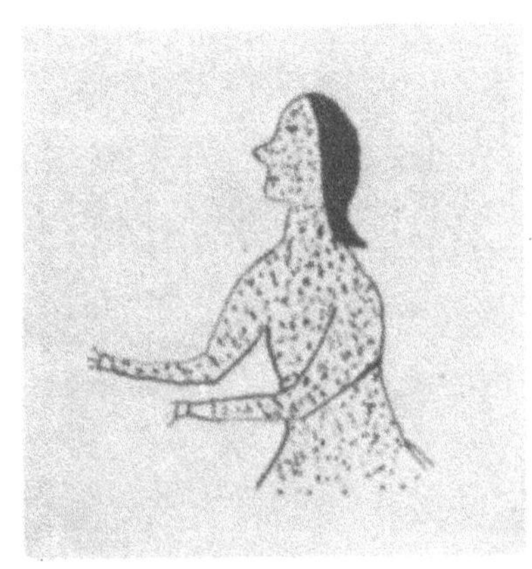

1845
They abandoned
Good Heron's younger
brother.

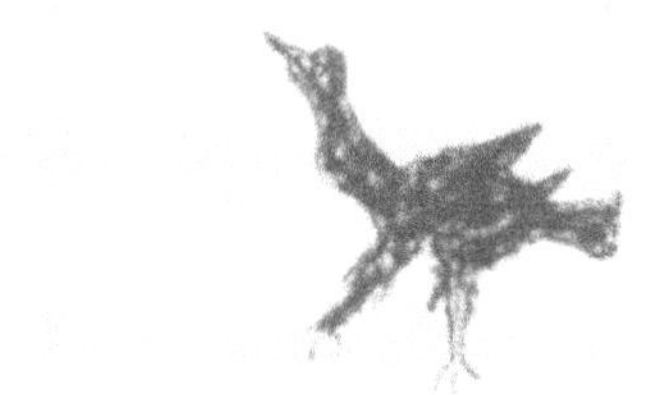

1846
Crow Eagle was stabbed.

1847
A transvestite was killed.

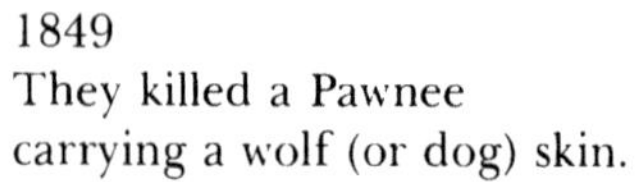

1848
Cramps

1849
They killed a Pawnee
carrying a wolf (or dog) skin.

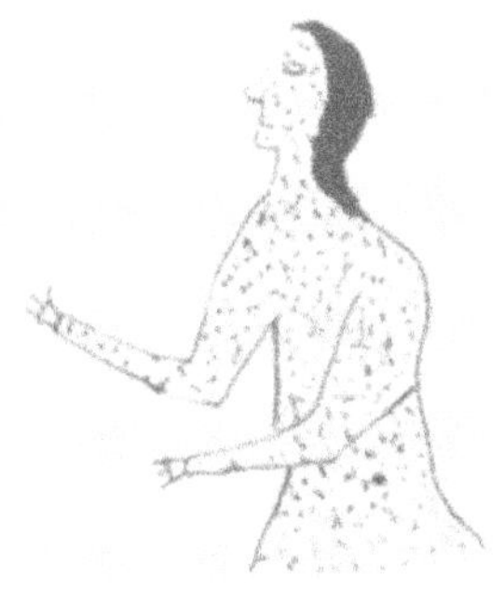

1850
Smallpox.

1851
Big distribution.

1852
Deep snow
during the winter.

1853
A bear stole a virgin.

1854
Thirty soldiers were killed.

1855
Striped Face [*Sic*, Wasp] retained them.

1856
Four Horns sang over someone (the *Hunka* ceremony).

1857
Good *Hunka* gave birth to a girl.

1858
Brown Robe was killed.

1859
Big Crow was killed.

1860
Many children died.

1861
Spotted Horse was killed.

1862
A boy was scalped.

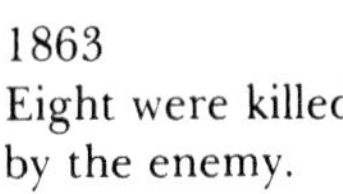

1863
Eight were killed by the enemy.

1864
Four Crow Indians were killed.

1865
Horses died off.

1866
One hundred
white men were killed.

1867
They surrounded
the white tents.

1868
They traded many mules.

1869
An old woman
was killed by a tree.

1870
Hump (High Back)
was killed by the enemy.

1871
Buffalo Hump was lost.

1872
They made
winter camp
without white men.

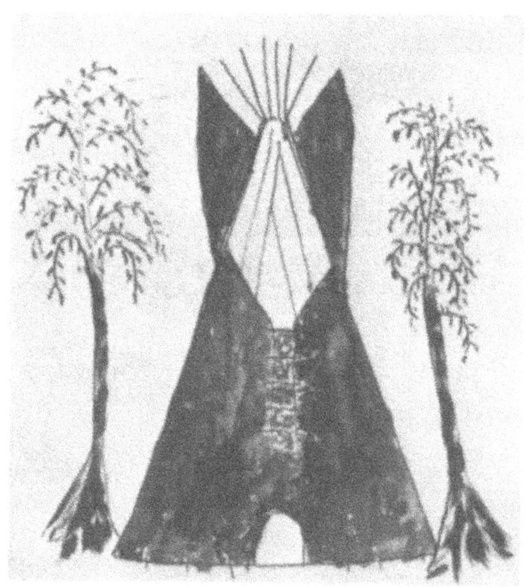

1873
Many Pawnees
were killed.

1874
They crossed
the river for
the last time.

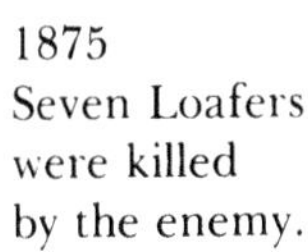

1875
Seven Loafers
were killed
by the enemy.

1876
Red Cloud's horses
were taken away.

1877
Crazy Horse
was killed.

1878
A *wakan* Cheyenne was killed.

1879
Spotted Wolf was killed.

1880
Spotted Testicles was killed.

1881
Spotted Tail was killed.

1882
Strong Heart
was imprisoned.

1883
The Oglalas
made for
themselves
a council
and leaders.

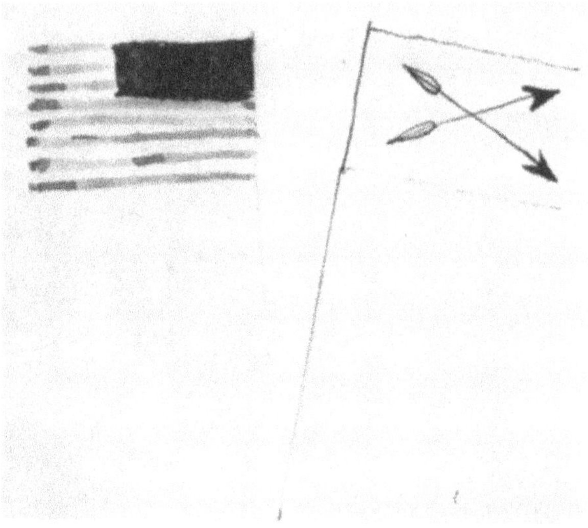

1884
The president
made a law against murder.

1885
Kills at Night
murdered them.

1886
They made a law
against seducing women.

1887
A blind Cheyenne was killed.

1888
Eclipse of the sun.

1889
Three Stars
made a treaty.

1890
Big Foot was killed.

1891
They were made
infantry soldiers.

1892
Has Two Sticks killed
some cowboys.

1893
Big school burned.

1894
Has Two Sticks
was hanged.

1895
The Oglalas cooked
one hundred dogs.

1896
White Bird died
during the winter.

1897
They burned down
the slaughterhouse.

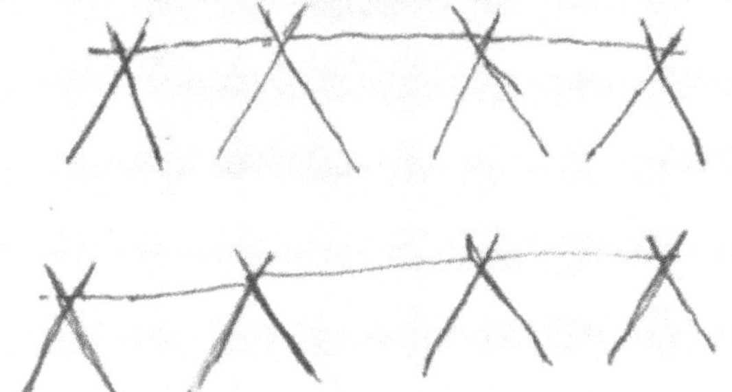

1898
First fences
were made.

1899
Glowing Coal
died during the winter.

1900
Issuing of annuities stopped.

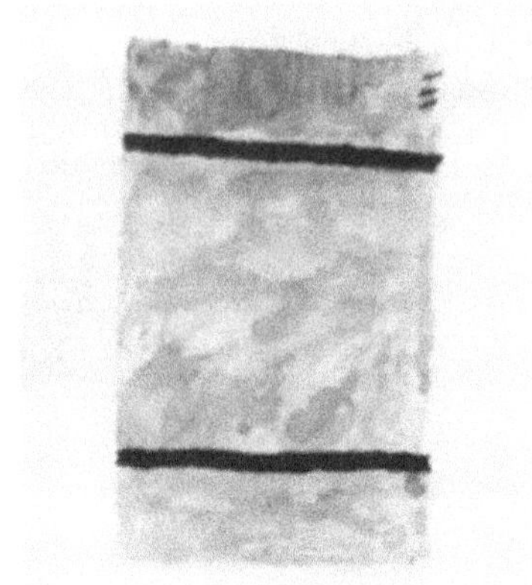

1901
Little Wound died.

1902
An old Crow woman disappeared.

1903
Some antelope
hunters were killed.

1904
The Oglalas took
the railroad and
were killed.

1905
A child
of Gray Warbonnet
committed suicide.

1906
Sword and
Standing Soldier
went together
to the city
(Washington, D.C.).

1907
Wagons were issued.

1908
American Horse
died during the winter.

1909
Red Cloud died
during the winter.

1910
Sword died
during the winter.

1911
Afraid of Bear died
during the winter.

1912
White Wolf died
during the winter.

Henry E. Maynadier, in command of the post, was known to the Lakotas as "Many Deer." See Hyde (1957:137–38) and Mallery (1886:144).

1866 NO EARS: *Waśicu opawinġe wicaktepi.* One hundred white men were killed.

The defeat of Lieutenant Colonel William J. Fetterman and his eighty men near Fort Phil Kearny, December 21, 1866. See Hyde (1957:148) and Olson (1965:50).

SHORT MAN: Same as No Ears.

IRON CROW: *Wahin wakpata waqin irpeyapi.* They abandoned their packs at Flint River.

Wissler commented: "Indians fleeing from soldiers." The night of April 14, 1866, a camp of Cheyennes and Lakotas led by Roman Nose and Pawnee Killer fled from U.S. troops under Major General Winfield Scott Hancock. They left their lodges standing on the bank of the Pawnee Fork of the Arkansas River, upstream from Fort Larned, Kansas. Hancock burned the village, destroying the lodges and supplies (Grinnell 1915: 238–46; Berthrong 1963:272–79). Flint River is the Cheyenne name for the Arkansas (Petter 1913–15:487).

1867 NO EARS: *Susuni wan ti hi ktepi.* A Shoshoni who entered the camp was killed.

SHORT MAN: *Ti ska naji yapi.* They surrounded the white tents.

The term *najiyapi* implies "standing them off," forcing them to fight. The reference is probably to the Wagon Box fight near Fort Phil Kearny, August 2, 1867. See Hyde (1957:159–60) and Olson (1965:63).

IRON CROW: *Pte om wani tipi.* Made winter camp with buffalo.

1868 NO EARS: *Wakinyan he ton irpeyapi.* Horned Thunder was abandoned.

John Colhoff suggested this referred to leaving the body of a dead warrior on the battlefield (Powers 1963:32).

The Kindle winter count agrees with this interpretation (Beckwith 1930:363).

SHORT MAN: *Sunsunla ota wiyopiwicakiyapi.* They traded many mules.

IRON CROW: [*Wa*] *Paha gleglega un wan ktepi.* They killed one wearing a striped warbonnet.

Wissler translated: "Wears Spotted War Bonnet killed (a Cheyenne Indian)." The reference is to the death of the Cheyenne chief Roman Nose at the Beecher Island fight, September 17, 1868. See Grinnell (1915:269). For an illustration of the warbonnet, see Walker (1980:275 and war insignia plate 4).

1869 NO EARS: *Winorcala wan can kte.* An old woman was killed by a tree.

SHORT MAN: Same as No Ears.

IRON CROW: *Tajontka owe kici ktepi.* They killed for animal kidneys.

Wissler translated: "Killed in quarrel over a kidney."

1870 NO EARS: *Canku wankantuya ahi ktepi.* Hump (High Back) was killed by the enemy.

Deloria commented: "Hump was a fearless fighter, older than Crazy Horse, but the two were constant war partners." See Hyde (1957:193).

SHORT MAN: Same as No Ears.

IRON CROW: *Canqin hi wicaktepi.* They killed some wood gatherers.

Wissler identified the victims as Pawnees.

1871 NO EARS: *Canrarake tanin śni.* Buffalo Hump was lost.

SHORT MAN: Same as No Ears.

IRON CROW: *Kipazo pte hi ko waniyetu.* Shows Them called buffalo during the winter.

Wissler translated: "Eagle Bull's promise of buffalo. (Promised them but did not come.)" According to Running Bear, *ptehiko* means "to perform ceremonies to attract the buffalo" (Buechel 1970:314).

1872 NO EARS: *Anog onze psa nonp wicakte.* Double Ass killed two Crow Indians.

Deloria translated the name "Anus at both ends (or sides) . . . or *unze* may mean simply buttocks," a vulgar nickname, probably bestowed by a *winkte* (transvestite). Colhoff's winter count gives the man's name as *Maȟpiya Peta,* Fire Cloud (Powers 1963:32), and Kindle's winter count gives it as *Natá ȟlóka,* Hollow Head (Hole in Head) (Beckwith 1930:363).

SHORT MAN: *Waśicu cola wani tipi.* They made winter camp without white men.

IRON CROW: *Ce talo scili wan kte waniyetu.* Raw Meat Penis killed a Pawnee during the winter.

Wissler translated the name "Buffalo Bull."

1873 NO EARS: *Omaha nonp wicaktepi.* Two Omaha Indians were killed.

SHORT MAN: *Sicili ota wicaktepi.* Many Pawnees were killed.

The event is discussed in Hyde (1957:202); he sets the number of dead at "over fifty."

IRON CROW: *Scili opawinge wicaktepi.* One hundred Pawnees were killed.

1874 NO EARS: *Ehake ko wakan tan* [i.e., *koakatan*] *ai.* They crossed the river for the last time.

The Oglalas crossed the Platte and spent the winter on the Republican River. This was their last tribal buffalo hunt. See Hyde (1957:229).

SHORT MAN: Same as No Ears.

IRON CROW: *Sapa wicaśa śungwanpi.* Ute Indians stole horses.

1875 NO EARS: *Wagluȟe śakowin ahi wicaktepi.* Seven Loafers were killed by the enemy.

The Loafers were a band of the Oglalas.

SHORT MAN: Same as No Ears.

IRON CROW: *Wakute maza ahi ktepi.* Shoots Iron was killed by the enemy.

1876 NO EARS: *Marpiya luta śunk ipi.* Red Cloud's horses were taken away.

The army confiscated the ponies from Red Cloud's people in October 1876. See Hyde (1957:285) and Olson (1965:233).

SHORT MAN: Same as No Ears.

IRON CROW: Same as No Ears.

1877 NO EARS: *Taśunka witko ktepi.* Crazy Horse was killed.

Crazy Horse died at Fort Robinson, Nebraska, on September 5, 1877. See Hyde (1957:298).

SHORT MAN: Same as No Ears.

IRON CROW: *Omaha toyanketa eyotaka.* They camped in the Omaha country.

This refers to the forced removal of the Oglalas from Red Cloud Agency near Fort Robinson to the Missouri River after the death of Crazy Horse. See Hyde (1957:299–301) and Olson (1965:247).

1878 NO EARS: *Śahiyela wakan wan ktepi.* A *wakan* Cheyenne was killed.

This refers to the death of Bullet Proof, who was killed during the Cheyenne outbreak from Fort Robinson, Nebraska, January 8, 1879. See Sandoz (1953:222).

SHORT MAN: Same as No Ears.

IRON CROW: *Ṡahiyela warlokapi ṡni wan ktepi.* A Cheyenne who could not be shot was killed.

1879 NO EARS: *Śunkmanitu gleśka ktepi.* Spotted Wolf was killed.

SHORT MAN: Same as No Ears.

IRON CROW: *Toka cankpe opi ed wani tipi.* First winter they lived at Wounded Knee (Creek).

The Oglalas returned from the Missouri River to the present location of Pine Ridge Reservation in October and November 1878. See Olson (1965:263).

1880 NO EARS: *Susu gleśka ktepi.* Spotted Testicles was killed.

SHORT MAN: Same as No Ears.

IRON CROW: *Siha blaska ti wicakte.* Flat Foot was murdered.

1881 NO EARS: *Sinte gleška ktepi.* Spotted Tail was killed.

The shooting of Spotted Tail by Crow Dog occurred August 5, 1881, near Rosebud Agency. See Hyde (1961:300).

SHORT MAN: Same as No Ears.

IRON CROW: *Sinte gleška ti ktepi.* Spotted Tail was murdered.

1882 NO EARS: *Cancega cinca wan içikte.* A child of Drum committed suicide.

Ķindle's winter count gives the name as *C'ánc'ega k'ínla,* "Packs the Drum" (Beckwith 1930:364).

SHORT MAN: *Conteri kaškapi.* Strong Heart was imprisoned.

The name is evidently *Cante tehi,* "Heart-strong."

IRON CROW: *Heca cinca wan içi kte.* A child of Buzzard committed suicide.

Wissler translated: "Bald Eagle, or Little Dog's Son, suicides."

1883 NO EARS: *Ite cangugu tahu pawega.* Burnt Wood Face broke his neck.

SHORT MAN: *Oglala kin mniciyapi na tancan içicagapi.* The Oglalas made for themselves a council and leaders.

Agent V. T. McGillycuddy, in his annual report for 1884, noted that the "more progressive" Oglalas had established "a permanent board of councilmen" on their own initiative. Young Man Afraid of His Horses was elected president, and other officials were also elected (Commissioner of Indian Affairs, *Annual Report* 1884:211).

IRON CROW: *Ite ceruru oha tahupawega.* Burnt Wood Sticking to Face broke his neck.

Wissler translated the name "Black Face," giving *ceruru* as "soot."

1884 NO EARS: *Tatanka ska tawicu kikte.* White Bull killed his wife. See Iron Crow.

SHORT MAN: *Tukanšilayapi tiwicakte šni wowasu kiye kaga.* The president made a law against murder.

This refers to the Major Crimes Act of March 3, 1885, giving federal courts jurisdiction over major crimes committed on Indian reservations. The act was passed in reaction to the Supreme Court's decision in the Crow Dog case that federal courts lacked jurisdiction for crimes committed by Indians against Indians on Indian reservations. See Prucha (1975:167–68).

IRON CROW: *Unkcemna tawicu wan kikte. Unkcemna* killed one of his wives.

Wissler translated: "White Bull kills his wife." The name *Unkcemna* might be translated "Fartsy." Deloria was told that the incident was an accident (Fire Thunder winter count for 1884).

1885 NO EARS: *Peta wicaśa wan irpeyapi.* A fire man was thrown out (of the reservation).

This refers to agent V. T. McGillycuddy's order ejecting Dr. T. A. Bland of the Indian Rights Association and publisher of the *Council Fire* from Pine Ridge Reservation. See Hyde (1956:96–98) and Olson (1965:294–96).

SHORT MAN: *Hanhepi wicakte tiwicakte.* Kills at Night murdered them.

IRON CROW: *Omniciye peta wan manil eirpeyapi.* A council fire man was thrown out.

1886 NO EARS: *Yuptanyan wanu ktepi.* Turns Over was accidentally killed.

SHORT MAN: *Win yapaya śni wasuyapi.* They made a law against seducing women.

Agent James M. Bell attempted to begin to get the Oglalas to marry in the white man's way, in order to prevent young men from engaging in temporary liaisons with a woman, then throwing her away and taking another (Commissioner of Indian Affairs, *Annual Report* 1886:77).

IRON CROW: *Wi ciqada talo kaksa kute.* Little Moon shot at Cut Meat (community).

Wissler commented: "Little Moon fires on a band of Sioux and kills a horse." Cut Meat is on the Rosebud Reservation.

1887 NO EARS: *Wakan wanu ktepi. Wakan* was accidentally killed.

Deloria commented: "Man must be named Holy—but

some think this and the preceding one are mixed up somehow. It is unlikely that two accidental killings would mark successive years."

SHORT MAN: *Śahiyela iśta ġunġan wan ktepi.* A blind Cheyenne was killed.

IRON CROW: *Cetan gi wanon wakaṭa iyeya.* Brown Hawk accidentally killed someone by hitting him.

1888 NO EARS: *Waparta yublecapi.* They opened bundles.

Agent H. D. Gallagher in his annual report for 1888 mentions his prohibition on the giving away of property at death, and hence on the "ghost keeping" bundles by which a soul could be kept with the people for a year. During that year goods for a large giveaway would be accumulated in order to send the spirit to the spirit world with honor. See Commissioner of Indian Affairs, *Annual Report* 1888:49 and Walker (1980:141).

SHORT MAN: *Anpa wi wan ṭe.* Eclipse of the sun.

Literally, "A sun died." A complete solar eclipse, January 1, 1889 (Miller 1959:286).

IRON CROW: *Waparta natakapi.* Bundles were forbidden.

1889 NO EARS: *Ogle śa tankśitku wan iċikte.* Red Shirt's younger sister committed suicide.

SHORT MAN: *Wicarpi yamini wolakota.* Three Stars made a treaty.

The 1889 agreement, negotiated with the Sioux by a commission headed by Major General George Crook, which broke up the Great Sioux Reservation. See Hyde (1956:202–28) and Olson (1965:313–18).

IRON CROW: *Ogleśa tankśitku rugnar iċiya.* Red Shirt's younger sister committed suicide by causing herself to be burned up.

1890 NO EARS: *Si tanka ktepi.* Big Foot was killed.

The Wounded Knee massacre, December 29, 1890. See Hyde (1956:300–302).

SHORT MAN: Same as No Ears.

IRON CROW: Same as No Ears.

1891 NO EARS: *Maka mani akicita wicakağapi.* They were made infantry soldiers.

This refers to the large number of Oglalas who were enlisted as Indian scouts during the Ghost Dance troubles. For lists of names and summary of activities, see copies of muster rolls in Pine Ridge Agency Records, Decimal classification 650, "Indians as Scouts," National Archives and Records Service, Kansas City Regional Branch, Record Group 75.

SHORT MAN: Same as No Ears.

IRON CROW: *Oglala kin makamani akicita wicakagapi.* The Oglalas were made infantry soldiers.

1892 NO EARS: *Can nonp yuha pte yuha eya wicakte.* Has Two Sticks killed some cowboys.

The incident is mentioned in Standing Bear (1928:237).

SHORT MAN: Same as No Ears.

IRON CROW: *Can noum yuha outapi.* Has Two Sticks shot them (with a gun).

1893 NO EARS: *Owayawa tanka ile.* Big school burned.

The Oglala Boarding School was destroyed by fire in February 1893 (Commissioner of Indian Affairs, *Annual Report* 1894:288).

SHORT MAN: Same as No Ears.

IRON CROW: *Wapaha sapa canpagmiyanyan naruruga.* Black Warbonnet was run over by a wagon.

1894 NO EARS: *Can nonp yuha panaksayapi.* Has Two Sticks was hanged.

The execution took place in Deadwood, South Dakota; the man's two sons, also implicated in the murder of the cowboys, were killed by Indian police. See Standing Bear (1928:237–39).

SHORT MAN: Same as No Ears.

IRON CROW: *Oglala canksa yuha wan ktepi.* The Oglalas killed a policeman.

1895 NO EARS: *Toka omniciye tanka kağapi.* They had the first big council.

All three counts refer to the council held in February 1896 at which delegates were elected to go to Washington, D.C., to confer about a variety of matters of interest to them; the Indians raised over eight hundred dollars to cover the costs of the trip. The delegation visited Washington during March and had talks with the commissioner of Indian Affairs (Letters Received by the Commissioner of Indian Affairs 7087–1896 and 10396–1896, Record Group 75, National Archives and Records Service).

SHORT MAN: *Oglala kin śunka opawinğe owicahanpi.* The Oglalas cooked one hundred dogs.

IRON CROW: *Karnir otanwaheta yewicayapi.* They selected delegates to send to Washington, D.C.

1896 NO EARS: *Zintkala ska ṭa waniyetu,* White Bird died during the winter.

SHORT MAN: Same as No Ears.

IRON CROW: Same as No Ears.

1897 NO EARS: *Talo tipi ileyapi.* They burned down the slaughterhouse.

Deloria recorded the following in connection with this event on the Fire Thunder winter count for 1897: "Up till now, the government had allowed the bands to stage a mock hunt at each issue of beef. The cattle would be turned loose and chased as in the olden days and butchered in the traditional way. But now an order came, putting a stop to this sport; meat was to be killed privately by butchers and cut in the white man's way, and issued out in hunks that cut right into the natural pieces which the women were used to leveling out into jerked meat. Besides, this cut short the enjoyment of raw entrails while still hot. The people resented the meat house, so one night somebody secretly set fire to it."

SHORT MAN: Same as No Ears.

IRON CROW: *Oglala kin talo tipi wan ilekiyapi.* The Oglalas set fire to a slaughterhouse.

1898 NO EARS: *Toka conkaške kağapi.* First fences were made.

Agent W. H. Clapp reported in 1899 that the boundary fence had been successful in keeping white ranchers' stock from trespassing on the Pine Ridge Reservation. In 1901, however, Agent W. R. Brennan noted that only the north line of the reservation was fenced (Commissioner of Indian Affairs, *Annual Report* 1899:335 and 1901:366)

SHORT MAN: Same as No Ears.

IRON CROW: *Ite orada tawicu glaruruga.* Speckled Face beat his wife (to death).

1899 NO EARS: *Peta ğa ṭa waniyetu.* Glowing Coal died during the winter.

SHORT MAN: Same as No Ears.

IRON CROW: *Ikce wicaša kin tahalo wicaqupi šni.* The Indians were not given their hides.

In 1901 agent W. R. Brennan reported that the hides from cattle issued to the Indians at Pine Ridge were shipped east for sale and the profits distributed to the Oglalas, amounting to about two dollars per capita each year (Commissioner of Indian Affairs, *Annual Report* 1901:363).

1900 NO EARS: *Wakpamni natakapi.* Issuing of annuities stopped.

By order of August 12, 1901, Oglalas who were judged self-sufficient (some 1,850, mostly tribal members who were mixed-bloods and whites) were removed from the ration list; as of July 5, 1902, rations were cut off for all able-bodied Indians, and the money was used instead to provide them with employment (Commissioner of Indian Affairs, *Annual Report* 1901:367, 1902:337). Standing Bear (1928:241) gives an Indian viewpoint on the effects of this policy.

SHORT MAN: Same as No Ears.

IRON CROW: *Oglala kin wokpamni wicaqupi šni.* The Oglalas were not given their annuities.

1901 NO EARS: *Wicaranran waniyetu.* Smallpox during the winter.

SHORT MAN: *Ta opi ciqala ṭa.* Little Wound died.

IRON CROW: *Taopi ciqala ṭa waniyetu.* Little Wound died during the winter.

1902 No Ears: *Winorcala wan tanin śni.* An old woman disappeared.

Short Man: *Winorcala kanǧi wan tanin śni.* An old Crow woman disappeared.

Iron Crow: *Tunkaśiyapi wan ktepi.* A president of the United States ("Grandfather") was killed.

The assasination of William McKinley, September 6, 1901. (Last entry in the Iron Crow winter count.)

1903 No Ears: *Tarca kute eya wicaktepi.* Some deer hunters were killed.

The conflict took place in Wyoming between a hunting party of Oglalas and some local whites. Documents concerning the event are printed as "Encounter between Sioux Indians of the Pine Ridge Agency, S. Dak., and a Sheriff's Posse of Wyoming," Sen. Doc. 128, 58th Cong. 2d sess., ser. 4589. See Kindle's winter count for 1903 (Beckwith 1930:366).

Short Man: *Tatokala kute eya wicaktepi.* Some antelope hunters were killed.

1904 No Ears: *Toka makiyutapi waniyetu.* First land allotment surveys during the winter.

Special alloting agent Charles H. Bates arrived at Pine Ridge August 26, 1904 (Commissioner of Indian Affairs, *Annual Report* 1904:58).

Short Man: *Oglala kin maza canku na wicakta.* The Oglalas took the railroad and were killed.

On April 7, 1903, a train carrying a group of Oglalas who were on their way to join Buffalo Bill's Wild West show collided with another train in Illinois, killing three and seriously injuring twenty-seven other Indians. See Standing Bear (1928:271).

1905 No Ears: *Wapaha rota cinca wan iċikte.* A child of Gray Warbonnet committed suicide.

Kindle's winter count gives *Wapáha Ḣóta cincá katíyékiya,* "Grey Warbonnet shot and killed his own son (when he was drunk)" (Beckwith 1930:366).

Short Man: Same as No Ears 1906.

1906 NO EARS: *Sapa wicaša owicayuspapi.* The Utes were captured.

A group of Ute Indians, following the opening of their reservation in 1905, fled to South Dakota during the summer of 1906 in the hope of finding refuge among the Sioux. They surrendered to the army at Fort Meade in November. In June 1907 they were transferred to Cheyenne River Reservation and in June 1908 they returned to Utah. See Laudenschlager (1979).

Deloria's copy of No Ears's winter count has *T'oká ptemák'òlotapi,* "First land leases for cattle grazing." In 1906, nine one-year grazing leases were issued for 969 head of cattle (Commissioner of Indian Affairs, *Annual Report* 1906:106). (This is the last entry in Deloria's copy.)

SHORT MAN: *Mi wakan na Akicita najin kici otuweton ipi.* Sword and Standing Soldier went together to the city (Washington, D.C.).

1907 NO EARS: *Makiyuta ki warpayeca icupi.* They received the land survey payments.

Both this and the Short Man entry evidently refer to the payment of fifty dollars cash and the issuance of livestock, wagons, and equipment to heads of families in conjunction with their land allotments (Annual Report of agent John R. Brennan, Pine Ridge, September 3, 1907, Letters Received by the Commissioner of Indian Affairs, 75216–1907 [file 031], Record Group 75, National Archives and Records Service, Washington, D.C.).

SHORT MAN: *Canpagmi wakpamnipi.* Wagons were issued.

1908 NO EARS: *Wašicu tašunka ṭe waniyetu.* American Horse died during the winter.

SHORT MAN: Same as No Ears.

1909 NO EARS: *Marpiya luta ṭe waniyetu.* (Dec. 10). Red Cloud died during the winter.

SHORT MAN: Same as No Ears.

1910 NO EARS: *Mi wakan ṭa waniyetu* (Nov. 18). Sword died during the winter.

SHORT MAN: Same as No Ears.

1911 NO EARS: *Mato kokipapi ṭa waniyetu.* Afraid of Bear died during the winter.

SHORT MAN: Same as No Ears.

1912 NO EARS: *Śungmanitu ska ṭa waniyetu.* White Wolf died during the winter.

SHORT MAN: Same as No Ears.

---

31. The Ghost Dance and Wounded Knee Fight. Beard. (CHS)

The buffalo were gone and all the Indians were hungry. I sat with my father in his tipi when a messenger came and told us that a Savior for the Indians had appeared to an Indian in the far land of the setting sun, and promised to come and bring again the buffalo and antelope and send the white man from all the land where the Indians hunted in the old times.

This messenger was holy and told us that if we would dance and pray to this Savior he would appear and show us things that were sacred. My father said, "My sons, we will go and see this thing." We went and saw the Indians dancing the ghost dance on the White Clay Creek and I and my father and all my brothers danced.

When we danced some Indians acted as if they died and some acted as if they were holy. When they did this they told that they saw mysterious things and some said they saw the Savior of the Indians and that he promised them to come and bring the good old times again. But I observed that it was bad Indians and Indians that no one used to pay any attention [to] and the medicine men who saw these things.

The spirit would not come to me nor to my father nor to my brothers and my father said, "My sons, I hear that they dance the ghost dance better away from here. We will go to the camps of the Indians on the Cheyenne [River] Agency and we may see the Holy One there. Kicking Bear also went with us, and my father and all his sons went to the camp of Big Foot who was on the Cheyenne [River] Reservation. The Indians were dancing the ghost dance there every day, but it was the same, and nothing mysterious [*wakan*] would come to any of my father's family.

One day, soon after we came to Big Foot's camp, some soldiers came and camped close by. There were about 500 of them. Big Foot went and counciled with the officer and said to him, "My friend, why do you come and camp so close to me?" The officer said, "You are dancing the ghost dance. I am afraid you will do something wrong." Big Foot said, "If my people dance and do nothing wrong, what harm is it to you or to anybody?" The officer said, "You must not dance the ghost dance." Big Foot said, "I go, and will take my people with me, and I do not want you to come after me. We will dance to the Holy Spirit and we will do no harm to anyone." The officer said, "If you go from the reservation you must have a pass for ten days." Then my father said to the officer, "My friend, do you get a paper from the Great Father at Washington when you pray to the white man's God? I think maybe the Great Spirit does not know you."

When the sun went down, Big Foot called us all together and told us to get ready in secret, and that night we all moved to Cherry Creek and all camped close together in a circle. The next day the soldiers came and camped near us again. Then the officer came to our camp and said to Big Foot, "You had better move back to your camp." Big Foot said, "I and my people are not cattle to be put in a pen. We do not want to go back now." Then the soldiers moved away. After they were gone Sitting Bull's old people and squaws and children came by riding bareback and we knew there was trouble gathering in Sitting Bull's camp. Big Foot said, "We will go back to our camp so the Great Father will know we do not belong to the bad Indians."

We moved back towards the Cheyenne, and many more soldiers came and camped near us. In the nighttime they came, so that when we got up in the morning they had a cannon pointing at our camp and the soldiers stood in a line with the guns in their hands. We came out of our tipis and looked at them and while we were looking a halfbreed came to us and said the officer wanted to talk with Big Foot.

Big Foot said, "He is welcome to our camp to talk, but why does he point his guns at us? I do not like that."

Then the offier came and said he wanted us to surrender. Big Foot told him that we were not hostiles and asked the officer to give him and his people something to eat and let him have a day to think over this. The officer and some of the headmen talked till afternoon. Big Foot promised the officer he would not go away before morning and that in the morning he would tell him what he would do.

The soldiers stayed nearby all night and in the morning they came in line again. The cannon was pointing at the camp, close by, and the officer sent word to Big Foot he would give him only a very little time to surrender, and that if he did not surrender before the sun was as high as his hand, the soldiers would fire the cannon and shoot the women and the children.

Big Foot said to his people, "We will go with this man." We all went with the soldiers. The next day some of the soldiers marched before the Indians and some of them marched behind and some marched alongside of the Indian wagons. Big Foot rode on a pony near the front and said nothing, and all the Indians watched him. In the afternoon he said to one of the braves, "Get ready." The brave rode back by all the Indians, and the squaws threw out the tipi poles one by one and threw away every heavy thing and scattered them for a long way.

The officer said to Big Foot, "Why are your people throwing away their things?" And Big Foot said, "The ponies are weak." When the sun was two fingers high, Big Foot said to the officer, "The ponies can go no farther. We will camp near here where there is good water." All the Indians turned out from among the soldiers and the soldiers looked foolish. By the time the soldiers had all gotten together, the Indians were all together and going up a creek and the soldiers came after them. Then Big Foot said, "We will camp here but do not let one pony get loose." The Indians all unhitched the ponies and built fires and began cooking, and the soldiers came near and stopped, for it was dark.

Then Big Foot told all the Indians who were riding on ponies to put blankets about them so they look like women, and to build small fires. He told the people in the wagon farthest from the soldiers to move on, and when it was gone a little time he told the next wagon to move on, and so with every wagon until the last. When the last two wagons moved, an under-officer came and asked where the wagons were, and Big Foot told him they had gone to the other side of the camp. He came again and Big Foot told him he would show him the wagons. Big Foot and all the Indians who stayed to build fires went with the under-officer, and when he saw them all gather together he ran back shouting that the Indians were attacking.

Then Big Foot told us to ride fast and when we came to the wagons he told them to drive fast, and he went ahead. We drove very fast all that night and were in the badlands the next day.

A half breed had told us that the General was at Pine Ridge Agency, and Big Foot said he would go to Red Cloud's camp at the Pine Ridge Agency. We all traveled together. One morning we came to a pass through the wall of the badlands through which we could go down to the valley of White River, but when we got there we saw soldiers marching in the valley of the White River. We lay in the badlands all day and watched them, and they camped that night at Cane Creek, north of White River. When they had passed the place where we lay, we went down in the valley and crossed the White River and camped on its banks the same night that the soldiers camped at Cane Creek. These soldiers were looking for us, and we were watching them.

The next morning Big Foot was sick and bleeding at the nose, but we moved on to what is now called Big Foot springs. The next day we moved to Red Water Creek. Big Foot was so sick he could go no farther, and we stayed there two days and two nights. All the time the young men were watching the soldiers, and saw them come up on the north side of the White River and get farther away from us, and we felt safe from them.

Then Big Foot said, "We will try to get to Red Cloud's camp before I die," and at sundown we broke camp and moved all night and camped on American Horse Creek opposite where [day] school no. 17 is now, and stayed there all day. The next day we moved up Yellow Thunder Creek and when we came opposite to Porcupine Butte we crossed over to Porcupine Creek and stopped for dinner, when we saw four Indian scouts. We called for them to come to us but they ran away as fast as their horses could go.

After noon we hitched up and started towards Porcupine Butte, and when near there, to the northeast of the butte, we saw soldiers coming to the northwest of the butte, and they had pack mules. Big Foot said, "Go and meet the soldiers." The soldiers formed in a line and set a cannon pointing at us, and it looked as if they were about to shoot at us. Then Big Foot said he would go ahead and meet the soldiers and tell them we only wanted to go to Red Cloud's camp at the agency.

Big Foot was so sick that he could not ride on a horse and he had been lying in a wagon ever since we left the Red Water. He had the wagon driven towards the soldiers, and the officer came to meet the wagon. I rode by the wagon with Big Foot and when the officer came near I said, "Do not shoot. We don't want to fight. We want to go to the agency."

The officer said, "Which is Big Foot?" An Indian said, "He is [in] that wagon. He is sick." The officer asked, "Is he able to talk?" The officer ran up to the wagon and pulled the blanket off of Big Foot's head and said, "Can you talk?" Big Foot said, "Yes." The officer said, "Where are you going?" Big Foot said, "We are going to our friends and relations at the Pine Ridge Agency." The officer said, "You will have to lay down your arms, Big Foot."

Big Foot said, "Yes. I am friendly and I will give up my arms. But I am afraid something will happen to me after I do this. Will you not wait until we get to the agency? I will go with you to the agency and my people will give you all their guns when we get to the agency. When we get there we will have a council with the General and we will understand everything. But now I do not understand and I am afraid something will happen to my people if they give up their guns now. I am sick, and I do not want to have any trouble."

The officer said, "Oh, I am glad to hear this. I have a good wagon here with four mules to draw it and I will put you in it." Big Foot said, "Yes, I will go in your wagon and you may do with me as you wish, but I put my people in your hands, and I wish you would see that no trouble comes on them."

The soldiers brought a sick wagon (ambulance), and four soldiers put Big Foot on two gray blankets like the soldiers have and they carried him and put him in the sick wagon. I was then afraid for Big Foot, for the officers laughed when they put Big

Foot in the wagon. Then the soldiers moved back towards Wounded Knee Creek with a guard around Big Foot and all the Indians followed.

I said to the medicine man, "My friend, you would better stop and dance the ghost dance for I am afraid there will trouble come to Big Foot."

One Indian wanted to shoot the officer but my father told him that that would do no good as the soldiers would only shoot at all the Indians and kill the women and children. Beside, it would only be worse for Big Foot.

I rode close to the soldiers with an Indian who could understand English, for I was troubled at the way the soldiers acted and I wanted to know what they said. We came to Wounded Knee Creek and the soldiers camped. They put Big Foot in a tent and kept him there with guards around him and all the Indians came up and put their tipis close to the camps of the soldiers. When the Indians put up their tipis an under-officer came with soldiers and put them as guards around the Indians.

My father said, "Why do you put guards around us? We would not have followed you if we had wished to run away." But the soldiers only laughed at us. Then my father called me and my brothers and said, "My sons, I am thinking some trouble will come to us. Whatever the soldiers tell you to do, I want you to do it, and do not do anything that will give the soldiers an excuse to do you any harm."

Then some of the Indians wanted to come on to the agency but the guards turned them back. This made all the Indians very uneasy so that they could not sleep. The guards were changed very often and a fast-shooting cannon [Hotchkiss gun] was put on a hill nearby and pointed at the camp with the Indians in it. The soldiers were working about this gun and we were afraid they were getting ready to fire on us.

In the night many more soldiers came and with the soldiers were some Indian scouts, but the soldiers would not let the scouts come to us and this made us very much afraid. About midnight, some of the Indians tried to get away to go to the General at the agency, but they found that a great many more guards were placed around us and they could not slip away. When we were told this, we felt that we were prisoners. Some of the soldiers told an Indian who could understand that we were to be disarmed and taken to the railroad and sent far away to the south where the ocean would be all around us.

Nobody in the Indian camp slept much that night except the children, for we were going from tipi to tipi talking about our situation. All agreed to give up their guns if they were asked to do so, but I intended to hide my gun and come and get it again. Some of the young men who had good guns, magazine guns that they had bought, would not say they would or they would not give them up.

Then my father asked the medicine man what he could do and told him that if his Messiah was of any account, now was the time to get his help. But the medicine man was sullen and would only say he would bring help when the time came for it.

When it was coming light the bugles sounded and we all came out and stood watching what the soldiers would do. Then the bugles sounded again and the soldiers surrounded the Indian camp. Some soldiers were on foot and they were nearest the Indians, and some were on horses and they were further away, out around the others. A half-breed named Phillip Wells interpreted for the officer and said, "All the Indians get in a ring and there will be a council." Then all the Indians sat in a ring except four men and the women and the children and Big Foot, who was still in the tent under guard.

Then the soldiers came up close around the Indians on three sides and the soldiers on the horses were farther away across a deep ditch. Some of the soldiers were about the cannon on the hill nearby and some were in a line by the camp of the soldiers. Then the interpreter said that the officer wanted the Indians to give up all their arms. An Indian asked what Big Foot said about this and the interpreter said that Big Foot said for the Indians to give up their guns to the officer.

Then the Indians all went into their tipis. I dug a hole in the ground and buried my gun, and when I came out a great many guns were piled nearby where the Indians were sitting. When I sat down there were soldiers behind me and soldiers on both sides of me. I was looking towards the hill at the cannon so I did not feel afraid. Then the officer said, "You have twenty-five more guns and I want you to bring them out. I know that you have more guns for we counted them yesterday. You have plenty of cartridges and knives and I want you to give them all up." But the Indians had piled nearly all their guns in the pile and not more than four or five had hidden their guns.

My father asked the officer if the Great Father would feed the Indians after he took all the guns away from them. The officer said, "I don't know anything about that. All I know is that I am going to get all the guns, and they are not all in that pile." But the Indians would not bring any more guns.

Then one of the four Indians who would not come into the circle at first came and sat down with the rest. The other three were the medicine man and two young men named Black Fox and Yellow Turtle. Black Fox and Yellow Turtle said they would not give up their guns and they held them in their hands. They told the officer they would give up all their cartridges and would carry their guns empty. But the officer said they must give up their guns and that he would go into the tipis and get all the rest of the guns. He went into a tipi and came out and went into another. While he was doing this an under-officer and four soldiers went towards Black Fox and Yellow Turtle who were standing by the tipis. There were soldiers behind them, and they began to walk away from the tipis towards the creek. The medicine man came and stood between the tipis and the Indians and my father said to him, "Give up your gun. Your ghost shirt will be all you need." The medicine man said, "My friend, I am afraid."

Then Phillip Wells came and said, "When the soldiers have all your guns, you Indians will all march past them and they will hold out their guns towards you." He meant they would hold their guns in front of them, but the Indians thought they would point their guns and take aim at them. My brother said, "When they point their guns at us they will shoot us." Then my father said to the medicine man, "You told us your Messiah could protect us from the white man's bullets. They will aim their guns at us. Now is the time for your Messiah to help us. See now if he can protect us. You stand there like an old woman."

The officer was talking very excitedly to the soldiers and the medicine man began to sing a prayer to the Great Spirit. Then an under-officer and two soldiers started towards Black Fox and Yellow Turtle. Yellow Turtle said to the soldiers, "My friends, do not come to me in that way for I do not want to hurt you." Then he said to Black Fox, "Now you will see if I am brave. Do not give up your gun." Black Fox said to the soldiers, "Keep away from me. I will die before I will let you have my gun, and if I die I will take some of you with me."

Then some of the Indians said, "They are going to shoot us. Let us get our guns and get to that ditch and get away." Then I looked away from the two young men and an old Indian said, "No, do not do that. It is the interpreter who is making all this trouble. If he brings trouble I will kill him with my knife."

My father said to the medicine man, "Now is the time for help. Now do your best." Then the medicine man stopped singing and began to cry to the Great Spirit, and gathered up a handful of dust and threw it towards the sky and waved his blanket under the dust, as they did in the ghost dance when they call for the Messiah. Just then the officer came out of a tipi with a gun in his hand, and I was looking at it for I thought it was my gun, and I heard a soldier cry out, "Look out! Look out! Run back!" And someone cried out in Indian, "Stop! Don't shoot!"

I turned and looked towards Black Fox and Yellow Turtle. They were holding their guns in their hands as if ready to raise them to shoot and were laughing at the under-officer and the two soldiers who were walking away from them very fast and looking back at them as if they were afraid. I was looking down the ditch towards the creek. I heard a gun fire behind me and up the ditch from where the two young men were, and the two soldiers and the under-officer were walking away from the ditch, and not towards where the gun was fired. Immediately, both Black Fox and Yellow Turtle turned and raised their guns and fired towards where I heard the first gunfire.

Then all the Indians jumped up. Some cried that we would all be killed and some cried "Get your guns and get away!" Several shots were fired by the soldiers on both sides of us, and both Black Fox and Yellow Turtle fell. Yellow Turtle began to sing his death song and, raised on his elbow, shot at the soldiers. It appeared to me that all the soldiers began to shoot and I saw Indians falling all around me. I was not expecting anything like this. It was like when a wagon wheel breaks in the road.

An Indian shouted in my ear, "Get your gun!" I was very

much frightened and started to run. I saw some soldiers running, and I ran that way. I ran into smoke so thick that I could not see anything. While I was running I took my knife out. The first thing I saw in the smoke was the brass buttons on a soldier's coat. A gun was thrust towards me and fired, and it was so close that it burnt my hair. I grabbed the gun and stabbed at the soldier with my knife. I stabbed him three times and he let go the gun. I tripped and fell and when I got up I found that I was among the soldiers, and I started to run back towards the ditch. I saw some soldiers aiming at me and I felt something hit me in the shoulder and I fell down.

I raised my head and saw a soldier aiming at me, but he missed me. I aimed at him with the gun I had taken from the soldier and snapped it, but I had forgotten to load it, so I quickly began to load it, and the soldier ran away. I began to breathe very hard and every breath hurt me very much. I got up and tried to run but could not, so I walked. I was strangling with something warm in my throat and mouth. I spit it out and looked at it, and it was blood, so I knew that I was shot.

Before I got to the ditch I saw some soldiers coming towards me and I charged towards them, for I thought I was dead anyway. They ran back into the smoke. I went on towards the ditch and came to a dead soldier and I stopped and cut off his belt of cartridges, for the cartridges I had would not fit the gun I had taken from the soldier. I tried to take his gun also, but I was too weak to carry it.

When I started for the ditch again I thought I stepped into a prairie dog hole for I fell, but when I tried to get up I could not do so, and I found that I was shot through the leg. So I sat there and loaded and fired towards the soldiers as fast as I could. When my cartridges were nearly all gone I broke a cartridge in the gun and could not use it any more. I then began to hop towards the ditch, and I could see nothing but dead women and children and dead soldiers were among them.

I got into the ditch and an Indian gave me a carbine he had taken from a dead soldier. Then the fast-firing cannon (Hotchkiss) began to fire and I began to crawl up the ditch. I met White Face, my wife, coming down the ditch. She was shot, the ball passing through her chin and shoulder. She said to me, "Let me go, you go on. We will die soon. I will get my mother. That is her body at the top of the bank." She went up to her mother's body and took it under the arms to lift it up when she fell dead, shot again. I came up on the bank for I thought I would as well die quickly.

Just as I got to the top of the bank, an Indian pulled me back, and as I fell back he was shot through the head. I took his cartridges, as they suited the carbine I had, and I started up the ditch again. I saw a woman coming towards me with a revolver in her hand. It looked like a soldier's revolver and I think she took it from a soldier, for she was very bloody. I started towards her and I saw some soldiers peep over the bank and shoot her. I shot at them and they ran back. I crawled up the ditch as fast as I could and I came to White Lance, my brother. He was sitting against the bank and another brother, Pursued, was lying by him. They were both wounded and Pursued was almost dead. He said, "My brothers, we will all be dead soon. But you must kill as many as you can before you die." They had three belts of cartridges taken from soldiers. When we saw that Pursued was dead, we went behind a little knoll where the ditch turns and where we could see the soldiers, and we fired at the soldiers. I looked and saw the Hotchkiss aiming at us. White Lance and I lay down close behind the knoll and the dirt and gravel scattered over us, thrown up by the Hotchkiss cannon. I got very sick and weak and thirsty and could shoot no more.

I could hear the soldiers coming close by me, and I saw a soldier peep over the bank. I fired at him, but I was too weak to take aim. The soldiers ran back and they fired the Hotchkiss again, and a shot from it cut Hawk Feather almost in two. Some soldiers were on a hill not far from the cannon, and they shot at me also. One of their bullets struck so near me that it threw the gravel in my face and I thought I was shot again. I lay very still and after a little while all quit shooting at me.

White Lance had gone on up the ditch and after a while I crawled on up the ditch to look for him. While I was crawling an Indian scout shot at me, and then ran away. I felt very sick and wanted to die as I crawled on top of the bank and shot at some soldiers, but I was too weak to stand up. They fired the Hotchkiss gun at me again and the balls passed very close to me so that I could almost feel the wind from the balls lift me from the ground. But I was too sick to stand up, so I lay very still. After a long time all the firing stopped. I crawled over the top of the hill and my brother, Yell At Them, and Jack LaPlant came to me with a horse, but I could not ride so they put their arms around me and took me away. But I was so sick I told my brother to go and leave me, but he said, "We have started for the agency and we will go there together or we will die together."

Then some of the Oglala Sioux came to us and they told us that all the Indians had gone from the agency to the hostiles' camp with Short Bull. So I went to Short Bull's camp, but when I got there I found that the Indians were not all there. But I was so badly wounded I could be taken no farther then. I learned while there that my father, whose name was Horn Cloud, my mother, whose name was Yellow Leaf, my wife, whose name was White Face, my child, whose name was White Foot, my brother, whose name was Pursued, and my sister, whose name was Her Horses had all been killed in the fight, and that my two brothers, White Lance and Enemy, were wounded.

When Big Foot was in the badlands we were very much closer to the camp of the hostile Indians than we were to the agency, and I sometimes think that if we had all gone and joined the hostiles instead of trying to go to the agency, my people would not have been shot down like wolves. But I remembered my father's words, and as soon as I could be hauled without danger to my life I was taken from Short Bull's camp and finally came to the agency.

Appendix I: The Authorities

The following list gives the names of Walker's informants and interpreters at Pine Ridge who contributed materials to this volume. Lakota names, reservation districts, and approximate birth dates are taken from the Pine Ridge censuses of 1896–1904 (National Archives and Record Service, Record Group 75, Microcopy M595, rolls 362–69). Some of these identifications are conjectural, since sometimes more than one person had the same name, or one individual used more than one name.

Bad Bear (Mato Sica). Wounded Knee district; b. ca. 1877.
Beard (Putinhin). Medicine Root district; b. ca. 1864.
John Blunt Horn (He Wotoka). Wounded Knee district; b. ca. 1857.
Charles Garnett. Medicine Root district; b. ca. 1876.
Antoine Herman. Medicine Root district; b. ca. 1861.
High Bear (Mato Wankatuya). Wakpamni district; b. ca. 1861. Wounded Knee district; b. ca. 1839. Medicine Root district; b. ca. 1835.
William Iron Crow (Kangi Maza). Wounded Knee district; b. ca. 1849.
Iron Tail (Sinte Maza). White Clay district; b. ca. 1860.
Nick S. Janis. Wakpamni district; b. ca. 1861. Nick L. Janis. Medicine Root district; b. ca. 1862.
Charles Nines. Not on the census rolls.
Richard Nines. Not on the census rolls. The Nines brothers were the sons of a quarter-blood Mohawk Indian from New York and a white woman. They were fluent in Lakota and for years were licensed Indian traders at Pine Ridge.
John No Ears (Nuge Wanica). White Clay district; b. ca. 1853.

Red Feather (Wiyaka Luta). White Clay district; b. ca. 1859.

Seven Rabbits (Mastincala Sakowin). Medicine Root district; b. ca. 1833.

Short Man (Short Bull No. 2) (Tatanka Ptecela). White Clay district; b. ca. 1847.

Spotted Elk (Onpan Gleska). White Clay district; b. ca. 1848. Medicine Root district; b. ca. 1857.

John Thunder Bear (Mato Wakinyan). Wounded Knee district; b. ca. 1847.

Thomas Tyon. White Clay district; b. ca. 1855.

Woman Dress (Winyan Cuwignaka). Wounded Knee district; b. ca. 1846.

Appendix II: Phonetic Key

In writing Lakota, Walker frequently omitted diacritical marks indicating phonetic values of the letters. Throughout this volume I have reproduced Walker's transcriptions exactly as he wrote them except that, to avoid confusion, I have supplied minimal diacritical marks. I have reproduced the Lakota of Thomas Tyon and Iron Crow exactly as they wrote it. In quotations from Ella Deloria, I have substituted *n* for the subscript hook indicating nasalization.

The phonetic symbols used in this book with special significance are the following:

c is pronounced *ch*

ġ is pronounced as Spanish pa*g*ar (frequently written as *r* or *ṙ* by Walker, Tyon, and Iron Crow)

g, preceding a vowel, is intended either for *ġ* or *k*

ȟ is pronounced as German a*ch* (sometimes written *r* by Walker, Tyon, and Iron Crow, sometimes *h*)

j is pronounced as the *s* in plea*s*ure (frequently written *ź* by Walker, always written *ż* by Deloria)

n, following a vowel, is not pronounced separately, but indicates that the preceding vowel is nasalized (frequently written *ŋ*)

š is pronounced *sh* (written *ś* by Walker; usually written *ṡ* by Iron Crow and Deloria; written *x* by Tyon)

Glottal stops are indicated by a subscript dot under the preceding consonant (for *c̣* and *ṭ* only) by Walker and Iron Crow; *k* followed by a glottal stop is written *q* by Walker, Tyon, and Iron Crow; Deloria indicates a glottal stop by a backwards superscript hook, e.g., *t*ʾ).

In quotations from Deloria, a period within consonant clusters (e.g., *g.l*, *m.n*) indicates an obscure vowel that is not ordinarily represented in other orthographies since it is always pronounced within such clusters. (In the word for 'water,' however, Walker always indicated this obscure vowel by writing an *i: mini.*) Deloria also uses a superscript hook (e.g., *c*', *t*') to indicate aspiration. Accent marks indicate stress.

For guides to the pronunciation of Lakota, see Eugene Buechel, *Lakota-English Dictionary,* and Allan R. Taylor, "The Colorado University System for Writing the Lakhóta Language."

Notes

Preface

1. For further discussion of the American Museum's plan of research on the plains, see James R. Walker, *Lakota Belief and Ritual,* ed. Raymond J. DeMallie and Elaine A. Jahner (Lincoln: University of Nebraska Press, 1980), pp. 13–15. In the end, other than the large amount of comparative data collected, the overall research plan met with mixed success. The formal summaries of the study are Clark Wissler, "General Discussion of Shamanistic and Dancing Societies," AMNH, *Anthropological Papers* 11, pt. 12 (1916): 853–76; Robert H. Lowie, "Plains Indian Age-Societies: Historical and Comparative Summary," AMNH, *Anthropological Papers* 11, pt. 13 (1916): 877–986; and Leslie Spier, "The Sun Dance of the Plains Indians: Its Development and Diffusion," AMNH, *Anthropological Papers* 16, pt. 7 (1921): 451–527. In a general sense, Robert H. Lowie's *Indians of the Plains,* AMNH, Anthropological Handbook no. 1, (New York: McGraw-Hill, 1954), serves as the summary statement of the research.

2. Clark Wissler to P. E. Goddard, correspondence files, Department of Anthropology, AMNH (filed under Wissler).

3. Clark Wissler's "Field Notes on the Dakota Indians, 1902," are in the archives of the Department of Anthropology, AMNH. Wissler's publications on the Sioux are listed in the bibliography for the present volume.

4. For fuller discussion of Walker's contributions see Walker, *Lakota Belief and Ritual,* pt. 1.

Part I. The Structure of Society

1. See H. Scudder Mekeel, "A Discussion of Culture Change as Illustrated by Material from a Teton-Dakota Community," *American Anthropologist* 34 (1932): 274–85; idem, "The Economy of a Modern

Teton Dakota Community," *Yale University Publications in Anthropology,* no. 6 (New Haven: Yale University Press, 1936); and idem, "A Short History of the Teton-Dakota," *North Dakota Historical Quarterly* 10 (1943): 136–205. More data are included in Mekeel's Ph.D. dissertation, "A Modern American Indian Community in the Light of Its Past: A Study in Culture Change" (Yale University, 1932). Copies of Mekeel's field notes from Pine Ridge in 1930 and 1931 are in the archives of the Department of Anthropology, AMNH. Collier's material on the Oglalas remains unpublished.

2. James R. Walker, "Oglala Kinship Terms," *American Anthropologist* 16 (1914): 97–98.

3. Correspondence is in the archives of the Department of Anthropology, AMNH. Walker's plan for arranging the kin terms is indicated in his letter to Wissler of December 22, 1914.

4. Walker, "Oglala Kinship Terms," pp. 100–101.

5. For a succinct discussion of Lakota society and kinship, see Raymond J. DeMallie, "Pine Ridge Economy: Cultural and Historical Perspectives," in *American Indian Economic Development,* ed. Sam Stanley (The Hague: Mouton, 1978), pp. 242–48.

6. John Parker, ed., *The Journals of Jonathan Carver and Related Documents 1766–1770* (St. Paul: Minnesota Historical Society Press, 1976), pp. 99–100; Reuben Gold Thwaites, ed., *Original Journals of the Lewis and Clark Expedition, 1804–1806,* 8 vols. (1904–1905; rpt., New York: Antiquarian Press, 1959) 6:93–99; Annie Heloise Abel, ed., *Tabeau's Narrative of Loisel's Expedition to the Upper Missouri* (1939; rpt., Norman: University of Oklahoma Press, 1968) pp. 101–23; William H. Keating, *Narrative of an Expedition to the Source of St. Peter's River,* 2 vols. (1824; rpt., Minneapolis: Ross and Haines, 1959) 1:392–406.

7. Raymond J. DeMallie, ed. and trans., "Nicollet's Notes on the Dakota," in *Joseph N. Nicollet on the Plains and Prairies,* ed. Edmund C. Bray and Martha Coleman Bray (St. Paul: Minnesota Historical Society Press, 1976), pp. 250–81; Edwin T. Denig, *Indian Tribes of the Upper Missouri,* ed. J. N. B. Hewitt, Smithsonian Institution, Bureau of American Ethnology, Annual Report 46 (1930), pp. 377–628; idem, *Five Indian Tribes of the Upper Missouri,* ed. John C. Ewers (Norman: University of Oklahoma Press, 1961), pp. 3–40; Thaddeus A. Culbertson, *Journal of an Expedition to the Mauvaises Terres and the Upper Missouri in 1850,* ed. John Francis McDermott, Smithsonian Institution, Bureau of American Ethnology, Bulletin 147 (1952), pp. 135–36; Ferdinand V. Hayden, *Contributions to the Ethnography and Philology of the Indian Tribes of the Missouri Valley* (Philadelphia: Sherman and Son, 1862), pp. 364–78. John C. Ewers's introduction to Denig's *Five Indian Tribes* (pp. xxxiv–xxxvi) discusses the relationship between Hayden's work and Denig's manuscripts.

8. Stephen Return Riggs, *Grammar and Dictionary of the Dakota Language,* Smithsonian Institution, Contributions to Knowledge, vol. 4, (1852), pp. vii–viii; idem, *Dakota Grammar, Texts, and Ethnography,* ed. J. Owen Dorsey, Contributions to North American Ethnology, vol. 9 (1893), pp. 155–64; James Owen Dorsey, "The Social Organization of the Siouan Tribes," *Journal of American Folk-Lore* 4 (1891): 257–63; idem, *Siouan Sociology: A Posthumous Paper,* Smithsonian Institution, Bureau of American Ethnology, Annual Report 15 (1897), pp. 215–22.

9. George E. Hyde, *Red Cloud's Folk: A History of the Oglala Sioux Indians* 1937; new ed., Norman: University of Oklahoma Press, 1957, pp. 308–15; Harry Anderson, "An Investigation of the Early Bands of the Saone Group of Teton Sioux," *Journal of the Washington Academy of Sciences* 46 (1956): 87–94.

10. William K. Powers, *Oglala Religion* (Lincoln: University of Nebraska Press, 1977), pp. 25–32; see Loretta K. Fowler's review of Powers's *Oglala Religion, American Ethnologist* 6 (1979): 404–6.

11. Lewis Henry Morgan, *Systems of Consanguinity and Affinity of the Human Family,* Smithsonian Institution, Contributions to Knowledge, vol. 17 (1871), pp. 283–382; Alexander Lesser, "Siouan Kinship," (Ph.D. diss., Columbia University, 1958 [originally written in 1929], pp. 14–65; Ruth Landes, *The Mystic Lake Sioux* (Madison: University of Wisconsin Press, 1968); Fred Eggan, "The Cheyenne and Arapaho Kinship System," in *Social Anthropology of North American Tribes,* ed. Fred Eggan (1937; enlarged ed. Chicago: University of Chicago Press, 1955), pp. 89–95; Jeannette Mirsky, "The Dakota," in *Cooperation and Competition among Primitive Peoples,* ed. Margaret Mead, (1937; new ed., Boston: Beacon Press, 1966), pp. 382–427.

12. Franz Boas and Ella Deloria, *Dakota Grammar,* Memoirs of the National Academy of Sciences, vol. 23, no. 2 (1941), pp. 129–131; Ella Deloria, *Speaking of Indians* (New York: Friendship Press, 1944); Royal B. Hassrick, "Teton Dakota Kinship System," *American Anthropologist* 46 (1944): 338–47; idem, *The Sioux: Life and Customs of a Warrior Society* (Norman: University of Oklahoma Press, 1964), pp. 97–111, 312–13.

13. Fred Eggan, "Social Anthropology: Methods and Results," in *Social Anthropology of North American Tribes,* ed. Fred Eggan (enlarged ed.; Chicago: University of Chicago Press, 1955), pp. 543–48; idem, *The American Indian: Perspectives for the Study of Social Change* (Chicago: Aldine Publishing Co., 1966), pp. 98–105; Raymond J. DeMallie, "Change in American Indian Kinship Systems: The Dakota," in *Currents in Anthropology: Essays in Honor of Sol Tax,* ed. Robert Hinshaw (The Hague: Mouton, 1979), pp. 221–41.

14. Eugene Buechel, S. J. *et al., Lakota Tales and Texts,* ed. Paul Manhart, S.J. (Pine Ridge, S. Dak.: Red Cloud Indian School, Lakota Language and Cultural Center, 1978).

15. Keating, *Narrative of An Expedition,* p. 442.

16. See Powers, *Oglala Relgion,* p. 5, for a modern interpretation that assumes historical reality for the Seven Council Fires.

17. DeMallie, "Nicollet's Notes on the Dakota," pp. 252–62.

18. Cf. Hassrick, *The Sioux,* p. 152.

19. Le Sueur's list of Sioux villages appears in Pierre Margry, ed., *Découvertes et Établissements des Français dans l'Ouest et dans le Sud de l'Amérique Septentrionale (1614–1754),* 6 vols. (Paris: Jouaust, 1875–86) 6:86–87.

20. Here Walker uses the Lakota forms. The Dakota designation for Sacred Lake is *Mdewakan* or *Bdewakan.*

21. The term *Dakota (Lakota)* is conventionally interpreted "allies." Although Powers, *Oglala Religion,* p. 12, dismisses Walker's interpretation "considered friends" as "purely fictional," it nevertheless seems to be a legitimate folk etymology current at Pine Ridge during Walker's time.

22. Powers, *Oglala Religion,* p. 4, argues that *oceti* should be interpreted "fireplace" rather than "fire." Walker's material indicates that the reference is to the fire itself, which was carefully preserved during marches from one campsite to the next and rekindled in the council lodge at each formal camp, symbolizing the autonomy of the camp. The term *oceti* does mean fireplace, not in the sense of a fixed location (as for the Iroquois—see Powers, *Oglala Religion,* p. 3), but rather in a relational sense, the center of the tipi, no matter where the tipi might be located. The council fire was called *peta omniciye,* literally, "council fire" (see document 6). It is important to emphasize here that Walker used the terms *gens (gentes), clan* and *band* synonymously. Today the term *band* is generally used to indicate subdivisions of the Sioux (i.e., *tiyošpaye*).

23. Walker fairly consistently treated the stories of the differentiation of the Seven Council Fires as legendary, rather than as historical. The existence of alternate versions of these stories demonstrates this to be the case. The purpose of the tales was to provide charters for the moral bonds among these related peoples, not to present a chronological history in the white man's sense.

24. Documentation for hostile encounters between various Lakota bands is given by Tabeau for ca. 1804. Horse stealing was evidently the cause of these altercations. See Abel, *Tabeau's Narrative,* pp. 105, 107, and 123.

25. See the legend "The Mysterious Lake" in Elaine Jahner's forthcoming work on Walker's Lakota myth.

26. Riggs, *Dakota Grammar, Texts, and Ethnography,* p. 157, makes the same interpretation, "Ki-yu-ksa, *Breakers of custom* or *law,* said to refer to marrying into their own gens." Nicollet made the same interpretation in 1838; DeMallie, "Nicollet's Notes on the Dakota," p. 255.

27. For a historian's interpretation of this conflict between the Sioux and Chippewa, see Gary Clayton Anderson, "Early Dakota Migration and Intertribal War: A Revision," *Western Historical Quarterly* 11 (1980): 17–36. For an anthropologist's perspective, see Harold Hickerson, *The Chippewas and Their Neighbors: A Study in Ethnohistory* (New York: Holt, Rinehart and Winston, 1970), pp. 64–119.

28. The reference here is to the emergence of the first Lakota people from their home beneath the earth. Iktomi and Double Face Woman *(Anog Ite)* tricked the Lakotas into coming out onto the world and led them to their first home in the region of the pines. James R. Walker, "The Sun Dance and Other Ceremonies of the Oglala Division of the Teton Dakota," AMNH, *Anthropological Papers* 16, pt. 2 (1917): 181–82.

29. In another similar document, "The Order of a Formal Camp of the Lakotas," Walker reverses the positions of the *Wak̇pekutetonwan* and the *Wak̇petonwan* (CHS MS file folder 49, no. 6).

30. *Pyabya* is more regularly given as *Payabya; Kiyuksa* is frequently given as *Kiyaksa,* "Bite in two;" *Waźaźa* is usually translated "Osage"; *Wagluk̇e* is usually translated "Loafers." Powers, *Oglala Religion,* p. 30–31, discusses the etymologies of these band names. See also Stephen E. Feraca, "The Political Status of the Early Bands and Modern Communities of the Oglala Dakota," W. H. Over *Museum News* 27 (1966): 1-26.

31. That is, Red Cloud's band usurped the place claimed by Little Wound's band, another aspect of the ongoing fued between these two rival factions into which the Oglalas had been divided at least since the murder of Bull Bear in 1841. The last public sun dance before Walker's time was in 1883.

32. The informant is evidently Little Wound.

33. The murder occurred in 1841. See Walker, *Lakota Belief and Ritual,* pp. 294 n. 1, 138, 195.

34. This year is so designated on the No Ears winter count (document 30). The "attack" mentioned here may refer to the dragoon expedition under Colonel Stephen W. Kearny which met the Oglalas and Brulés in council at Fort Laramie on June 16, 1845. The troops fired howitzers and a rocket to impress the Sioux with the army's might. See S. W. Kearney, "Report of a Summer Campaign to the Rocky Mountains, &c., in 1845," Senate Exec. Doc. 1, 29th Cong. 1st sess., (serial set no. 470, pp. 210–13.

35. Evidently the last four bands named belonged to Little Wound's faction and the previous six to Red Cloud's faction. This suggests that the *Ḣokayuta* band was split between the two factions.

36. This is one of many explanations for the origin of the name Oglala. However, what is generally interpreted as a version of the name

was recorded as early as 1701 by Le Sueur, who established Fort l'Huillier on the Blue Earth River in present-day Minnesota. He gives "Oujatespouitons—Village dispersé en plusieurs petites bandes [village dispersed in several small bands]," in Margry, *Découvertes et Établissements,* 6:87. For discussion of Le Sueur's data on Sioux groups, see Mildred Mott Wedel, "Le Sueur and the Dakota Sioux," in *Aspects of Upper Great Lakes Anthropology: Papers in Honor of Lloyd A. Wilford,* ed. Elden Johnson (St. Paul: Minnesota Historical Society Press, 1974), pp. 157–71.

37. Ĉf. discussion in Riggs, *Dakota Grammar, Texts, and Ethnography,* pp. 195–96, 200–202.

38. For the symbolism of ash wood, see document 11, p. 31.

39. This document was used in Clark Wissler, "Societies and Ceremonial Associations in the Oglala Division of the Teton-Dakota," AMNH, *Anthropological Papers* 11, pt. 1 (1912): 10, 13. See also discussion of *akicita* societies in Walker, *Lakota Belief and Ritual,* documents 87–92.

40. Walker, "Sun Dance," p. 96, mentions the appointment of marshals specifically for the sun dance camp.

41. This document was used in Wissler, "Societies and Ceremonial Associations," pp. 36–37, 40.

42. According to Red Feather, *naca* is an older term for chief than the more commonly used *itancan,* Eugene Buechel, S.J., *A Dictionary of the Teton Dakota Sioux Language: Lakota-English, English-Lakota,* ed. Paul Manhart, S.J. (Pine Ridge, S. Dak.: Red Cloud Indian School, 1970), p. 342. The term *naca* does not seem to be Siouan and may have been borrowed from the Arapaho word for chief, *nééčee.* The doubled vowels indicate length, accent marks indicate high tone. See Zdeněk Salzmann, "Arapaho VI: Noun," *International Journal of American Linguistics* 31 (1965): 149. The closely related Gros Ventres (Atsina) word used by men for "chief" is *nätcä.* See Regina Flannery, *The Gros Ventres of Montana: Part I, Social Life,* Catholic University of America Anthropological Series No. 15 (1953), p. 31, n. 4.

43. This obviously reflects a Lakota bias!

44. This document was used in Wissler, "Societies and Ceremonial Associations," pp. 11, 21.

45. Probably Conquering Bear; see document 30, 1854.

46. This document was used in Wissler, "Societies and Ceremonial Associations," pp. 7–8, 10.

47. The term is *išteca,* "to be ashamed"; cf. Riggs, *Dakota Grammar, Texts, and Ethnography,* p. 204.

48. The friend relationship between men known as *kola* was as binding as kin relationships. Cf. Riggs, *Dakota Grammar, Texts, and Ethnography,* p. 196.

49. Walker repeatedly wrote that by marrying the oldest sister, a man gained rights over the younger sisters. See document 22.

50. That is, there is no Lakota term meaning "wife" abstractly, without an affix indicating *whose* wife, e.g., *mitawin,* my wife, *tawicu,* his wife. The same point is made in Riggs, *Dakota Grammar, Texts, and Ethnography,* p. 203.

51. *Oh̄anhanhan,* "to do badly," Stephen R. Riggs, *A Dakota-English Dictionary,* ed. J. Owen Dorsey, Contributions to North American Ethnology, vol. 7 (1890).

52. *Yuza,* "to take a wife," Riggs, *Dakota-English Dictionary.*

53. This text was printed in Walker, "Oglala Kinship Terms," pp. 104–109, but is marred by many typographical errors and mistranslations. This is a new translation by the editor, made from the original typescript of Tyon's Lakota text in AMNH. Tyon uses *x* for *š.*

54. This document is composed of material taken from Walker, "Oglala Kinship Terms." Typographical errors have been corrected, diacritical marks added, and the material reorganized according to Walker's original manuscript. Cf. Boas and Deloria, *Dakota Grammar,* pp. 129–34.

55. Walker, "Oglala Kinship Terms," p. 101, gives *Ta-yak* and *Mita-yak,* obviously typographical errors. The final *-k* is an abbreviated form of the suffix *-ku,* "his."

56. According to Riggs, *Dakota-English Dictionary,* the term *winu* was used by the Dakota speakers, whereas the Lakota speakers used *wiwayaka,* literally, "woman-captive."

57. Cf. Riggs, *Dakota Grammar, Texts, and Ethnography,* p. 45, which gives *Winona* for first-born daughter, *Hapistinna* for third-born daughter, and *Wanske* for fourth-born daughter. The forms as given by Walker may simply be erroneous. *Witokape,* Walker's term for first-born daughter, is particularly confusing because Riggs, *Dakota-English Dictionary,* gives *witoka* as the Lakota form for female captive (literally "woman-enemy"). Powers, *Oglala Religion,* pp. 38–39, discusses birth-order names and makes etymological conjectures.

58. This document is a composite from four separate drafts in the Walker collection, CHS, entitled "The Social Organization of the Sioux," "Social Customs of the Oglala Sioux," "Sociality of the Oglala Sioux Indians," and "The Plains Indians, Their Medicines and Myths" (MS folders 55, no. 1, 54, no. 4, 54, no. 3, and 69, no. 1). These all seem to have been written as public lectures. I have taken greater editorial liberty here in combining material from each of them in order to present the substantive data from each draft without needless repetition. In conjunction with this document the reader could consult Walker, "Oglala Kinship Terms," pp. 98–100, which gives a condensation of material presented here on courtship, marriage, and divorce.

59. Although from the perspective of Western culture buying a wife seems degrading to women, Walker wrote that the Lakota woman saw it

as a mark of esteem; "She could afterwards proudly make the boast that her man had paid the price for her" ("Sun Dance," p. 148).

60. The instrument was actually a flageolet, made of cedar. See Hassrick, *The Sioux,* pp. 116, 146–47. For Double Face *(Anog Ite),* see Walker, "Sun Dance," p. 91.

61. For the Buffalo and *Hunka* ceremonies, see Walker, "Sun Dance," pp. 122–51, and idem, *Lakota Belief and Ritual,* documents 79–86.

62. The term is *wicawoȟa,* which Walker interprets as *wica,* "man," + *woȟa,* "something buried, a cache." Ella C. Deloria, *Dakota Texts,* Publications of the American Ethnological Society, vol. 14 (New York: G. E. Stechert & Co., 1932), p. 14, n. 4, felt this etymology to be linguistically incorrect. She suggested the term was, more fully, *wic'áwoȟan-hi,* indicating a man who has come and who stays "from attraction." The reverse term, used for a woman living in her husband's family's lodge, is *wiwóȟa.*

63. According to Walker, "Oglala Kinship Terms," p. 100, the term is *wino-wanžica,* literally, "woman-one."

64. That is, there are no special kin terms for grandparents' parents or grandchildren's children, the terms for grandparents and grandchildren simply being extended generationally as far as needed.

65. Although Lakota men's societies were not strictly age-graded like those of many other plains tribes, Walker's data suggest that in a general sense there was age-grading between different groups of societies (i.e., boys' societies, *akicita* societies, headmen's societies, chiefs' society). James H. Howard (personal communication) has also recorded information that suggests some age-grading in Oglala men's societies. Cf. Wissler, "Societies and Ceremonial Associations," pp. 65–66.

66. These societies for women are discussed in Wissler, "Societies and Ceremonial Associations," pp. 75–80.

67. For games, see Walker, "Sioux Games," *Journal of American Folk-Lore* 18 (1905): 277–90, 19 (1906): 29–36; J. Owen Dorsey, "Games of Teton Dakota Children," *American Anthropologist,* o.s. 4 (1891): 329–45; Louis L. Meeker, "Ogalala Games," *Bulletin* of the Free Museum of Science and Art (Philadelphia) no. 3 (1901): 23–46; Stewart Culin, *Games of the North American Indians.* Smithsonian Institution, Bureau of American Ethnology, Annual Report 24 (1907): 1–846.

68. See "The Four Great Virtues" in Walker, "Sun Dance," pp. 160–61.

Part II. Hunting, War, Ceremony, and Art

1. Tabeau, "La Cerne ou Chasse en Commun," in Abel, *Tabeau's Narrative,* pp. 245–48. Denig's major discussion of hunting is in his "Indian Tribes of the Upper Missouri," pp. 530–43. Frances Densmore's

material on buffalo hunting is in her *Teton Sioux Music*, Smithsonian Institution, Bureau of American Ethnology, Bulletin 61 (1918), pp. 436–47.

2. Stanley Vestal's primary works on the Sioux are *Sitting Bull: Champion of the Sioux* (1932; new ed., Norman: University of Oklahoma Press, 1957); *Warpath: The True Story of the Fighting Sioux Told in a Biography of Chief White Bull* (Boston: Houghton Mifflin, 1934); and *New Sources of Indian History, 1850–1891* (Norman: University of Oklahoma Press, 1934). The pictorial autobiographies of Sitting Bull and White Bull are reproduced in Vestal's biographies. For Sitting Bull's pictorial autobiographies, see also M. W. Stirling, "Three Pictographic Autobiographies of Sitting Bull," *Smithsonian Miscellaneous Collections* 97 (1938) and Alexis Praus, "A New Pictographic Autobiography of Sitting Bull," *Smithsonian Miscellaneous Collections* 123 (1955). For White Bull's pictorial autobiographies also see James H. Howard, *The Warrior Who Killed Custer: The Personal Narrative of Chief Joseph White Bull* (Lincoln: University of Nebraska Press, 1968). Amos Bad Heart Bull's drawings are in his *A Pictographic History of the Oglala Sioux* (Lincoln: University of Nebraska Press, 1967). George Sword's manuscripts are currently being translated and edited for publication by Raymond J. DeMallie.

3. The most relevant of Clark Wissler's publications are "Symbolism in the Decorative Art of the Sioux," International Congress of Americanists, *Proceedings*, vol. 13 (1902), pp. 339–45; "Decorative Art of the Sioux Indians," AMNH, *Bulletin* 18 (1905), pp. 231–75; "Some Protective Designs of the Dakota," AMNH, *Anthropological Papers* 1, pt. 2 (1907), pp. 21–53; and "Costumes of the Plains Indians," AMNH, *Anthropological Papers* 17, pt. 2 (1915), pp. 39–91. For Densmore's material see her *Teton Sioux Music* and "A Collection of Specimens from the Teton Sioux," *Indian Notes and Monographs*, vol. 11, pt. 3 (1948), pp. 163–204. For a more positive interpretation of the power of the Double Woman Dreamers see Mable Morrow, *Indian Rawhide: An American Folk Art* (Norman: University of Oklahoma Press, 1975), p. 145.

4. There are two drafts of this document. The earlier version is entitled "Communal Chase of the Buffalo and Marshalls of the Chase," and the later, much longer version, is entitled "Communal Chase of the Buffalo" (CHS MS folders 51, no. 1 and 50 no. 1). I give here the text of the longer version, but I have also integrated into it material from the earlier version that Walker did not include in the later one. In an introductory note to the earlier version, Walker wrote: "This paper is based on a description written by George Sword, a full blood Oglala, in the Oglala Dialect of the Lakota, and rewritten and translated into English by Clarence Three-stars, a full blood Oglala, to which are additions gotten from information given by Oglalas who probably knew of such matters."

5. Nicollet, writing in 1838, made the same distinction between *akicita*, "soldiers," and *zuyes'a*, "warriors." DeMallie, "Nicollet's Notes," p. 224.

6. Cf. the discussion of head *akicita* in Wissler, "Societies and Ceremonial Associations," pp. 9–10.

7. For information on plains Indian sign language see W. P. Clark, *The Indian Sign Language* (Philadelphia: L. R. Hamersly, 1885), and Garrick Mallery, *Sign Language among North American Indians Compared with that among Other Peoples and Deaf-mutes*, Smithsonian Institution, Bureau of American Ethnology Annual Report 1 (1881): 263–552.

8. This is a mistranslation. The Lakota text actually reads "Two of Little Thunder's younger brothers were killed." See document 30.

9. According to a myth recorded by Wissler, the hoop-and-pole game was taught to the Lakotas by the buffalo as a sacred means to call buffalo in times of necessity. See Walker, "Sioux Games," pp. 281–83, 286–88. *Heȟaka*, "elk," is a type of hoop-and-pole game using a branched pole.

10. Cf. the account by High Bear in Wissler, "Societies and Ceremonial Associations," pp. 8–9.

11. See Alice C. Fletcher, "The White Buffalo Festival of the Uncpapas," *Reports of the Peabody Museum of American Archaeology and Ethnology*, vol. 3 (1884): 260–75.

12. This document was used in Wissler, "Societies and Ceremonial Associations," p. 91 (cf. also pp. 53, 55). For symbolism of the wolf, see Densmore, *Teton Sioux Music*, pp. 179–84, and Walker, *Lakota Belief and Ritual*, p. 160. Note the reference to the use of a wolf skin in war in Short Man's winter count for 1849 (document 30).

13. From a manuscript on the Badger society. The informant may have been Thunder Bear.

14. Walker consulted this document in writing his "Sun Dance." It presents the perspective of a warrior, not a holy man.

15. This document is the text of a public address delivered by Walker. It is in part a conjectural reconstruction of Lakota art before contact with Europeans. Walker wrote: "I shall speak only of aboriginal decorative arts, for since their contact with white people the distinctive arts of the Sioux have lost their significations and become mere matters for adornment or of commerce." The general introductory paragraphs are omitted here.

16. Cf. color symbolism in the discussion of war insignia in Walker, *Lakota Belief and Ritual*, document 92. Also see Walker's discussion of the symbolism of the *itazipa wakan* ("sacred bow") in Lothar Dräger, ed., "Die Aursrüstung der Kriegsanführer bei den Ogalala-Dakota, Nach Aufzeichnungen von F. Weygold und J. R. Walker," *Jahrbuch des Museums*

für Völkerkunde zu Leipzig (East Berlin) 24 (1967): 182–85.

17. For painting techniques, see John C. Ewers, *Plains Indian Painting* (Stanford: Stanford University Press, 1939), pp. 3–7. James H. Howard noted (personal communication) that the patellae of animals were also used as paint brushes.

18. Walker's statements that moccasins and other items of clothing were aboriginally painted in the same manner as they were later decorated with quillwork or beadwork is purely conjectural. Since no museum specimens substantiate this use of painting, Walker's reconstruction must be rejected as historically incorrect, although it is possible that this was a Lakota folk belief about the historical development of their art.

19. Nonetheless, numerous Lakota war shirts in museum collections are painted blue.

20. Again, Walker's discussion of warbonnets fails to agree with what is known from museum collections and information collected by anthropologists. James H. Howard pointed out (personal communication) that Walker's material here seems to be "white man's Indian lore." Howard wrote: "The number of feathers on a plains warbonnet is almost always a standard thirty-one feathers, not the varying number we might expect if there was a definite correlation between the number of feathers and the coups of the wearer." Similarly, Howard dismisses Walker's contention that only holy men could use buffalo horns or hair to decorate their warbonnets, noting that many early paintings and drawings of plains Indians by such artists as George Catlin, Karl Bodmer, and Paul Kane depict chiefs wearing buffalo split-horn bonnets. However, in using the term "holy men" Walker probably intended to designate any man with vision powers (which would include all chiefs), not to limit the term to shamans only.

21. No examples of painted leglets or dresses of the type suggested by Walker are known from museum collections. The only painted dresses are those made for the ghost dance. Elk teeth, used to decorate dresses, are highly valued by the Lakotas. According to Shooter, "In observing the carcass of an elk it is found that two teeth remain after everything else has crumbled to dust. These teeth will last longer than the life of a man, and for that reason the elk tooth has become the emblem of long life." (Densmore, *Teton Sioux Music,* p. 176).

22. These effigies contain the infant's umbilical cord. See J. Owen Dorsey, *A Study of Siouan Cults,* Smithsonian Institution, Bureau of American Ethnology, Annual Report 11 (1894), p. 482. No examples of painted effigies are found in museum collections; all are quilled or beaded.

23. See Walker, *Lakota Belief and Ritual,* pp. 270–72.

24. For discussion of face and body paints see Reginald and Gladys

Laubin, *Indian Dances of North America: Their Importance to Indian Life* (Norman: University of Oklahoma Press, 1977), pp. 116–22 and color plate 8.

25. For dyes, see Carrie A. Lyford, *Quill and Beadwork of the Western Sioux,* Indian Handicrafts Pamphlet 1 (Lawrence, Kansas: Haskell Press, 1940), pp. 42–43. Contrary to Walker's suggestion, painted, quilled, and beaded designs were distinct from one another.

26. These headdresses, known as roaches, are usually made of porcupine guard hair and deer-tail hair. See Laubins, *Indian Dances,* pp. 146–47. For symbolism of the roach, see Walker, *Lakota Belief and Ritual,* p. 273.

27. James H. Howard pointed out (personal communication) that Lakota pyrographic work was usually done with a heated metal file. This is another example of Walker's "upstreaming" to conjecture what the aboriginal practice might have been.

28. For the carving of pipes and pipestems, see John C. Ewers, *Indian Art in Pipestone: George Catlin's Portfolio in the British Museum* (Washington, D.C.: British Museum Publications and Smithsonian Institution Press, 1979).

29. Painted and beaded designs, contrary to Walker's account, were in most cases distinct from one another.

30. Walker's description of the lazy-stitch and loomwork techniques is confusing at best. See Lyford, *Quill and Beadwork,* pp. 61–65. According to Lyford, loom beading was introduced to the Lakotas by white teachers in the Indian schools. James H. Howard suggests (personal communication) that although contemporary Lakotas believe that loom beadwork is a recent innovation, it may be an old Lakota technique, which he has traced back at least as far as the 1840s.

Part III. Time and History

1. The best known of these generation pictographs are those of Battiste Good published in Garrick Mallery, *Picture-Writing of the American Indians,* Smithsonian Institution, Bureau of American Ethnology, Annual Report 10 (1893): 287–93.

2. Martha Warren Beckwith, "Mythology of the Oglala Dakota," *Journal of American Folk-Lore* 43 (1930): 363.

3. William K. Powers, "A Winter Count of the Oglala," *American Indian Tradition* 52 (1953): 33.

4. Corbusier's winter counts are reproduced in Mallery, *Pictographs of the North American Indians,* Smithsonian Institution, Bureau of American Ethnology, Annual Report 4 (1886): 127–46.

5. Walker's copy of the No Ears count is in CHS, MS. folder 59.

6. The Short Man winter count is in the archives of the Department of Anthropology, AMNH, filed with the Nines brothers' manuscripts. Walker first mentioned this winter count to Wissler in a letter of November 5, 1913, suggesting that if Wissler would send some water colors and brushes, the keeper—whom he calls "Short-bull No. 2, an old Oglala"—would make a copy for the museum. In a letter of December 27, 1913, Walker reported that "Short-bull No. 2" was progressing well with the copy. Walker sent the completed copy of the count to Wissler on January 22, 1914, now referring to the keeper as "Short-man," whom he paid ten dollars for his work in making the copy. Evidently the man was known by both names.

7. White Cow Killer's winter count is published in part in Mallery, *Pictographs of the North American Indians,* pp. 127–46.

8. Iron Crow's winter count is in the archives of the Department of Anthropology, AMNH, accession file 1902–72.

9. Wounded Bear's winter count is published in Stephen E. Feraca, "The Discovery of a Sioux Indian Calendar," *New Europe* 3, no. 10 (1974): 4–10.

10. The Red Horse Owner winter count is published in Joseph S. Karol, S.J., *Red Horse Owner's Winter Count* (Martin, S.D.: Booster Publishing Co., 1969).

11. Deloria's copy of the Fire Thunder (Red Horse Owner) winter count is entitled "Oglala Year Count" in her "Old Dakota Legends," MS 30X8a.21 (I–6a), ca. 1937, Boas Collection, American Philosophical Society Library, Philadelphia.

12. Both Cloud Shield's and American Horse's winter counts are published in Mallery, *Pictographs of the North American Indians,* pp. 127–46.

13. Deloria's copy of the No Ears winter count is entitled "An Old Oglala Year Count from 1759–1906," in her "Old Dakota Legends," MS. 30X8a.21 (I–6b), ca. 1937, Boas Collection, American Philosophical Society Library, Philadelphia.

14. M. L. McCreight, *Firewater and Forked Tongues: A Sioux Chief Interprets U.S. History* (Pasadena: Trails End Publishing Co., 1947), pp. 163–70.

15. James H. Howard, "Two Teton Dakota Winter Count Texts," *North Dakota History* 27 (1960): 64–79.

16. The Garnier count is in the Nebraska State Historical Society, Lincoln, and is published in Robert T. Grange, "The Garnier Oglala Winter Count," *Plains Anthropologist* 8 (1963): 77–79.

17. Bureau of American Ethnology Collection, National Anthropological Archives, Smithsonian Institution, MS. 2261.

18. Fred B. Hackett's copy of the No Ears winter count was pub-

lished in an edition of fifty copies (Hackett to DeMallie February 28, 1964).

19. Martha Warren Beckwith, "Mythology of the Oglala Dakota," *Journal of American Folk-Lore* 43 (1930): 349–67; reprinted in Frederick W. Turner III, *The Portable North American Indian Reader* (New York: Viking Press, 1974), pp. 135–57.

20. William K. Powers, "A Winter Count of the Oglala," *American Indian Tradition* 52 (1963): 27–37.

21. Comprehensive listings of winter counts are given in James H. Howard, *Yanktonai Ethnohistory and the John K. Bear Winter Count,* Memoir 11, Plains Anthropologist 21, no. 73 (1976):65–78 and idem, *The British Museum Winter Count,* British Museum Occasional Paper 4 (1979): 97–119.

22. Buechel's *Lakota-English Dictionary* gives "Pawnee" for *Palani* and "Skidi Pawnee" for *Scili;* contemporary Lakotas, however, usually translate *Palani* as "Arikara" and *Scili* as "Pawnee." Buechel, following Riggs, *A Dakota-English Dictionary,* gives "Kutenais" for *Škutani,* which seems unlikely; the translation "Gros Ventres (Atsinas)" comes from James Mooney, *The Ghost-Dance Religion and the Sioux Outbreak of 1890,* Smithsonian Institution, Bureau of American Ethnology, Annual Report 14, pt. 2 (1896): 955.

23. James H. McGregor, *The Wounded Knee Massacre from Viewpoint of the Sioux* (Baltimore: Wirth Brothers, 1940), pp. 103–107.

Bibliography

Abel, Annie Heloise, ed. *Tabeau's Narrative of Loisel's Expedition to the Upper Missouri.* 1939. Reprint ed., Norman: University of Oklahoma Press, 1968.

Anderson, Gary Clayton. "Early Dakota Migration and Intertribal War: A Revision." *Western Historical Quarterly* 11 (1980): 17–36.

Anderson, Harry. "An Investigation of the Early Bands of the Saone Group of Teton Sioux." *Journal of the Washington Academy of Sciences* 46 (1956): 87–94.

Bad Heart Bull, Amos. *A Pictographic History of the Oglala Sioux.* Lincoln: University of Nebraska Press, 1967.

Beckwith, Martha Warren. "Mythology of the Oglala Dakota." *Journal of American Folk-Lore* 43 (1930): 339–442.

Berthrong, Donald J. *The Southern Cheyennes.* Norman: University of Oklahoma Press, 1963.

Boas, Franz, and Deloria, Ella. *Dakota Grammar.* Memoirs of the National Academy of Sciences, vol. 23, no. 2 (1941).

Buechel, Eugene, S.J. *A Dictionary of the Teton Dakota Sioux Language: Lakota-English, English-Lakota.* Edited by Paul Manhart, S.J. Pine Ridge, S.Dak.: Red Cloud Indian School, 1970.

Buechel, Eugene, S.J., et al. *Lakota Tales and Texts.* Edited by Paul Manhart, S.J. Pine Ridge, S.Dak.: Red Cloud Indian School, Lakota Language and Cultural Center, 1978.

Catlin, George. *North American Indians: Being Letters and Notes on Their Manners, Customs, and Conditions, Written During Eight Years' Travel amongst the Wildest Tribes of Indians in North America, 1832–1839.* 2 vols. 1841. Reprint ed., Edinburgh: John Grant, 1926.

Clark, W. P. *The Indian Sign Language.* Philadelphia: L. R. Hamersly, 1885.

Collier, Donald. Field notes from Pine Ridge Reservation, February–March 1939. Copy loaned by the author.

Commissioner of Indian Affairs. *Annual Reports,* 1884–1906. Washington, D.C.: Government Printing Office.

Culbertson, Thaddeus A. *Journal of an Expedition to the Mauvaises Terres and the Upper Missouri in 1850.* Edited by John Francis McDermott. Smithsonian Institution, Bureau of American Ethnology, Bulletin 147, 1952.

Culin, Stewart. *Games of the North American Indians.* Smithsonian Institution, Bureau of American Ethnology, Annual Report 24, 1907.

Deloria, Ella C. *Dakota Texts.* Publications of the American Ethnological Society, vol. 14. New York: G. E. Stechert & Co., 1932.

———. "Old Dakota Legends." MS 30X8a.21, ca. 1937, Boas Collection, American Philosophical Society Library, Philadelphia.

———. *Speaking of Indians.* New York: Friendship Press, 1944.

DeMallie, Raymond J. "Pine Ridge Economy: Cultural and Historical Perspectives." In *American Indian Economic Development,* edited by Sam Stanley, pp. 237–312. The Hague: Mouton, 1978.

———. "Change in American Indian Kinship Systems: The Dakota." In *Currents in Anthropology: Essays in Honor of Sol Tax,* edited by Robert Hinshaw, pp. 221–41. The Hague: Mouton, 1979.

DeMallie, Raymond J., ed. and trans. "Nicollet's Notes on the Dakota." In *Joseph N. Nicollet on the Plains and Prairies,* edited by Edmund C. Bray and Martha Coleman Bray, pp. 250–81. St. Paul: Minnesota Historical Society Press, 1976.

Denig, Edwin T. *Indian Tribes of the Upper Missouri.* Edited by J. N. B. Hewitt. Smithsonian Institution, Bureau of American Ethnology, Annual Report 46, 1930, pp. 377–628.

———. *Five Indian Tribes of the Upper Missouri.* Edited by John C. Ewers. Norman: University of Oklahoma Press, 1961.

Densmore, Frances. *Teton Sioux Music.* Smithsonian Institution, Bureau of American Ethnology, Bulletin 61, 1918.

———. "A Collection of Specimens from the Teton Sioux." *Indian Notes and Monographs,* vol. 11, pt. 3 (1948): 163–204.

Dorsey, James Owen. "Games of Teton Dakota Children." *American Anthropologist,* o.s. 4 (1891): 329–45.

———. "The Social Organization of the Siouan Tribes." *Journal of American Folk-Lore* 4 (1891): 257–63.

———. *A Study of Siouan Cults.* Smithsonian Institution, Bureau of American Ethnology, Annual Report 11, 1894, pp. 351–544.

———. *Siouan Sociology: A Posthumous Paper.* Smithsonian Institution, Bureau of American Ethnology, Annual Report 15, 1897, pp. 207–44.

Dräger, Lothar, ed. "Die Ausrüstung der Kriegsanführer bei den Ogalala-Dakota, Nach Aufzeichnungen von F. Weygold und J. R.

Walker." *Jahrbuch des Museums für Volkerkunde zu Leipzig* (East Berlin) 24 (1967): 158–86.

Eggan, Fred. "The Cheyenne and Arapaho Kinship System." In *Social Anthropology of North American Tribes.* Edited by Fred Eggan, pp. 33–95. 1937. Enlarged ed., Chicago: University of Chicago Press, 1955.

———. "Social Anthropology: Methods and Results." In *Social Anthropology of North American Tribes.* Edited by Fred Eggan, pp. 485–551. Enlarged ed., Chicago: University of Chicago Press, 1955.

———. *The American Indian: Perspectives for the Study of Social Change.* Chicago: Aldine Publishing Co., 1966.

Ewers, John C. *Plains Indian Painting.* Stanford: Stanford University Press, 1939.

———. *The Horse in Blackfoot Indian Culture with Comparative Material from Other Western Tribes.* Smithsonian Institution, Bureau of American Ethnology, Bulletin 159, 1955.

———. *Indian Art in Pipestone: George Catlin's Portfolio in the British Museum.* Washington, D.C.: British Museum Publications and Smithsonian Institution Press, 1979.

Feraca, Stephen E. "The Political Status of the Early Bands and Modern Communities of the Oglala Dakota." W. H. Over *Museum News* 27 (1966): 1–26.

———. "The Discovery of a Sioux Indian Calendar." *New Europe* 3, no. 10 (1974): 4–10.

Flannery, Regina. *The Gros Ventres of Montana: Part I, Social Life.* Catholic University of America Anthropological Series no. 15, 1953.

Fletcher, Alice C. "The White Buffalo Festival of the Uncpapas." In *Report of the Peabody Museum of American Archaeology and Ethnology*, vol. 3, Salem, Mass.: Salem Press, 1884, pp. 260–75.

Fowler, Loretta. Review of William K. Powers's *Oglala Religion, American Ethnologist* 6 (1979): 404–6.

Grange, Robert T. "The Garnier Oglala Winter Count." *Plains Anthropologist* 8 (1963): 77–79.

Grinnell, George Bird. *The Fighting Cheyennes.* New York: Charles Scribner's Sons, 1915.

Hassrick, Royal B. "Teton Dakota Kinship System." *American Anthropologist* 46 (1944): 338–47.

———. *The Sioux: Life and Customs of a Warrior Society.* Norman: University of Oklahoma Press, 1964.

Hayden, Ferdinand V. *Contributions to the Ethnography and Philology of the Indian Tribes of the Missouri Valley.* Philadelphia: Sherman and Son, 1862.

Hickerson, Harold. *The Chippewas and Their Neighbors: A Study in*

Ethnohistory. New York: Holt, Rinehart and Winston, 1970.

Howard, James H. "Two Teton Dakota Winter Count Texts." *North Dakota History* 27 (1960): 64–79.

———. *The Warrior Who Killed Custer: The Personal Narrative of Chief Joseph White Bull*. Lincoln: University of Nebraska Press, 1968.

———. *Yanktonai Ethnohistory and the John K. Bear Winter Count*. Memoir 11, Plains Anthropologist 21 (73), 1976.

———. *The British Museum Winter Count*. British Museum Occasional Paper 4, 1979.

Hyde, George E. *A Sioux Chronicle*. Norman: University of Oklahoma Press, 1956.

———. *Red Cloud's Folk: A History of the Oglala Sioux Indians*. 1937. New ed., Norman: University of Oklahoma Press, 1957.

———. *Spotted Tail's Folk: A History of the Brulé Sioux*. Norman: University of Oklahoma Press, 1961.

Karol, Joseph S., S.J. *Red Horse Owner's Winter Count*. Martin, S.Dak.: Booster Publishing Co., 1969.

Kearney, S. W. "Report of a Summer Campaign to the Rocky Mountains, &c., in 1845." Senate Executive Document no. 1, 29th Cong., 1st sess., serial set no. 470, pp. 210–13.

Keating, William H. *Narrative of An Expedition to the Source of St. Peter's River*. 2 vols. 1824. Reprint ed., Minneapolis: Ross & Haines, 1959.

Kroeber, Alfred L. *The Arapaho*. Bulletin of the American Museum of Natural History, vol. 18 (1902–1907), pp. 1–229, 279–454.

Landes, Ruth. *The Mystic Lake Sioux*. Madison: University of Wisconsin Press, 1968.

Laubin, Reginald and Gladys. *Indian Dances of North America: Their Importance to Indian Life*. Norman: University of Oklahoma Press, 1977.

Laudenschlager, David D. "The Utes in South Dakota, 1906–1908." *South Dakota History* 9 (1979): 233–47.

Lesser, Alexander. "Siouan Kinship." Ph.D. dissertation. Columbia University, 1958 [1929].

Lowie, Robert H. "Plains Indian Age-Societies: Historical and Comparative Summary." American Museum of Natural History, *Anthropological Papers* 11, pt. 13 (1916): 877–986.

———. *Indians of the Plains*. American Museum of Natural History, Anthropological Handbook 1. New York: McGraw-Hill, 1954.

Lyford, Carrie A. *Quill and Beadwork of the Western Sioux*. Indian Handicrafts Pamphlet 1. Lawrence, Kansas: Haskell Press, 1940.

McCreight, M. L. *Firewater and Forked Tongues: A Sioux Chief Interprets U.S. History*. Pasadena: Trail's End Publishing Co., 1947.

McGregor, James H. *The Wounded Knee Massacre from Viewpoint of the Sioux*. Baltimore: Wirth Brothers, 1940.

Mallery, Garrick. *Sign Language among North American Indians Compared with That among Other Peoples and Deaf-Mutes.* Smithsonian Institution, Bureau of American Ethnology, Annual Report 1, 1881, pp. 263–552.

———. *Pictographs of the North American Indians.* Smithsonian Institution, Bureau of American Ethnology, Annual Report 4, 1886, pp. 1–256.

———. *Picture-Writing of the American Indians.* Smithsonian Institution, Bureau of American Ethnology, Annual Report 10, 1893.

Margry, Pierre, ed. *Découvertes et Établissements des Français dans l'Ouest et dans le Sud de l'Amérique Septentrionale (1614–1754).* 6 vols. Paris: Jouaust, 1875–86.

Mekeel, Haviland Scudder. "Field notes from Pine Ridge Reservation, summers 1930, 1931." Department of Anthropology, AMNH, New York.

———. "A Discussion of Culture Change as Illustrated by Material from a Teton-Dakota Community." *American Anthropologist* 34 (1932): 274–85.

———. "A Modern American Indian Community in the Light of Its Past: A Study in Culture Change." Ph.D. dissertation. Yale University, 1932.

———. "The Economy of a Modern Teton Dakota Community." *Yale University Publications in Anthropology,* no. 6. New Haven: Yale University Press, 1936.

———. "A Short History of the Teton-Dakota." *North Dakota Historical Quarterly* 10 (1943): 136–205.

Meeker, Louis L. "Ogalala Games." *Bulletin* of the Free Museum of Science and Art (Philadelphia), no. 3 (1901): 23–46.

Miller, David Humphreys. *Ghost Dance.* New York: Duell, Sloan, and Pearce, 1959.

Mirsky, Jeannette. "The Dakota." In *Cooperation and Competition among Primitive Peoples,* edited by Margaret Mead, pp. 382–427. 1937. New ed., Boston: Beacon Press, 1966.

Mooney, James. *The Ghost-Dance Religion and the Sioux Outbreak of 1890.* Smithsonian Institution, Bureau of American Ethnology, Annual Report 14, pt. 2, 1896.

Morgan, Lewis Henry. *Systems of Consanguinity and Affinity of the Human Family.* Smithsonian Institution, Contributions to Knowledge, vol. 17, 1871.

Morrow, Mable. *Indian Rawhide: An American Folk Art.* Norman: University of Oklahoma Press, 1975.

Nasatir, A. P. *Before Lewis and Clark: Documents Illustrating the History of the Missouri, 1785–1804.* 2 vols. St. Louis: St. Louis Historical Documents Foundation, 1952.

Olson, James C. *Red Cloud and the Sioux Problem.* Lincoln: University of Nebraska Press, 1965.

Parker, John, ed. *The Journals of Jonathan Carver and Related Documents 1766–1770*. St. Paul: Minnesota Historical Society Press, 1976.

Petter, Rev. Rudolphe. *English-Cheyenne Dictionary*. Kettle Falls, Wash., 1913–15.

Powers, William K. "A Winter Count of the Oglala." *American Indian Tradition* 52 (1963): 27–37.

———. *Oglala Religion*. Lincoln: University of Nebraska Press, 1977.

Praus, Alexis. "A New Pictographic Autobiography of Sitting Bull." *Smithsonian Miscellaneous Collections* 123, 1955.

Prucha, Francis Paul, S.J., ed. *Documents of United States Indian Policy*. Lincoln: University of Nebraska Press, 1975.

Ricker, Eli. Interview with Dewey Beard, February 20, 1907. MS. Tablet 30, Ricker Collection, Nebraska State Historical Society, Lincoln.

Riggs, Stephen Return. *Grammar and Dictionary of the Dakota Language*. Smithsonian Institution, Contributions to Knowledge, vol. 4, 1852.

———. *A Dakota-English Dictionary*. Edited by J. Owen Dorsey. Contributions to North American Ethnology, vol. 7, Washington, D.C.: Government Printing Office, 1890.

———. *Dakota Grammar, Texts, and Ethnography*. Edited by J. Owen Dorsey. Contributions to North American Ethnology, vol. 9. Washington, D.C.: Government Printing Office, 1893.

Robinson, Doane. *A History of the Dakota or Sioux Indians*. South Dakota Historical Collections, vol. 2. Pierre, S.Dak., 1904.

Salzmann, Zdeněk. "Arapaho VI: Noun." *International Journal of American Linguistics* 31 (1965): 136–51.

Sandoz, Mari. *Cheyenne Autumn*. New York: McGraw-Hill, 1953.

Spier, Leslie. "The Sun Dance of the Plains Indians: Its Development and Diffusion." American Museum of Natural History, *Anthropological Papers* 16, pt. 7 (1921): 451–527.

Standing Bear, Luther. *My People, the Sioux*. Boston: Houghton Mifflin, 1928. Reprint ed., Lincoln: University of Nebraska Press, 1975.

Stirling, M. W. "Three Pictographic Autobiographies of Sitting Bull." *Smithsonian Miscellaneous Collections* 97 (1938): 1–57.

Taylor, Allan R. "The Colorado University System for Writing the Lakhóta Language." *American Indian Culture and Research Journal* 1 (1975): 3–12.

Thwaites, Reuben Gold, ed. *Original Journals of the Lewis and Clark Expedition, 1804–1806*. 8 vols. 1904–1905. Reprint ed., New York: Antiquarian Press, 1959.

Turner, Frederick W. III. *The Portable North American Indian Reader*. New York: Viking Press, 1974.

U.S. Congress. *Encounter between Sioux Indians of the Pine Ridge Agency,*

S.Dak., and a Sheriff's Posse of Wyoming. January 27, 1904. Senate Document 128, 58th Cong., 2d. sess., serial set no. 4589.

Vestal, Stanley. *New Sources of Indian History, 1850–1891.* Norman: University of Oklahoma Press, 1934a.

———. *Warpath: The True Story of the Fighting Sioux Told in a Biography of Chief White Bull.* Boston: Houghton Mifflin, 1934b.

——— *Sitting Bull: Champion of the Sioux.* 1932. New ed., Norman: University of Oklahoma Press, 1957.

Walker, James R. "Sioux Games." *Journal of American Folk-Lore* 18 (1905): 277–90, 19 (1906): 29–36.

———. "Oglala Kinship Terms." *American Anthropologist* 16 (1914): 96–109.

———. "The Sun Dance and Other Ceremonies of the Oglala Division of the Teton Dakota." American Museum of Natural History, *Anthropological Papers* 16, pt. 2 (1917): 50–221.

———. *Lakota Belief and Ritual.* Edited by Raymond J. DeMallie and Elaine A. Jahner. Lincoln: University of Nebraska Press, 1980.

Wedel, Mildred Mott. "Le Sueur and the Dakota Sioux." In *Aspects of Upper Great Lakes Anthropology: Essays in Honor of Lloyd A. Wilford.* Edited by Elden Johnson, pp. 157–171. St. Paul: Minnesota Historical Society Press, 1974.

Wissler, Clark. "Field Notes on the Dakota Indians, 1902." AMNH, New York.

———. "Symbolism in the Decorative Art of the Sioux." International Congress of Americanists, *Proceedings,* 13 (1902): 339–45.

———. "Decorative Art of the Sioux Indians." AMNH, *Bulletin* 18 (1905): 231–75.

———. "The Whirlwind and the Elk in the Mythology of the Dakota." *Journal of American Folk-Lore* 18 (1905): 257–68.

———. "Some Dakota Myths." *Journal of American Folk-Lore* 20 (1907): 121–31, 195–206.

———. "Some Protective Designs of the Dakota." AMNH, *Anthropological Papers,* 1, pt. 2 (1907): 21–53.

———. "Societies and Ceremonial Associations in the Oglala Division of the Teton-Dakota." AMNH, *Anthropological Papers* 11, pt. 1 (1912): 1–99.

——. "Costumes of the Plains Indians." AMNH, *Anthropological Papers* 17, pt. 2 (1915): 39–91.

———. "General Discussion of Shamanistic and Dancing Societies," AMNH, *Anthropological Papers* 11, pt. 12 (1916): 853–76.

Index

www.ingramcontent.com/pod-product-compliance
Ingram Content Group UK Ltd.
Pitfield, Milton Keynes, MK11 3LW, UK
UKHW022222290425
458005UK00005B/56

9 780803 297371